VIOLENCE AND
THE MEDIA

ISSUES in CULTURAL and MEDIA STUDIES

Series editor: Stuart Allan

Published titles

Media, Risk and Science
Stuart Allan

News Culture
Stuart Allan

Television, Globalization and Cultural Identities
Chris Barker

Cultures of Popular Music
Andy Bennett

Masculinities and Culture
John Beynon

Cinema and Cultural Modernity
Gill Branston

Violence and the Media
Cynthia Carter and C. Kay Weaver

Ethnic Minorities and the Media
Edited by Simon Cottle

Moral Panics and the Media
Chas Critcher

Modernity and Postmodern Culture
Jim McGuigan

Sport, Culture and the Media
David Rowe

Cities and Urban Cultures
Deborah Stevenson

Compassion, Morality and the Media
Keith Tester

VIOLENCE AND THE MEDIA

Cynthia Carter and C. Kay Weaver

OPEN UNIVERSITY PRESS

Buckingham · Philadelphia

Open University Press
Celtic Court
22 Ballmoor
Buckingham
MK18 1XW

email: enquiries@openup.co.uk
world wide web: www.openup.co.uk

and
325 Chestnut Street
Philadelphia, PA 19106, USA

First Published 2003

A catalogue record of this book is available from the British Library

ISBN 0 335 20505 4 (pbk)   0 335 20506 2 (hbk)

Library of Congress Cataloging-in-Publication Data
Carter, Cynthia, 1959–
    Violence and the media/Cynthia Carter and C. Kay Weaver.
       p. cm. – (Issues in cultural and media studies)
    Includes bibliographical references and index.
    ISBN 0-335-20506-2 – ISBN 0-335-20505-4 (pbk.)
       1. Violence in mass media. I. Weaver, C. Kay, 1964–. II. Title. III. Series.

P96.V5 C37 2003
303.6–dc21

                                                                          2002030373

Typeset by Type Study, Scarborough
Printed in Great Britain by Biddles Limited, Guildford and King's Lynn

CONTENTS

SERIES EDITOR'S FOREWORD

Over the centuries, the heralding of each new medium of communication – whether it be the printing press, the cinema, radio, television or the Internet – has been accompanied by a host of popular anxieties about the cultural influence of its content. In each instance, the depiction of violence has been singled out as a matter of urgent public concern, with impassioned disputes unfolding over questions of taste, decency, morality and (never far behind) censorship. Each medium continues to pose diverse challenges for those engaging with media representations of violence today, not least with respect to the familiar problem of how best to differentiate the public interest from what interests the public. Precisely how this distinction is made, of course, will necessarily invite strong reactions from those with deeply-felt convictions about the possible consequences of violent imagery for our society.

In this light, it is not surprising that Cynthia Carter and C. Kay Weaver's *Violence and the Media* addresses from the outset the cacophony of claims and counter-claims about the effects of violent imagery on media audiences. This field of debate, as they show, is sharply polarised between those who insist that media content has a decisive impact on people's behaviour, and those who refuse to accept that any such correlation can be upheld at all. In seeking to elaborate a third position, Carter and Weaver provide an evaluative assessment of the varied definitions of violence, as well as the main theoretical frameworks, employed in a wide variety of media analyses. Each chapter delves into a distinct area of enquiry, from news accounts of violence, to cinematic portrayals, televisual representations (especially those directed at children), pornography, advertising and cyberspace. Researchers, Carter and Weaver suggest, need to focus greater attention 'on the extent to which everyday representations of violence in the media help, over time, to normalize and legitimize the presence and use of violence in society.' In their view, it is by examining how violent imagery is implicated in the structural hegemony of powerful groups that further insights can be gained into how these processes are sustained (or not) in ideological terms. All in all, this is a bold attempt to take stock of current research while, at the same time, striving to recast the orientation of future work.

The *Issues in Cultural and Media Studies* series aims to facilitate a diverse range of critical investigations into pressing questions considered to be central to current thinking and research. In light of the remarkable speed at which the conceptual agendas of cultural and media studies are changing, the authors are committed to contributing to what is an ongoing process of re-evaluation and critique. Each of the books is intended to provide a lively, innovative and comprehensive introduction to a specific topical issue from a fresh perspective. The reader is offered a thorough grounding in the most salient debates indicative of the book's subject, as well as important insights into how new modes of enquiry may be established for future explorations. Taken as a whole, then, the series is designed to cover the core components of cultural and media studies courses in an imaginatively distinctive and engaging manner.

Stuart Allan

ACKNOWLEDGEMENTS

Writing this book has been both a pleasure and a challenge. One of the greatest pleasures has been sharing ideas and developing our arguments on media violence, a subject that we view as one of the most important in cultural and media studies today. One of the challenges has been to do this while living on opposite sides of the world – made possible because of the many communication technologies we are both very fortunate to have at our disposal. Pleasures and challenges aside, we would not have completed this book without the endless encouragement and support of Stuart Allan, our series editor. His editorial interventions, good humour and generosities are appreciated more than he knows. Our warmest thanks also go to Justin Vaughan and Miriam Selwyn and their colleagues at Open University Press for their enthusiasm for the project and extraordinary patience in waiting for us to deliver.

We would each like to take this opportunity to acknowledge various people who have given us advice and inspiration along the way.

Cynthia
I offer sincere appreciation to the following people: Barbara Adam, Nawal Masri Asad, Gill Branston, Rod Brookes, Carolyn Byerly, Máire Messenger Davies, Peter Garrett, John Hartley, Patricia Holland, Dafna Lemish, Myra Macdonald, Lisa McLaughlin, David Miller, Roberta Pearson, Lana Rakow, Karen Ross, Muna Sha'ath, Elizabeth Stanko, Linda Steiner, Christine Trevitt, John Tulloch, Brian Winston and Maggie Wykes. I am very grateful for study leave from the School of Journalism, Media and Cultural Studies, Cardiff University, during which I was able to finish this book and especially

thankful for colleagues' support. On a more personal note, I would like to thank Nancy Carl, Margaret Carter, Robert Carter, Bill Daly, Marion Mac-Millan, Jeri Owen and Meta Stairs for their love and encouragement. Last, but most certainly not least, I am deeply indebted to Stuart and Geoffrey. It is your unconditional love and infinite patience that enabled me to see this project through to completion.

Kay
Many people and institutions have provided invaluable support during my involvement with *Violence and the Media*. John Hartley facilitated our developing the original proposal for the book by inviting me to the Tom Hopkinson Centre for Media Research at Cardiff University in 1998. Alice Kessler-Harris and the Institute for Research on Women and Gender at Columbia University generously gifted me with time, space and access to vast research resources in supporting my Visiting Scholarship during late 2000 through to early 2001. Ted Zorn, Juliet Roper and my colleagues in Management Communication at the University of Waikato, as well as Olive Jones, Liz Lake, Ruth Laing, David Miller, Sean Russell, Jane Williams, Ann Hardy, Judy Motion, Bevin Yeatman, my parents Diana Weaver and Ian Weaver, and brothers Alan and Duncan, have all provided wonderful friendship and encouragement over many years. Finally, a very special thank you to Nan Seuffert for her enduring support, understanding and gloriously indulgent distractions.

Introduction
VIOLENCE AND THE MEDIA

Violence in drama and news demonstrates power. It portrays victims as well as victimizers. It intimidates more than it incites. It paralyzes more than it incites. It defines majority might and minority risk. It shows one's place in the 'pecking order' that runs society.

(Nancy Snow 2001: 24)

The deepest sources of murderous American violence are stupefying inequality, terrible poverty, a nihilistic drug-saturated culture, and an easy recourse to guns. TV's contribution is a target of convenience for a political culture that makes it difficult to grow up with a sense of belonging to a decent society.

(Todd Gitlin 2002)

What is 'media violence'?

- Why is there so much violence in the media?
- Does violent media content lead to violent behaviour in audiences?
- Can violent images desensitize us to real violence?
- What do members of the public think about media violence?
- What meanings about our social and cultural environment are communicated by media **representations** of violence?
- What, if anything, is to be done about it?

Questions such as these have long been sources of controversy and debate in media and **cultural studies** research. Ultimately what has been at issue is whether the media have the power to directly influence audiences' perceptions of the seriousness of human violence. If the media portray violence as a 'normal' and acceptable way of dealing with problems, do they encourage or at least lend justification to certain forms of violent behaviour?

Starker (1989) notes how from the earliest days of the popular press in North America and Britain there was widespread public concern around reporting sex and violence which, it was felt, were undermining cultural morals and desensitizing the social sensibility of readers (see also Murdock 2001). Similar concerns were voiced in the early days of cinema, radio and television, and then again with the advent of video games and music videos (Petley 2001). More recently, public anxieties have surfaced around the use of the extent to which the Internet is used to widely distribute 'snuff' images and child pornography (Craig and Petley 2001). For almost a century now, the apparent ability of the media to negatively affect individual behaviour has been one of the foremost concerns around media violence for government officials, pressure groups, media scholars and citizens. Typical questions posed by such constituencies have been:

- Do some forms of violent media content directly or indirectly cause actual violent behaviour to occur?
- Is it possible to empirically measure and prove that there is a causal link between exposure to media violence and increased levels of real violence?
- Is western society becoming more violent and, if so, is this partly because the mass media portray violence as inevitable and even sometimes as desirable?
- Is it now widely seen to be 'cool' (especially among young people) to enjoy violent media content?

All of these are questions about media effects. They are also questions that deeply divide media and cultural studies researchers into two broad camps – those who agree that there is strong evidence of media effects, and those who refute this evidence. As we discuss further below, which camp researchers inhabit in this debate depends on their politics. But before we explore that issue, we first need to explore the arguments about the definitions of violence used in media research.

As US media effects scholar Potter (1999) argues, the question 'what is media violence?' is a deceptively simple one. Each one of us thinks that we know what we mean by the term 'violence' because 'we know it when we see it'. However, Potter (1999: 63) astutely points out that, 'When we have to write a definition, it is difficult to translate our understanding into words. Instead of using a formal definition, we usually define violence ostensively: We point to examples'.

In an effort to define violence Potter (1999: 80) states that 'Violence is a violation of a character's physical or emotional well-being. It includes two key elements – intentionality and harm – at least one of which must be present'. However, many researchers do not necessarily share this view of violence. Indeed, attempts to define what we mean by violence have long been the source of fierce debate in media and cultural studies. Most obviously, definitions often vary from geographic place to place, group to group, across cultures and time. In the USA, as Ali (2002) notes, widely accepted cultural definitions of media violence have substantially changed with the passing of each decade. In the 1930s, for example, many parents objected to films such as *Boo-Boop-a-Doop* (1932) and *Little Orphan Annie* (1932) because there was a feeling that they contained 'too much violence and suspense. In the 1990s, some movies with lenient, PG ratings (e.g. *Dick Tracy* [1990]) had higher body counts than films that were judged to be "really violent" (e.g. *Death Wish* [1974]) in the 1970s' that were 'R' rated (Ali 2002) (see Chapter 2).

Definitions of violence are also affected by questions of *how* violence is *represented*. For example, the National Television Violence Study (1997) in the US assessed types of media violence that were believed to be particularly problematic where child audiences are concerned. It identified four types of media representations that are thought to encourage children to underestimate the seriousness of real human violence:

- *Unpunished violence*: it is said that around one-third of violent programmes on US television feature villains who are not punished or are punished only at the end of the story. It is felt that this form of representation does not alert young viewers to the fact that violence is wrong and that we should not be violent.
- *Painless violence*: almost half of all television violence does not show victims to be in pain. It is argued that the message promoted by this presentation of violence is that violence does not result in serious injury, pain or death.
- *Happy violence*: this type of violence often occurs in children's cartoons, where characters who are repeatedly hurt become the points of humour. It is thought that 'happy violence' desensitizes children to the seriousness of violence and tells them that violence is funny.
- *Heroic violence*: around 40 per cent of all acts of violence on US television are initiated by characters who are presented as positive role models. It is said that this kind of portrayal encourages children to emulate violent behaviour. Violence used by a good guy for a positive reason (to protect someone or save the world) may well be more problematic than violence initiated by a 'bad guy' who does not ultimately gain from their violent actions.

While the UCLA Television Violence Monitoring Report (1995) used these four types of violence to classify television representations, not everyone will necessarily agree that the representations to which the researchers refer *are* violent. What is more, many media and cultural studies researchers utterly reject the notion that such representations have an effect on the behaviour of children or adult audiences.

For example, the British cultural studies scholar Martin Barker (2001) is adamant that effects arguments have had nothing useful to say about media violence (see also Gauntlett 1998). Barker (2001) asserts:

> *There simply is no category 'media violence' which can be researched; that is why over seventy years of research into this supposed topic have produced nothing worthy of note . . .* Hard though it may be to accept that an entire research tradition is based on thin air, this is my case.
>
> (Barker 2001: 42–3, emphasis in the original)

Barker and Petley (2001: 4) argue that the mere presence of violent content in the media is not the key issue that should concern media scholars. Instead, they state, 'It is its purposes and meanings, both within individual media items and the wider circuits and currents of feelings and ideas that accompany it, that have to be examined.' Other critical researchers have reached similar conclusions. Schlesinger et al. (1992), for example, argue for the need to shift from trying to prove causal effects on the behaviour of potential perpetrators to the fears that it can instill in women about real violence. They elaborate:

> Are women likely to feel more vulnerable, less safe or less valued members of our society if, as a category, they are with some frequency depicted as those who are subjected to abuse? If so, the portrayal of violence against women may be seen as negative, even if women viewers have never experienced such violence and/or its likelihood is not increased.
>
> (Schlesinger et al. 1992: 170)

For these researchers then, media effects are considered in broader social terms of influence and perception, rather than the narrow psychological terms that traditional media effects have been concerned with in their focus on individual behaviour.

Once it is appreciated that arguments about media violence and its effects can be informed by either psychological or social/sociological perspectives, among others, it becomes apparent that researchers' theoretical and political orientations are crucial to what questions they ask about media violence and how they conceive its influence.

In statistical studies of media violence, which in media effects research is a preferred method of psychologists, researchers claim to be able to present objective facts about, for example, the *quantifiable* effect on behaviour of watching television. However, critical media scholars are quick to point out that media effects theories are far from objective and that the effects tradition developed out of research concerned with making communication systems *more* 'effective'. Effects researchers originally focused on the issue of communication effectiveness because they were investigating how to ensure the steady and expanding flow of ideas, goods and capital, particularly from the period just after the Second World War. The media were considered crucial to the maintenance of this flow: they 'advertise' what is on sale, from specific consumer goods to lifestyles that are built around consumption. Thus, effects research is underpinned by the ideological assumption that free-market capitalism is desirable and needs to be supported by effective communications systems (Murdock 2001).

Appreciating the importance of this ideological assumption to effects research, it is easier to see why scholars in this tradition are concerned about media violence. Media violence, however it is defined, sends out strong messages about economic and social hierarchies in capitalist society in a way that legitimizes and polices inequalities based on class difference, 'race', gender, sexuality, and so on. At times, however, the messages of media violence are publicly deemed to be 'too strong' and to have gone 'too far'. What going 'too far' means is that the media are perceived to be in the invidious position of contributing to the delegitimization of free-market capitalism (Murdock 2001).

For example, capitalism is undermined when the media show that the pursuit of capital is actually the impetus for violence. If the media are seen to be enabling audiences to blame capitalism for the various forms of violence that it inevitably fosters, then the whole system might come into disrepute. However, when the media are regarded as having gone 'too far', they are not blamed for consciously and deliberately delegitimizing capitalism, but are instead accused of unconsciously and inadvertently contributing to worsening levels of violence in society (Starker 1989). It is the media's incitement to violence and not capitalism then that is criticized for fostering social and economic instability (you know it is really bad when people are too afraid to go to the mall). This is where effects research comes into its own. It is an approach that documents if and where media violence messages are 'too strong' (by demonstrating links between media violence and violent behaviour) so as to reign in the media and re-establish their 'proper' legitimizing function within capitalism. This is precisely the main bone of contention that critical media researchers have with effects research on media violence. Critics argue that the main objective of effects research on media violence is to legitimize capitalism rather than to demonstrate any genuine concern about human violence or coming up with any real insights into it (Barker 2001).

While media effects theories have dominated research into media violence, researchers using other perspectives have also argued for the importance of studying this phenomenon. We shall now turn our attention to four key conceptual approaches that have been used to study media violence – including that of media effects, and explain the claims that each of these makes about the audience's relationship to that violence.

Approaches to research into media violence

Research on media violence can be broadly divided into four different theories (most of which have been developed to talk about television and film violence although they have also been applied to the study of the press, cartoons, computer games, and so on). They are 'behavioural effects theory', **'desensitization theory'**, **'cultivation theory'** and 'the limited effects argument'. As we shall now explain, each of these proposes quite a different understanding of media violence.

Behavioural effects theory

Behavioural effects theory, initially so called because it concentrated on 'measuring changes in [individuals'] behaviour after they were exposed to violent media material' has expended over 70 years and over 10,000 research studies investigating possible links between viewing violence and inclinations to aggressive behaviour (Cunningham 1992: 67). Effects theorists argue that this research proves that viewers learn from television to consider violence appropriate behaviour, and that this applies to viewers from pre-school through to adult ages (Paik and Comstock 1994; Wilson et al. 1998a).

A considerable proportion of the research conducted from within this perspective includes laboratory studies where children or adults are shown violent imagery and their subsequent behaviour observed. Changes in behaviour are quantified in terms of increases in violent or aggressive play, or propensity to administer pain to another person (for two classic studies using this approach see Bandura et al. 1963; Berkowitz and Rawlings 1963). Studies of this kind found that when media audiences are shown content in which the initiator of violence is rewarded, there is often an increased likelihood of audience members exhibiting aggressive behaviour. **Longitudinal studies** on television violence, for example, have concluded that the effects can last over time and that 'approximately 10 percent of the variability in later criminal behaviour can be attributed to television violence' (Paik and

Comstock 1994; Wilson et al. 1998a: 19). While researchers conclude that there is a positive correlation or link between consumption of media violence and aggressive and violent behaviour in audiences, how, exactly, have they explained that correlation?

From a **cognitive perspective**, television researchers have argued that 'observation of violence on television provides material for the learning of complex behavioural scripts' (Geen 1994: 7). That is, in watching a violent scenario, and then later finding themselves in a situation with some degree of similarity (a situation of conflict for example), the viewer uses the media representation as a script to guide their behaviour (Huesmann 1986). A slightly different explanation for the positive correlation argues that watching violence primes the viewer to have aggressive ideas. That is, the violent imagery can 'engender a complex of associations consisting of aggressive ideas, emotions related to violence, and the impetus for aggressive acts' (Geen 1994: 158). Further, researchers have found that identification with a violent hero, perception of the violent act as justified and rewarded, and the perception of the violence as realistic and/or factual all increase the likelihood of aggressive behaviour in children and adult viewers (Wilson et al. 1998a). Consequently, some scholars have argued that 'certain depictions of violence pose more of a risk for viewers than others' (Wilson et al. 1998a: 45). However, others have claimed that aggression in audiences 'is most likely to occur when [they have] been provoked in some way and is therefore relatively likely to aggress' (Geen 1994: 152). This suggests that audiences are more likely to apply what they learn from the media when in a situation where aggression is a potential response anyway, rather than a random unmotivated act.

Behavioural effects theories have gained wide acceptance among politicians, broadcasting regulators and media watchdog groups. However, some critics maintain that politicians and government policy accept arguments about media effects because it avoids their having to scrutinize how violence in society might be caused by wider structural inequalities between people in society and political decision-making. For broadcast regulators, supporting the conclusions of traditional effects research has been used to demonstrate a serious commitment to communication research (Rowland 1983). Yet effects studies have been highly criticized on the grounds that they offer an 'impoverished view' of media content. As Cunningham (1992) argues, these studies largely fail to appreciate that media violence is a many splendoured thing. In other words, it takes 'many styles and forms' and it is produced and consumed in a range of different ways (Cunningham 1992: 68). Laboratory experiments into the effects of television viewing have especially been challenged on 'grounds of low external validity created, for example, by their artificial circumstances, the absence of the possibility of retaliation by a victim, brevity of the television exposure, and immediacy of the measurement of effect' (Paik and Comstock 1994: 2).

Additionally, critics of effects research have charged researchers with employing weak and inconsistent methods, downplaying studies where no effects of viewing violence are found, and for failing to take into account that aggressive behaviour can be caused by many factors other than watching violence (Gauntlett 1995, 1998). Other commentators of the approach have warned against assuming that the media have the power to encourage violent behaviour. Cumberbatch (1989), for example, argues that there is a significant difference between learning from the media and putting that learning into action. He suggests, 'We may learn how to rape, rob or murder from what we see in films or on television but the barriers to our performing these acts in everyday life are more motivational than knowledge based' (Cumberbatch 1989: 36). From this perspective, how media messages are responded to has to be considered within the context of social and cultural forces beyond the text such as the type of violence and who committed it. This will determine whether the violence is deemed to be acceptable, or unacceptable.

However, there is a need to be cautious in accepting some criticisms of behavioural effects theory. Critics often fail to take into account the ways in which the everydayness of media violence influences audience perceptions about the meaning and acceptability of violence in society (Miller and Philo 1996). Further, there is a tendency to caricature effects research and neglect to consider the complex ways in which it researches and theorizes effects (Gerbner 1983; Lang and Lang 1983; Curran 1990; McLeod et al. 1991; Potter 1999). It is also important to remember that effects theories are highly influential in the formation of media policy and regulation. In the USA, many researchers, especially cognitive psychologists, continue to assert that there is conclusive evidence to prove a link between children and adolescents watching violence on television and subsequent aggressive behaviour (Paik and Comstock 1994). These arguments are taken very seriously by media regulators and often form the basis of new communications policies (for a recent example, see Jeffrey G. Johnson, cited in Kolata 2002). Therefore the tradition needs to be engaged with intelligently, rather than rejected out of hand as ill informed.

Desensitization theory

Desensitization theory, which is also a theory of media effects, proposes that consuming a constant diet of media violence can 'undermine feelings of concern, empathy, or sympathy viewers [or readers] might have toward victims of actual violence' (Wilson et al. 1998a: 22). In the important research conducted by Dietz et al. (1982), for example, it was concluded that men who watch slasher films containing rape depictions show less sympathy toward actual rape victims. They also consider rape attacks to be less violent than men who did not view the diet of violent film imagery. A study by Linz et al. (1984) claims that with increased viewing of violent imagery viewers become more comfortable with it. Desensitization theorists also believe that with the proliferation of media depictions of violence, and their increased realism, has come a significant rise in the effects of desensitization. According to Thoman (1993), 'One expert believed that of the 25,000 murders committed in the United States every year . . . at least half are due to the influence and desensitizing effects of media violence'.

Deborah Prothrow-Stith, MD and Dean of Harvard University's School of Public Health, has cautioned that there is now a 'growing crisis of violence as public health issue in [US] society' (cited in Thoman 1993). Recounting the story of a young gunshot victim treated in a Boston hospital emergency room, Prothrow-Stith indicated that because the boy had been desensitized by portrayals of violence in the media, he had 'expressed surprise that his wound would actually hurt'. Prothrow-Stith recalled:

> I thought, boy, he's really stupid, anybody knows that if you get shot, it's going to hurt. But it dawned on me that what he sees on television is that when the superhero gets shot in the arm, he uses that arm to hold onto a truck going 85 miles an hour around a corner. He overcomes the driver and shoots a couple of hundred people while he's at it.
>
> (cited in Thoman 1993)

This is of course only one incidence of alleged desensitization to media violence, and is not sufficient to prove the theory.

Proving desensitization theories of media effects is indeed problematic. This is largely due to the difficulty of conducting research that requires screening a television diet of violent imagery to research participants and later testing their responses to real acts of violence. These responses would then have to be compared with participants whose viewing includes much less or no violent imagery. Because of the obvious difficulty of showing participants real acts of violence, researchers have shown either video footage of what they tell participants are real acts of violence or mock trials which are identified as real. Participants are then asked to make judgements about the victim and severity of the crime (Linz et al. 1984; Krafka and Linz 1997). However, such research tends to be criticized on the grounds of being contrived (Fowles 1999).

Critical media scholars who are generally highly wary of effects research are often willing to actually agree with desensitization theory, at least in part. Instead of going along with the notion that audiences are easily manipulated and numbed by media violence, they want to talk about the ways in which audiences are invited to read in preferred ways. Carter (1998), for example, makes a similar point in relation to the representation of sexual violence in the British press. She suggests that it operates ideologically through its discursive construction of sexual violence as ostensibly 'normal', 'inevitable' and 'ordinary'. However, critical media researchers tend to disagree with desensitization effects theorists' argument that any decline in sensitivity to either media violence or real acts of violence is directly and only attributable to media representations.

Cultivation theory

A different approach to theorizing the effects of media violence is presented within cultivation theory. According to an important early study by Gerbner and Gross (1976) that helped to set out the broad parameters in which research would take place over the following decades, 'cultivation analysis, as we call that method, inquires into the assumption television cultivates about the facts, norms and values of society' (Gerbner and Gross 1976: 182). The cultivation analysis approach does not assume that media violence *causes* social violence. Rather, researchers argue that media representations of violence constitute a means of social control in that they 'vividly dramatize the preferred power relations and cultivate fear, dependence on authority, and the desire for security rather than social change' (White 1983: 287). For Gerbner and Gross (1976: 182), television violence is the 'simplest and cheapest dramatic means available to demonstrate the rules of the power game'.

The **Cultural Indicators Project** initiated by Gerbner and his colleagues in 1967 (from which cultivation theory derives) has based its theoretical conclusions on quantitative content analysis of US prime-time television programming. The aim has been to identify how much violence appears in television programming, who are the victims, and who are the perpetrators. For example, its early analyses of character types most likely to be portrayed as perpetrators and victims of violence found that 'of the 20 most victimized groups . . . all but three are composed of women' (Gerbner et al. 1978: 191). It is said that television's repeated portrayal of certain groups as victims represents a symbolic expression of those victim types' social impotence in society (Gerbner and Gross 1976: 82). In terms of the audience, such symbolic imagery is theorized as cultivating social conceptions about 'who are the aggressors and who are the victims' where 'there is a relationship between the roles of the violent and the victim. Both roles are there to be learned by viewers' (Gerbner et al. 1979: 180). Additionally, the more heavily television is watched, the more vulnerable is the viewer to this learning (Gerbner and Gross 1976).

More recently, Gerbner (1994) has developed what he refers to as the 'mean world' thesis. This thesis suggests that heavy users of television, in particular, tend to 'overestimate their chances of involvement in violence . . . believe that their neighborhoods are unsafe . . . state that fear of crime is a very serious problem [and] assume that crime is rising, regardless of the facts of the case' (Gerbner 1994). Critical researchers have equally expressed concerns of this kind. For example, television crime reality programmes have been accused of creating exaggerated fears of crime (Grade 1989: 32–4; Sweeney 1992; Culf 1994) and encouraging public support for tougher policies on law and order (Schlesinger and Tumber 1993; Anderson 1995; Osborne 1995).

As with all media effects theories, the cultivation approach has been widely criticized. Its conclusions are indeed problematic given that they are largely based on content analyses of the media that tend to make no distinction between the types of programmes in which violence is shown. Violence in children's cartoons, for example, is often equated with violence in realist drama and horror movies (Cumberbatch 1989; Barker 2001). A related concern is that cultivation research sometimes overemphasizes individualistic responses to media violence, thus under-assessing the significance of the ways in which representations of violence in the media contribute to the (re)production of structural social inequalities (see Feilitzen 1998; Linné and Wartella 1998). As such, it tends to 'abstract the relationship of message content and individual perceptions from the historical, political, and economic conditions which influence both' (White 1983: 288). This clearly suggests a need to examine how factors outside of the media effect how audiences interpret media content.

How viewers *interpret* violent portrayals is a question that largely has been side-stepped by cultivation theorists. In the mid-1980s, Gunter (1985) purported that cultivation analysis simply *assumes* there is a link between what is shown on television and how individuals understand the world around them. He says, 'no evidence is presented to show whether or not 'messages' identified through content analysis are actually perceived and learned by viewers' (Gunter 1985: 33). About five years later, researchers began to explore the extent to which fear of violence was linked to heavy television viewing. One study found no correlation between fear of violent attack and quantities of viewing (Docherty 1990). Herein lies a further problem. The theory of media effects espoused by cultivation theorists is largely based on textual analyses of media content. Theorists then speculate as to how that content might affect behaviour, attitudes, and so on. To date, there has been little research that has foregrounded how audiences negotiate media violence in the context of their everyday lives.

This point is pursued by Lupton and Tulloch (1999), who have concluded that to understand the relationship between representations of media violence and people's fears of crime, it is not enough to argue that such representations cultivate fears of victimhood (particularly in so-called heavy television viewers). Instead, what is needed is grounded research that explores how audiences make sense of media violence and 'the ways in which media products interact with other sources of meaning in constructing perceptions of crime' (Lupton and Tulloch 1999: 512). Here, Lupton and Tulloch's concern has been to 'investigate the basis and meaning of [audiences'] fear, and its location in everyday experiences and narratives' (1999: 515).

The limited (or no causal) effects argument

As the criticisms of media effects research detailed above indicate, there are many critics who refute claims that media violence has a direct, negative impact on viewers' behaviour and attitudes toward others, or their perceptions of the world beyond the television, newspaper, film or computer screen. Scholars critical of media effects theories tend to stress the inadequacies of the research on which they are based. Some of them advocate sociological understandings of behaviour over the psychological theories that tend to dominate effects research, while others object to the sheer weight of influence which effects researchers place on the media as determinants of human behaviour. Buckingham (2000), for example, argues that behaviourist effects research

> fails to prove its central hypothesis: that media violence makes people more aggressive *than they would otherwise have been*, or that it causes them to commit violent acts *they would not otherwise have committed*. It may influence the form or style of those acts, but it is not in itself sufficient cause to provoke them. Sociological research on real-life violence consistently suggests that its causes are multifactorial; and it rarely gives much credence to exaggerated claims about the impact of the media. In this context, to seek for evidence of 'the effects of media violence' is to persist in asking simplistic questions about complex social issues.
>
> (Buckingham 2000: 130, emphasis in the original)

This argument is typical of sociological and cultural theorists' response to media effects research. However, a related criticism of effects arguments is that the research methods on which they are based fail to examine how viewers interpret representations of violence. Miller and Philo (1996) make this point when they state that behavioural effects research is

> unable to study the processes of sense-making which inevitably occur between the media and their audiences: these accounts tend to remain innocent of the notion of 'culture' in which representations circulate, and by which audiences understand and interpret meaning.
>
> (Miller and Philo 1996: 18)

Audience reception research, which examines how audiences make sense of media texts, has consistently demonstrated that they engage with and interpret media content in complex ways. Audiences are capable of reading media content critically, subverting and 'resisting' **dominant ideological readings** of that content, and gaining pleasure from viewing television through 'cognitive processes of "recognition" and "identification"' (Nightingale 1996: 119). In theorizing pleasure, some cultural scholars have conceptualized fictional media content as providing viewers with a fantasy escape from their everyday lives and as having relatively little direct impact how their social or political reality, or their discursive understanding of the world. Thus, in an often-quoted saying, media studies moved the focus from the question of what the media do to people, to what people do with the media.

However, this trend in media research and theory is not without its own weaknesses. In recent years, it has been criticized for promoting a **populist view of audiences** as sovereign consumers responsible for constructing the meaning of media content and an understanding of that content as absolved of **ideology** (Nightingale 1996: 12). Some maintain that this populist view denies that television has any direct influence over viewers' understanding of the world and their position and experiences within it. However, recent research that explores how television audiences interpret programmes about specific issues, such as AIDS, the nuclear debate, and crime and violence, has found that how texts present that material can have a significant impact on viewers' understanding of issues (Corner et al. 1990; Weaver 1995; Miller et al. 1998). Consequently, some cultural and sociological theorists are beginning to demonstrate a new willingness to revisit research exploring how images of violence might influence audiences (see Barker and Petley 2001: 4).

Efforts by cultural and media studies researchers to determine the influence or effects (direct and indirect) of media violence have often centred on attempts to establish causal relationships between representations of violence and situations of violent action in which real people are harmed.

Gauntlett (1998) argues that after several decades of effects research, causal links between violent media content and violent human behaviour still have not been proved. The reason for this failure, he contends, is either that there are none or, alternatively, that media researchers have used the wrong approach in their examinations of the media and audiences. Instead, he suggests, research should focus on '*influences* and *perceptions* rather than *effects* and *behaviour*' (Gauntlett 1998: 128, original emphasis). In his view, recent qualitative media research on audiences which listens to what audiences have to say about media content is the only way out of the binaristic terms of debate initially set out by the effects model (Gauntlett 1998: 128). Since very few studies (if any) appear to be able to empirically establish such causal links, some critics have been led to the conclusion that media violence has little or no effect on audiences. And if no cause and effect can be firmly established, as some proponents of this latter view insist, then following this argument to its logical conclusion leads to an intellectual cul-de-sac: it becomes impossible to object to media violence. Or does it?

It is true that attempts to prove and measure direct relationships between media violence and human behaviour often tend to neglect asking more difficult questions about the contexts in which audiences make sense of media violence. In turn, they fail to consider how media violence shapes audiences' sense of identity and relationships in the social world (see Lupton and Tulloch 1999). Effects research has also failed to come to grips with the complex ways in which, over time, media violence can contribute to the construction of wider (increasingly global) social sensibilities and expectations related to gender, ethnicity, sexuality, class, nationality and so on (see Kamalipour and Rampal 2001). Nevertheless, simply to dismiss research that seeks to address widespread concerns around media violence and its relationship to violence in society takes us back to the rather untenable position of claiming expertise to speak on behalf of media audiences (thereby marginalizing if not silencing those voices). There are very real and often times deeply felt public concerns and fears associated with media violence. To casually or impatiently dismiss these concerns (even when they come from so-called 'moral campaigners') and imply that 'claims about the possible "effects of violent media" are not just false, they range from the daft to the mischievous' misses a crucial point (Barker and Petley 2001: 1). As early as 1990, for example, researchers such as Young (1990) have argued that when assessing women's fears of becoming victims of violent crime, it is important to remember that such fears are not just 'fantasies impressed upon them by the mass media' (Young 1990: 337). Instead, as Lupton and Tulloch (1999) have suggested:

If, for example, women are more afraid of some crimes than men, then this is because they are subjected to higher levels of harassment and threatening behaviours in their everyday lives than appear in official crime statistics . . . Perceived risk may reflect real experiences of assault or harassment. Women's fears should not, therefore, be discounted as 'irrational' but rather be viewed as rational responses to lived situations they find frightening. Likewise, the nonchalance of some men is represented as 'irrational' because they do not adequately assess the higher risk to which they are exposed as being a victim of crime.

(Lupton and Tulloch 1999: 509–10)

In the final section of this introduction, we turn to a consideration of the politics shaping the terms of public debate (including academic) around media violence. What we are suggesting is that there is always something at stake, politically speaking, in choosing to adopt one stance over another.

The politics of the media violence debate

As we have indicated so far in this introduction, the 'media violence debate' has largely presented us with a binaristic model – you are either with 'us' or you are one of 'them'. To argue that there may be both short or longer term negative cultural influences of media violence tends to be met by some media critics with a derisory dismissal or accusations of cultural conservatism. Those who might want to identify with media influence approaches, however critical they might be in their political views, sometimes have been discredited with the labels 'witch hunters' and 'moralists' (Barker and Petley 2001). Such a view urges us to accept that most people 'enjoy and enthusiastically participate in the movies, TV programmes, video games or whatever that the moralists are so certain are "harmful"' (Barker and Petley 2001: 2).

While we would agree that direct, causal effects are difficult, if not impossible (or always desirable) to relate directly to violent media content, we would argue for the continuing import of media effects research that is critically informed (such as that of some cultivation theorists). If there is not support for this kind of work (even if we do not particularly want to do it ourselves), we may well find ourselves in a situation in which we turn a collective blind eye to any and all potential cultural harms cultivated by media violence.

Far too often, the media violence debate is characterized as a zero sum dynamic, in which media and cultural studies scholars are left with only two options. On the one hand, one can try to prove that media violence directly or indirectly affects individuals, encouraging them to behave more violently. The apparent conclusion to be drawn is that media violence is one of the main contributors to our increasingly violent societies. We would then have to agree with US psychologist Johnson that 'by decreasing exposure to media violence, we may be able to prevent millions of Americans from being raped and murdered' (cited in Kolata 2002). On the other hand, one can seek to support the line of argument that media violence has no (or very few) negative effects on audiences. Here the conclusion is that media violence is not a problem since audiences do not by and large mimic the behaviour of those they see or read about in the media. If society is now more violent than it was in the past – a big 'if' in their eyes – the media have had little or nothing to do with it.

One of the reasons we wanted to write this book is that we believe that the conceptual and methodological redevelopment of media violence research is now long overdue. What is urgently needed is a radical rethink of the terms of a debate that has become intransigently binaristic. We reject all attempts to force researchers into opposing camps. Let us be quite clear, however. We do not agree with the view that media violence in itself is the sole or predominant cause of social violence. We regard this position as intellectually inadequate (of course, there will always be specific incidents when violent content in the media is the catalyst behind specific violent acts – so-called 'copycat' crimes).

In our view, it would be wrong to conclude, however, that there is no cause for concern about media violence and that it never or rarely has any effect (negative or otherwise) on anyone. Although it is not possible and often not productive to try to prove that violent representations directly lead to violent action in a chain of cause and effect, there are certainly fundamental and intricate connections between representation and human attitudes. Representations are not the same as 'the real' or people's lived experiences in everyday life – we certainly appreciate the distinction. However, such connections demand that we continue to take media representation seriously. The range, availability and accessibility of media in western societies grew enormously over the course of the twentieth century. The media play an increasingly important role in shaping us all both individually and collectively in society. We may not know exactly what types of influence the media have on us, but it is still worth trying to find out how the media might contribute to shaping our perceptions of ourselves and others and our hierarchical relations to each other in the world.

Of course, as Barker and Petley (2001) suggest, what each of us means by 'violence' varies, sometimes enormously. This point seems rather obvious; it is not possible to view media violence as a singular 'thing'. However, we do not agree that so-called 'moral campaigners' as well as 'effects researchers' always view violence in this way – as something that 'might grow cumulatively like poison inside people' (Barker and Petley 2001: 3). We find it hard to understand how it is possible to simultaneously argue for the multi-accentuality of the sign 'violence' (that there is no one definition) while at the same time defining 'moral campaigners' and 'effects researchers' as homogeneous groups who also display homogeneity across groups. We find such a binarism to be intellectually unproductive.

We are also puzzled as to how it might be possible to separate out the meaning of violence in the media from the 'moral codes that different audiences bring to bear as they watch' (Barker and Petley 2001: 7). It seems to us that this argument rests upon an assumption that moral codes somehow develop independently from representations of media violence (and other types of representation). We unequivocally accept that media violence must be understood in the context of audience sense-making practices, but disagree that there is little to be gained from trying to comprehend certain preferred (ideological/hierarchical) meanings that are inscribed via media texts. In our view, understanding how the media contribute ideologically to the hegemonic (re)production of unequal distributions of social power within and across societies media remains a crucial task for critical media and cultural studies research.

One of the things we are trying to do with this book is to contribute to the work of cutting a critically informed path between the 'limited or no media effects' and 'powerful media effects' models that have long held considerable sway in media and cultural studies research. To go beyond these models requires an intellectual reorientation and a repoliticization of the entire field of study, rather than thinking that it is probably good enough to simply retheorize what we mean by media violence. In our view, media researchers now need to focus on the extent to which everyday representations of violence in the media help, over time, to normalize and legitimize the presence and use of violence in society. Media violence can never be simply reduced to the representation of individual acts of violence and individual responses. We argue that researchers should examine how media violence is implicated in the structural legitimization of the place and position of dominant groups in society.

In seeking to contribute to the development of this political critique, our inquiry begins in Chapter 1 with an evaluative assessment of certain key issues in media and cultural studies research on the news and journalism. In its more critical forms, a central concern of this research has been to understand how news reports of violence help to shape public conceptions of the world as a place that is consistently, even inevitably violent. Some researchers have argued that such conceptions contribute, in turn, to the legitimization of various forms of state sanctioned 'social control'. We have selected three substantive areas of research into news reporting through which to explore these issues. The first one critically assesses research on war examining how journalists have contributed to a sanitization of state violence. This is followed by an overview of studies investigating social struggles, where we look at analyses of news reporting of racially motivated police brutality, 'race riots' and the anti-globalization movement. We end the chapter with a review of research on news accounts of sexual violence.

Film violence is the focus of Chapter 2. Filmmakers have always encouraged audiences to enjoy cinema's ability to show larger than life and spectacular scenes of violence. Our chapter on violence in film considers how cinema's violent imagination has evolved over time, along with attendant changes to its regulation. We also consider debates about how film depictions of violence inflect, and respond to, changing social and political attitudes and ideologies, especially with regard to concerns about the effects of watching violence on film viewers. What quickly becomes apparent in this discussion is that not all film violence is considered to be equally dangerous for all viewers. Portrayals of violence against cherished social institutions, such as the police and the state, for example, are likely to be considered to have the potential to induce violent behaviour in viewers. Yet, the portrayal of violence against women and people of colour, for example, is not seen as having the same worrying outcomes.

Turning to television, Chapter 3 examines why representations of violence in this medium have aroused concern, especially in relation to the alleged effects on children. We examine how children's programmes have been criticized for their violent content, and explore research into how children interpret images of violence. Placing concerns about the impacts of television on children in a wider context, we then outline the argument that these concerns are actually less about television than they are about protecting and constructing notions of childhood innocence. As we show, television broadcasting policy is increasingly likely to be built around these notions. Moving to consider adult television content, we assess how police crime drama, reality crime shows and sports programming variously construct violence and what meanings viewers are encouraged to take from representations of violence in these genres. Research into how adults engage with television violence has found that it can play a significant role in how people understand their lives and relate to their social environments. As we explain, research has especially identified television violence as impacting differently on men and women.

Attention turns in Chapter 4 to an examination of research on pornography and violence. The chapter starts with a brief discussion about efforts to define pornography and some of the ideological assumptions underpinning these definitions. From there we outline various conceptual frameworks that have informed research in this area. First, we look at libertarian concerns around the protection of pornography as a form of free speech. We then examine conservative perspectives that view pornography as a dangerous incitement to violence against women. From there we move on to consider the views of anti-pornography radical feminists who regard pornography as a form of violence against women (and children). Finally, we take a look at certain cultural studies perspectives making the case for the wider development of feminist sexual expression (even violent pornography in the form of sadomasochism or **SM**) as a way of challenging the violence of the phallic imagery.

In Chapter 5, we investigate studies into the portrayal of violence in advertising. In the context of what appears to be an increasing trend toward the inclusion of violent imagery in advertising texts, it is important to consider how advertising contributes to violent media content more generally. This chapter briefly outlines how the pursuit of advertising revenue provides the basis for the screening of violent programmes because they are thought to attract substantial audiences. We then turn to consider the extent to which advertisements themselves contain violent imagery, as well as how – even when they do not contain explicit violence – they have been theorized as promoting gendered **power relations** which support men's violence against women. We also look at how advertising is used in efforts to promote anti-violence messages, and in campaigns to prevent violence against women. We end this chapter with a brief exploration of one of the latest controversies to hit the advertising and marketing industries, their involvement in the promotion of violent films, music, and computer or video games to children.

In Chapter 6, we outline recent research exploring violence and cyberspace. The chapter begins with a brief discussion about risk and modernity in order to provide a context in which to understand how people are responding to 'cyberviolence'. From there we look at violent computer games, one of the earliest public concerns around computer-mediated violence that goes back to the 1970s but remains relevant today. We then turn to a consideration of what we call cybersexploitation where we assess feminist studies into cybersexual harassment, **flaming** and cyberstalking all of which have threatened to curtail women's democratic participation on the Internet. This discussion is followed by a response to suggestions that the Internet may be a powerful tool that provides **paedophiles** with easier access to child victims. From there we critically assess research on the presence of racist groups on the Internet and their hate websites. The chapter concludes with a short overview of selected legislative responses to cyberviolence in the USA and in Europe. Here we consider how state, police, pressure group and commercial representatives have sought to regulate violent Internet content, as well as and how others have challenged such efforts as being infringements on 'free speech'.

In the book's conclusion (Chapter 7), we return to our argument for the importance of further investigations into the key beneficiaries of the existing system of production, representation and consumption of media violence. We contend that what is now needed is a more nuanced and politically aware understanding of the complex ways in which the growing 'normalcy', 'banality' and 'everydayness' of media violence influence our relationships with each other in the world. At both the local or everyday level, as well as in terms of the level of global interconnections between people, the need for more critically informed research on media violence is, in our view, more urgent than ever.

1 | GRIM NEWS

Events portrayed on television news have generated copycat crimes including mass murder, terrorism . . . workplace violence . . . hate crimes and suicide . . . The notoriety perpetrators receive can itself be a motivating factor for others to imitate violent acts.

(Paul Klite 1999)

President Bush says this is a war between good and evil. You are either with us or against us. But that's exactly what bin Laden says. Isn't it worth pointing this out and asking where it leads?

(Robert Fisk 2001)

Introduction

It is something of a journalistic cliché that if something 'bleeds, it leads'. Historically speaking, Hartley (2000) suggests, western journalism has been a 'profession of violence', its occupational ideology based on the presupposition that 'truth is violence, reality is war, news is conflict . . . Journalism is combat' (Hartley 2000: 40). *New York Times* columnist Michael Wolff shares a similar stance, arguing that some US journalists responded with much enthusiasm to the 2001 bombing campaign in Afghanistan, primarily because it provided them with something 'serious' to report. In his view, these journalists were thinking 'Oh God! Thank God . . . a war . . . It's a real story. It's real journalism. It's a nation challenged' (cited in CNN 2001b).

Wolff appears to be suggesting that what counts as 'real' journalism revolves around violence, particularly with regard to the reporting of war. If this is true, is it possible to discern patterns or trends in the ways the news media cover violence? Is their reporting predominantly fair and balanced? Do journalists typically avoid taking sides? According to some media commentators, questions such as these ones help to pinpoint important tensions worthy of serious attention (see Gitlin 1980; Herman and Chomsky 1988; Naureckas 1990; Walker 1991; Allan 1999; Miller 2000; Rockwell 2000). A key problem, some have pointed out, is that most journalists operate without a well-developed ethical framework for covering violence (Klite 1999; Lynch and McGoldrick 2000; Schechter 2001; Lynch 2002). As a result, it follows, there is a risk that their reporting will contribute to public misunderstandings of the complexities of violent situations.

Researchers investigating these dynamics include Galtung (cited in Schechter 2001). Speaking at a conference devoted to the attendant issues, he outlined a twelve-point list of important factors. Taken together, these points not only highlight where he thinks the reporting of violence has gone wrong, but also indicate a basis for efforts to improve it:

- Decontextualizing violence: focusing on the irrational without looking at the reasons for unresolved conflicts and polarization.
- Dualism: reducing the number of parties in a conflict to two, when often more are involved. Stories that just focus on internal developments often ignore such outside or 'external' forces as foreign governments and transnational companies.
- Manichaenism: portraying one side as good and demonizing the other as 'evil'.
- Armageddon: presenting violence as inevitable, omitting alternatives.
- Focusing on individual acts of violence while avoiding structural causes, like poverty, government neglect and military or police oppression.
- Confusion: focusing only on the conflict area (that is the battlefield or location of violent incidents) but not on the forces and factors that influence the violence.
- Excluding or omitting the bereaved, thus never explaining why there are acts of revenge and spirals of violence.
- Failure to explore the causes of escalation and the impact of media coverage itself.
- Failure to explore the goals of outside interventionists, especially big powers.
- Failure to explore peace proposals and offer images of peaceful outcomes.
- Confusing cease-fires and negotiations without actual peace.
- Omitting reconciliation: conflicts tend to reemerge if attention is not paid to efforts to heal fractured societies. When news about attempts

to resolve conflicts are absent, fatalism is reinforced. That can help engender even more violence, when people have no images or information about possible peaceful outcomes and the promise of healing.

(cited in Schechter 2001)

In general terms, then, what Galtung is arguing is that journalists have often been complicit in making certain violent situations worse, not least because their stories have sometimes been simplistic and unreflexive. If journalists were to address these deficiencies, he suggests, then their reporting would be more socially responsible.

This issue of social responsibility is of central importance, informing as it does the work of a wide range of media scholars attempting to rethink familiar assumptions. Of particular significance, some argue, is the marked tendency in western journalism to assume that certain types of violence (namely those types perpetrated by the military and police representing 'us') are 'legitimate', while other types are deemed to be 'illegitimate' (violence associated with 'them', namely those who challenge 'our' norms, values and beliefs). To pursue this and related lines of critique, this chapter will first provide an overview of what some media researchers have had to say about news reporting of war. In later sections, the discussion will turn to examine news coverage of 'race riots', the anti-globalization movement and, finally, sexual violence.

Sanitizing war

Military and state officials have long believed, as Knightly ([1975] 1999) observes, that it is vitally important to direct public opinion by sanitizing violence, namely so as to maintain public support for military efforts in times of war. When reporters began to cover war from the battlefield in the mid-nineteenth century, he argues, they could see what was happening first hand rather than simply relying on information from government or military sources. Ever since it has been increasingly difficult to hide the horrors of war from the public. Media commentators today frequently point to the news coverage of the war in Vietnam as a turning point. Dubbed the first 'television war', US reporters broadcast the daily realities of battle directly into the nation's living rooms. This type of coverage helped to capture in stark visual terms the growing human costs of the war, and as such was praised – as well as blamed – for helping to erode public support for the conflict (Gitlin 1980; Hallin 1986; Young and Jesser 1997). In the summer of 1965, for example, 61 per cent of US citizens reportedly thought that their government was right to send troops to Vietnam. Three years later, barely 35 per cent held this view (Young and Jesser 1997: 84–5). Some commentators at the time believed that the main lesson the US military took away from Vietnam was that it would never again provide journalists with unlimited access. The horrific realities of battlefield violence, it seemed, were too much for the public to handle.

Researchers have been quick to point out, however, that the mainstream news media largely went along with official definitions about what was happening, and in so doing actually sanitized much of the violence in their daily reports. For example, after the My Lai massacre of March 1968 which left hundreds of Vietnamese civilians dead, Cohen (2001) maintains, 'not one [news] outlet would touch the story'. Journalists sanitized the violence because they feared that failure to do so might offend the families of the soldiers involved. This process of sanitization, it follows, was 'a result of media coziness with government and military sources and network TV policies'. Pictures of US casualties were rarely aired, but those of Vietnamese civilian victims were virtually non-existent. Even when the news media became more critical in its coverage, Cohen maintains, much of the reporting failed to call into question 'the war's morality or its effects on the Vietnamese population, two million of whom were ultimately killed.' Instead, many journalists were preoccupied with the issue of whether or not the war was 'winnable'.

British news coverage of the Falklands/Malvinas war in 1982 provides another telling example of the sanitization of state-legitimized violence. During this conflict with Argentina over the ownership of the islands, the UK government under Prime Minister Margaret Thatcher took direct control of communications and censored anything that she and her officials felt might undermine British military efforts. According to Young and Jesser (1997: 98), the British government used 'deception, misinformation, disinformation and media manipulation' to support its war aims. A typical form of deception was to misrepresent the number of casualties suffered by both sides, thereby making the conflict seem much less violent than it actually was (see also Morrison and Tumber 1988).

This is not to suggest, however, that the relationship between the government and journalists was always harmonious. On 3 May 1982, for example, Conservative Member of Parliament (MP) John Page accused BBC2 *Newsnight* journalist Peter Snow of being 'unacceptably even handed' in his reporting of the conflict. In the 'offending' programme, Snow said:

> There is a stage in the coverage of any conflict where you can begin to discern the level of accuracy of the claims and counter-claims of either

side. Tonight, after two days, we cannot demonstrate that the British have lied to us so far. But the Argentines clearly have ... Until the British are demonstrated either to be deceiving us or to be concealing losses, we can only tend to give a lot more credence to the British version of events.

(cited in Morrison and Tumber 1988: 228)

Page's criticism was shared by his leader, Margaret Thatcher. She was reportedly furious with Snow, accusing him in a House of Commons speech of causing 'offence and ... great emotion among many people' (quoted in Morrison and Tumber 1988: 229). The *Sun* followed up this point on 7 May with the headline:

DARE CALL IT TREASON: THERE ARE TRAITORS IN OUR MIDST

By questioning the government's handling of events, Snow and others like him were being called unpatriotic, even treasonous. After the conflict was over, journalists and officials alike publicly affirmed that there was a need to learn from this event. Both sides shared the perception that public trust had been undermined by misinformation, lies and jingoism. Much was made at the time about the importance of being more open and honest with the public in reporting future conflicts.

By the time of the 'Gulf War' in 1991, however, Young and Jesser (1997: 159) maintain that it had become clear that 'despite the promises of greater media freedom and increased cooperation, the military and the politicians in the US and UK had developed a firm appreciation and acceptance of the benefits of an ever tighter media control'. This time around, the British Army devised a 'press pool' system that submitted journalists to a vetting system by 'Media Response Teams' (MRTs). Those journalists who agreed to uphold the conditions laid down by military officials were allowed into the area of the conflict and given daily briefings. Pool journalists tended to reproduce in their accounts claims that the allied aircraft were imparting 'surgical strikes' with 'pin point precision bombing' so as to leave intact civilian buildings and people. Examples to the contrary were more often than not simply reported as instances of 'collateral damage' (see also Taylor 1995).

The ideological alignment of journalistic definitions of reality with those espoused by government and military officials was established from the outset of the conflict, and only rarely tested. On 22 November 1990, in his speech to American troops stationed in Saudi Arabia, former US President George Bush declared that the invasion of Kuwait was a 'clear act of international aggression to which the world must respond, if necessary by force' (quoted in Wolfsfeld 1997: 171). Bush further claimed that Saddam Hussein was guilty of heinous acts of barbarism, including mass hangings, pulling babies from incubators, shooting children for not displaying his photo, and unleashing a horror on the people of Kuwait. Most of the Republican President's counterparts in the Democratic Party adopted a similar line. Early in 1991, with the US bombing of Iraq underway, Senator Joseph Lieberman confirmed Bush's assessment. Responding to allegations regarding the numbers of Iraqi civilians being killed, he insisted that 'Iraqi propaganda' was at work. In Lieberman's words:

> Journalists are shown what Iraq claims is damage to civilian homes and businesses in Iraq, but they're not shown the horrendous damage that Iraq did to Kuwait. We see Iraqi babies being pulled from the wreckage of a military target in Baghdad, but we never saw Kuwaiti babies being tossed out of incubators in Kuwait.
>
> (cited in Miller 2000)

Some reporters on the scene insisted that Iraqi civilian homes and businesses were being targeted by the US military (which US officials later confirmed, admitting that they had deliberately targeted resources like electricity and water supplies so as to demoralize the civilian population). However, the reason why the world never saw Iraqi soldiers pull Kuwaiti babies from incubators 'is that it never happened – like other nightmarish atrocities ascribed to the Iraqi army by our propagandists' (Miller 2000).

Wolfsfeld (1997) is one of several commentators who have sought to demonstrate how news reports recurrently contributed to the officially sanctioned demonization of Saddam Hussein as a Hitler figure (see also Naureckas 1990). Similarly important in this context was the official definition of the allied military effort as a defensive 'response' to 'Iraqi aggression'. By framing the conflict in these terms, Wolfsfeld (1997: 187) contends, the news story 'met all three criteria for journalistic resonance: it was dramatic [violent], simple, and familiar'. It was a story told within the limits of a good versus evil dynamic, as Kuwait was rescued from an evil dictator and 'democracy' restored in the region. Violence was safely packaged in formats that were palatable to home audiences, thereby shielding them from the harsh realities of death and destruction which might have encouraged awkward questions to be asked about the factors behind the conflict.

Director of the US Institute for Peace and International Security at the Massachusetts Institute of Technology (MIT), Walker (1991) concurs with this line of argument, contending that:

> The first images of the 42-day Mideast war mesmerized most viewers. Iraqi buildings and bunkers ... being surgically destroyed by

precision-guided bombs dropped by stealthy aircraft . . . Hundreds of military news reporters in the Saudi briefing room laughed with nervous interest as if viewing Nintendo games, although thousands of individuals were killed, possibly, by that weapon. High-tech warfare had, indeed, come of age.

(Walker 1991)

In Walker's view, it was such images that invited people in the USA to believe that the war was a 'remote, bloodless, pushbutton battle in which only military targets were assumed destroyed'. Not only was violence against Iraqis being sanitized, however. US casualities and injuries were also largely kept from the public. As Miller (2000) notes:

Eager to idealize high-tech warfare, the Pentagon not only downplayed . . . unheroic incidents [such as US soldiers killed by 'friendly fire'], but hid our wounded from the public. Disfigured troops allege that they were not allowed to join the postwar victory parades in Washington and New York City.

(Miller 2000)

Former US Colonel David Hackworth, working as a journalist during the Gulf War, has argued that the stage management was so successful that it represented a 'media triumph for the military and the administration – a lovely, bloodless, corpseless war, just the sort the politicians love' (cited in Young and Jesser 1997: 181).

Significant in this context is the decision made by the UK Sunday newspaper the *Observer* to publish a photograph of a charred Iraqi soldier in its 1 March 1991 edition. As Taylor (1998: 181) notes, the photograph 'was a horrifying, raw picture of a burned corpse, which the paper captioned 'the real face of war'. The image dispelled the air of unreality about a war with almost no pictorial evidence of death'. Yet the *Observer* was largely alone in deciding to publish such pictures of the US attack on the Iraqi army – most UK newspapers instead chose to publish pictures of charred vehicles shot at some distance so that bodies could not be discerned. No US newspapers picked up the photograph in question. One editor after the next evidently saw it come over the wire and promptly deemed it unsuitable. As Taylor (1998: 183) observes, images that capture the brutality and violence of such horrific attacks do not form part of the 'public record of a "clean" and necessary war'.

Ten years later, western journalists were again facing the prospect of reporting on the horrors of war, this time the 'war on terrorism' following the attacks in New York, Washington DC and Pennsylvania on September 11 2001. Why, then, asked reporter Robert Fisk (2001) at the time, are journalists in both the UK and USA 'falling back on the same sheep-like conformity that we adopted in the 1991 Gulf war and the 1999 Kosovo war? Here we go again'. In Fisk's view, the lessons learned in those two previous wars had apparently been all but forgotten by the time of the bombing campaign of Afghanistan. Journalists were once again using 'soldier-speak' terms like 'collateral damage' to refer to civilian deaths, seemingly without a thought as to how that helps to sanitize the violence. News coverage of the first US missile attacks on Afghanistan avoided the subject of possible civilian deaths, focusing instead on the humanitarian aid (mainly in the form of food packages) being dropped (Fisk 2001).

At stake here, several media commentators have pointed out, is the extent to which journalists are willing to uphold a normative order whereby official distinctions between 'legitimate' and 'illegitimate' violence are normalized (see CNN 2001a). More often than not, the line between the two is hierarchically drawn in strict ideological terms. In western countries many citizens appear to have, at best, a sketchy understanding of the factors underlying the attacks, in part due to the steady decline in the amount of international news coverage available in mainstream media (see Gitlin 2001; Said 2001; Zelizer and Allan 2002). Even a glance at much of the reporting to date suggests that there has been an over-reliance on official definitions of the crisis, thereby leading to the marginalization – if not outright silencing – of alternative voices of dissent. Such restricted forms of reporting have served George W. Bush's administration well. At the time of writing, there appears to be overwhelming public support for the use of military violence to respond to the attacks (92 per cent in a poll taken in October 2001 cited in Said 2001).

Reporting 'violent' social struggles

News researchers have examined a wide array of social struggles, such as strikes (Glasgow University Media Group 1976, 1980, 1982; Philo 1990), anti-nuclear demonstrations (Hollingsworth 1986; Herman and Chomsky 1988; Cummings 1992) and environmental protests (Hansen 1993; Anderson 1997; Allan et al. 2000), among others. A common finding across these studies is that the news media often play a crucial role in constructing such struggles as being inherently threatening to the status quo, whether they actually are or not in practice. Time after time, a minor incident where some form of violence is involved has been used to discredit the aims and objectives of those raising their voices in protest.

Similar strategies are sometimes in play with regard to the reporting of 'racial' conflict. Looking at how ethnic minorities are represented in news **discourse**, Allan (1999: 166) argues that journalists often implicitly link issues around 'race' with those of 'law and order' (see also Lewis 1982; Cottle 1993, 2000). As Allan points out, US Governor Otto Kerner made a similar argument in 1968 in his report to the US National Advisory Commission on Civil Disorders that was struck to investigate the reasons behind the 'race riots' of the mid-1960s. Kerner concluded that the media were complicit in 'exacerbating racial conflicts' during the 'race riots' of the mid-1960s. In his view, journalists 'report and write from the standpoint of a white man's world' and thus contribute to the 'slights and indignities [that] are part of the Negro's daily life' (cited in Allan 1999: 167). Kerner went on to urge US citizens to consider the 'overall treatment by the media of the Negro ghettos, community relations, racial attitudes, urban and rural poverty – day by day and month by month, year in and year out' (cited in Wilson 2000: 86).

Published about ten years later, Hall et al.'s (1978) groundbreaking analysis of UK news reporting of crime and civil unrest came to similar conclusions. One of the important findings of the study was that the press at the time was recurrently labelling certain groups (ethnic minorities, working classes and so on) and their activities as being threatening to the 'moral order', even on occasion violently so. These labels were operating ideologically so as to lend greater authority to state institutions, especially those charged with public responsibility for 'law and order'. As Hall et al. argue:

> Crime issues are clear-cut; political conflicts are double-edged. But a governing class, which can assure the people that a political demonstration will end in a mob riot against life and property has a good deal going for it – including popular support for 'tough measures'. Hence, the 'criminalisation' of political and economic conflicts is a central aspect of the exercise of social control. It is often accompanied by heavy ideological 'work', required to shift labels about until they stick, extending and widening their reference, or trying to win over one labelled section against another.
>
> (Hall et al. 1978: 189)

From the 1970s, critics began to document how the news media consistently constructed the activities of certain ethnic minority groups as potential 'threats' to social stability and the 'legitimate' exercise of power by the state and its representatives (police, courts, etc.). Clearly, it is the daily repetition of this message that has had a far-reaching negative influence on social attitudes around 'race'.

Moving ahead to the 1990s, one particularly infamous event stands out in many people's recollections about the ways in which the news media report ethnic minorities. On 3 March 1991, 21 Los Angeles Police Department (LAPD) officers, as well as 4 California Highway Patrol (CHIP) officers, either took part in or watched as fellow officers brutally beat an unarmed African-American man, Rodney King, after he was stopped for speeding. King was reportedly given 56 baton blows, 6 kicks and several taser shocks in a period of 2 minutes, resulting in 11 skull fractures, as well as brain and kidney damage. This shockingly violent incident became a major, international media event, primarily because a man named George Holliday, who was standing on a balcony of a nearby building, captured it on videotape. The following day, Holliday gave his 81-second tape to Los Angeles TV Channel 5 (after having tried to give it to the LAPD, which allegedly refused to accept it). By the end of the day, it was being broadcast worldwide. According to Cannon (1998), the 'short, brutal clip riveted the nation and became an instant symbol of racism and police brutality in America'.

By 15 March 1991, four police officers were arrested and charged with assault with a deadly weapon and use of excessive force – all pleaded not guilty. At the request of the defence, the trial was moved out of South Central Los Angeles, which is the multicultural community where the incident occurred, to the predominantly white, middle-class suburb of Simi Valley where many people have friends or family who are police officers. Court officials dismissed as irrelevant the charge of the 'pro-police bias' of the area. At the same time, no challenge was raised to the fact that none of the jurors was African-American. Not surprisingly, the videotape became a crucial bit of evidence in the trial. Jurors soon discovered, however, that the news media were playing only an edited version. Evidently the first three seconds of the unedited version of the tape apparently showed King charging toward one of the police officers. As Cannon (1998) notes:

> the prosecution in Simi Valley was put at a definite disadvantage by the prior editing of the videotape on television. When the full videotape was played during the trial, it reinforced the perception of conservative jurors that the media had not told the full story of Rodney King.
>
> (cited in Leibovich 1998)

After seeing the unedited tape, jurors were apparently shocked, since all of them had only ever seen the edited version on television. According to Cannon, the jurors sat with 'mouths . . . agape. They are saying the mental equivalent of "ah-ha" ' (cited in Leibovich 1998). Of course they assumed, wrongly in our view, that the tape somehow proved that King had provoked the attack, perhaps due in part to their feelings of being betrayed and manipulated by the media's edited version. On 29 April 1992, the jury acquitted the four police officers.

Almost immediately, thousands of people in South Central Los Angeles responded angrily to the verdict. So-called 'rioting' started in South Central and spread to other areas of the city over the following days. City officials called upon federal troops and the California National Guard in order to contain the crowds. After 6 days, 54 people were dead, 2383 injured and 13,212 arrested. Estimates of property damage range to figures as high as $900 million (Cannon 1998). 'Rioting' also occurred in several other cities around the USA but none as serious as those in Los Angeles.

More than one commentator has argued that the US news media were partly to blame for racist responses to the full videotape. The ways in which Channel 5, in particular, edited Holliday's videotape not only highlighted the brutality of the violence, but also made it more sensational and inexplicable. In effect, the edits helped to make the violence more 'newsworthy' while, at the same time, making its legal significance more difficult to interpret. Regarding the latter point, the shortened version of the tape not only contributed to the bewilderment and outrage many felt about the verdict of the trial, but also would eventually undermine King's claim of police brutality.

It is worth noting that a 1992 task force report on the news media coverage of the LA 'riots' undertaken by the National Association of Black Journalists concluded that 'in only relatively few cases did Black journalists direct coverage or participate in front-page decisions' (cited in Wilson 2000: 98). One Latino journalist, Hector Torbar, was asked to write the first front-page story reporting on the 'riots' for the *Los Angeles Times* where he had been working as a general reporter for several years. However, Torbar claims that his editor removed all of the references to 'race' from the lead of his story (Torbar tried to make a connection between King's beating, the 'riots' and the institutional racism of the police) because of the 'climate' at the time (cited in Williams 2001). Looking back at what he reported on the first day of the LA 'riots', Hector writes:

Re-reading the story over the years, I noticed that there is a sort of an inverted pyramid of sources. The official sources of the story rise to the top, the unofficial sources, witnesses, civil rights activists fall over in the story. That to me is a function of the power relations in place in shaping how news is formed. Part of it is, my own self-conscious, internal editor aware of the peculiar suspicions, skepticism in the way we write about minority communities. The other is the way the editor came to edit it.

(cited in D. Williams 2001)

What is clear is that a generation after the Kerner Report in 1968, in the 1990s, journalists of colour still had relatively few opportunities to challenge the dominant white, hegemonic view of the world that informs most western journalism despite their increased visibility, particularly in television news. As Rhodes (2001) concludes, 'covert racial discrimination is still alive and well in the newsroom' (2001: 51). Has this incident had any lasting effects on the ways in which the news media report on ethnic minorities? Most major news organizations still largely comprise white journalists writing from the standpoint of a white world. In making the argument that the reporting of minorities has not improved since the Rodney King incident, African-American journalist Earl Caldwell states:

> In my mind, it hasn't changed. It's just as bad. It might even be worse. The media cover minority communities on the basis that they covered Rodney King, only for extraordinary things. Day to day stuff, they write things largely as they did in 1968, like it's a white man's world. Nothing's changed.
>
> (cited in Sutherlin 2001a)

Fellow journalist Austin Long-Scott agrees, saying that: 'So the big question to me is OK, we hear about the big ones, what's going on out there everyday that we don't hear about?' (cited in Sutherlin 2001b; see also hooks 1992; Hunt 1997; McLaughlin 1998; Wilson 2000; Rhodes 2001).

From our discussion around news reporting of 'race' and violence, we now turn our attention to the ways in which the news media have reported the contemporary anti-globalization movement. Here, as we shall see, much of the coverage assumes that protests against the state or corporations will be violent, even before they actually take place.

To understand how and why much of the news coverage of the anti-globalization movement is currently being framed, it is helpful to briefly look back at some of the lessons learned from journalists' coverage of the anti-Vietnam war movement in the 1960s. Gitlin (1980) has noted in his groundbreaking study of the US anti-war organization, the Students for a Democratic Society (SDS), that while initially the press had pretty much ignored them, in the Spring of 1965 'deprecatory themes began to emerge, then to recur and reverberate' (Gitlin 1980: 27). One of those themes was an 'emphasis on violence', a framing device that eventually meant that the movement was:

> Bit by bit . . . surrounded by a firebreak of discrediting images, images partly but *only* partly of its own making. The specter of violence hovered over media representations before it became a popular movement

itself. But the media, with their agenda-setting power, are not simply prophetic; their images can be, in important measure, self-fulfilling.

(Gitlin 1980: 183, original emphasis)

For example, on 7 May 1967, the *New York Times* ran a story by Paul Hoffman headlined:

THE NEW LEFT TURNS TO MOOD OF VIOLENCE IN PLACE OF PROTEST

(cited in Gitlin 1980: 183)

In the article, Hoffman interpreted SDS leader Gregory Calvert's call for student 'sedition' to mean 'violence' when Calvert merely meant he was asking students to become more radicalized in their opposition to the war. Calvert later noted that Hoffman's article was a deliberate effort to 'raise the spectre of violence on the part of the "radical" movement' so as to discredit its aims (cited in Gitlin 1980: 184). In discrediting the movement as violent, Gitlin (1980: 183) argues, the media thus applied the 'full weight of its credibility to containment-through-innuendo'. That containment, of course, served the purposes of the ruling elite who used the media to assure 'the country that, in the end, the system had worked' (Gitlin 1980: 192).

Is the media's coverage of today's anti-globalization movement much different from that of the anti-war movement in the 1960s? To address this issue, we shall begin by outlining how and why the anti-globalization movement has emerged before moving on to look at the ways in which the media have reported its activities.

The 1990s saw the emergence of anti-globalization groups who began to stage large-scale (as well as many smaller, localized) demonstrations against capitalism (Figure 1.1). According to Klein (2000), from the mid-1990s there was a growing political backlash, particularly among young people, to the 'brutalities of free-market globalization' (Klein 2000: 445). By the late 1990s, various groups around the world had made connections with each other, often via the Internet, realizing that while their individual struggles may differ, they shared a belief in the need to seize globalization from the hands of multinational corporations. The message that anti-globalization protesters were trying to make clear, almost always by peaceful means, was that they felt global corporations were responsible for widening gaps between rich and poor in the world.

In the UK, anti-globalization demonstrations came about partly through a coalition of various groups who were protesting over the implementation of a new Criminal Justice Act in 1994. The Act made raves illegal, gave police more powers to evict squatters and to crack down on nomadic New

Protests erupt in violence

'Guerrilla gardening' action turns ugly with looted shops and battles with police

Will Woodward, Paul Kelso and John Vidal

A protest against capitalism in central London involving 4,000 people descended into ugly scenes of violence yesterday when shops were looted and bricks and bottles were hurled at police.

For the first three hours of the "guerrilla gardening" action protesters did not intervene as activists dug up the grassy area of Parliament Square and daubed paint and graffiti on monuments including the Cenotaph and a statue of Sir Winston Churchill. But hundreds of officers in riot gear were brought in to break up the demonstrators after a McDonald's restaurant and a bureau de change on Whitehall were broken into and wrecked shortly after 2pm.

Police contained the protests in Parliament Square and Trafalgar Square for several hours before allowing protesters to leave. But fighting between demonstrators and police continued into the evening. The windows of a Carphone Warehouse and a Rymans store were smashed along the Strand. Officers followed a group of about 400 from Parliament Square to Kennington Park, south London, where, after stones were thrown, they once again surrounded them.

Tony Blair last night said the perpetrators were "beneath contempt". He added: "The people responsible for the damage caused in London today are an absolute disgrace. Their actions have got nothing to do with convictions or beliefs and everything to do with mindless thuggery."

The Metropolitan police said its operation, the biggest in the capital for a political demonstration for 30 years, had been "professional and proportionate".

Police made 42 arrests. Nine members of the public and one policeman, who was hit in the face by a brick, were taken to hospital. Eight other police were injured. But the violence and damage were nowhere near the scale of the assault on the City on June 18 last year, which had caught police unawares.

The violence this afternoon was not about peaceful and lawful protest, and we have had to change our policing style accordingly to ensure both officer and public safety," said Michael Todd, deputy assistant commissioner of the Metropolitan police.

From 11am police stood back as supporters of the Reclaim the Streets "dis-organisation" took over Parliament Square. Activists dug up most of the grassy area of the square opposite the Commons, putting down plants and seeds and digging ponds. Turf was ripped up and put on the road. Protesters hung banners from lamp-posts and forced police to block through traffic.

At about 1.40pm most of the demonstrators' headed up Whitehall, where bottles were thrown at riot police guarding Downing Street.

Further on, a group of 13 police officers, some with cameras, was forced back by a small group of demonstrators and at 2.05pm a small McDonald's restaurant at the north end of the road on Whitehall, which was closed, was smashed and looted.

Staff fled to safety at the back of the building as, to cheers from the crowd, two protesters pounded the windows until they smashed and then one protester, wearing a black scarf over his face, smashed the McDonald's sign. Paint was thrown over the yellow "M" sign, and smoke bombs were let off inside the building. There were roars as a demonstrator brought out the till, wielding it above his head, and then food was thrown into the street.

Shortly after, a store next door, both a souvenir shop and a bureau de change, had its windows smashed with staff still inside. Goods from the shop were thrown to the crowd.

At 2.30pm riot police charged the crowd. In a well-practised manoeuvre similar to that used at a Reclaim the Streets protest at Euston sta-

tion on November 30 last year, police rushed in from a side road and split the demonstration, pushing about 3,000 towards Trafalgar Square and the rest towards Parliament Square.

Other police in riot gear sealed off the exits to both squares, which at Trafalgar Square included several hundred tourists.

Entrances to Westminster and Charing Cross underground stations were closed, as was the National Gallery. Demonstrators threw bottles and cans at riot police and an officer was punched. Trafalgar Square was daubed with graffiti. Some tried to storm St Martin's-in-the-Fields church.

By 4.20pm Whitehall was cleared of demonstrators. Shortly afterwards, following an 11-minute stand-off, police began to allow the crowd to leave Parliament Square. At about 6pm, police "retook" Nelson's Column.

The "guerrilla gardening" action was on the fourth day of a series of events over the May Day holiday in opposition to global capitalism. Yesterday's event was the most heavily advertised and, as protesters had acknowledged, some violence was expected.

Some 5,500 officers policed yesterday's event, with 9,000 on duty elsewhere. But no more than a sprinkling of officers were in Parliament Square for the start of the protest. They did not react when a protester jumped on a police van and intervened only to help a woman whose car had been surrounded in Great George Street.

In Manchester city centre about 200 Reclaim the Streets supporters tried to storm the Arndale centre. Eight people were arrested.

Three people were arrested yesterday by British Transport police at their home addresses in Bedfordshire in connection with the riot at Euston on November 30.

> 'The people responsible for the damage in London today are an absolute disgrace. Their actions have got nothing to do with convictions or beliefs and everything to do with mindless thuggery'
>
> Tony Blair

Austin

YOU'RE UNDER ARREST.

Riot police with batons try to break up the May Day demonstration in Trafalgar Square Photograph: Dylan Martinez

Figure 1.1. 'Protests Erupt in Violence', Will Woodward, Paul Kelso and John Vidal, cartoon by Austin, and photograph by Dylan Martinez.

Source: © *Guardian*, 2 May 2000.

Age travellers, as well as eco-warriors who were fighting new road-building schemes (see Wykes 2000). It was the coming together of these and other 'single issue' groups that eventually led to the formation of what Klein (2000: 312) refers to as the 'fastest growing political movement since Paris '68: Reclaim the Streets (RTS)'. In May 1995, about 500 people showed up to the first RTS party/protest in London to 'dance to a bicycle-powered sound system, drums and whistles' while they challenged the growing power of multinational corporations. The following year about 3000 attended the event.

In 1997, the RTS party/protest attracted over 20,000 people to Trafalgar Square in central London. Partly a victim of its own success, there were a few protesters who reacted angrily to police when they attempted to impound a van that housed a sound system. RTSer John Jordan stated to the *Daily Telegraph* at the time, 'I saw some of our people actually trying to stop yobbos who had got tanked up on beer and were mindlessly throwing bottles and rocks. A few of our contingent actually put themselves into the firing line and one was beaten up' (cited in Klein 2000: 318). While some newspapers were able to make the distinction between the majority of peaceful protesters and the minority 'yobbos', many journalists took the opportunity to brand the RTS event as a violent demonstration. Thus, for example, the *Daily Express* headline on 13 April 1997 was:

RIOT FRENZY – ANARCHIST THUGS BRING TERROR TO LONDON

Ever since, some elements of the press have remained interested in these events mainly for their potential to offer stories of violent protest rather than to take seriously what RTSers and other groups are trying to say about the nefariousness of global capitalism.

For example, on 2 May 2000, the press reacted in a similar fashion to a largely peaceful protest occurring in London during the previous day's Mayday celebrations. After three days of collective action against global capitalism, the *Guardian* defined the Mayday events with the following headline:

PROTESTS ERUPT IN VIOLENCE: 'GUERRILLA GARDENING' ACTION TURNS UGLY WITH LOOTED SHOPS AND BATTLES WITH POLICE

The Independent's front-page headline read:

VIOLENCE FLARES IN LONDON AS MAY DAY PROTESTS TURN UGLY

Looking across the press coverage, reports by and large tended to focus on the aggressive activities of a very small number of people. A man who took part in the May Day event remarked on this when interviewed the following day on BBC Radio 4's pre-eminent morning news programme *Today*. There he suggested that it was only when violence erupted that the news media became interested in the event.

Sexual violence and the politics of blame

In their influential study *The Lust to Kill*, Cameron and Frazer (1987) argue that representations of sexual violence are endemic to western culture, having roots deeply embedded in **patriarchy**. In their view, the popular press has long drawn upon a traditional (male) fascination with sexual violence, symbolized by figures like 'Jack the Ripper' in the nineteenth century and Peter Sutcliffe (the 'Yorkshire Ripper') in the 1980s. Significantly, they argue, such men have become 'cultural heroes' by some accounts (both men having 'cleaned up the streets' of prostitutes). In addition to countless news stories, the number of books, films and even websites devoted to their crimes continues to proliferate. As Cameron and Frazer (1987) maintain, media portrayals of the actions of serial sexual murders function on multiple levels, namely because of their perceived entertainment value.

Particularly pertinent here, as Cameron and Frazer observe, are the ways in which news narratives about sexual murder mark out the boundaries of 'acceptable' behaviour for each gender, typically putting women firmly in a subordinate position to men. If women remain fearful of physical violence from men, they are less likely to demand wide-ranging changes to gendered power relations. The often sensationalized ways in which sexual violence is reported, Cameron and Frazer suggest, helps to reproduce women's fears of victimization, thereby encouraging them to feel a sense of diminished power in their relationships with men (see also Weaver et al. 2000). This line of argument finds an echo in Soothill and Walby's (1991) research, where they agree that sensationalized reporting of sexual violence has long been a staple feature of the British press. Comparing sex crimes stories from the 1950s through to the 1980s, the authors found that in the 1950s and 1960s, most sex crime stories appeared in the popular press but that from the 1970s 'quality' newspapers began to show a marked interest in printing them. They partly explain this shift by suggesting the period of their study was marked by an enormous increase in competition between newspaper titles. As competition increased, they believe, sexual violence stories have tended to become more common features in all newspapers as they have also become more explicit and horrific in detail.

In the fiercely competitive news culture of the USA, Benedict's (1992) examination of sex crimes news reaches similar conclusions. Analysing the content and language that journalists use in these stories, she found that women are typically blamed for the violence used against them. However, not all victims are reported in the same way. Benedict's analysis discerned that white, middle-class victims are more favourably described than working-class women and women of colour. Another important finding of her study was that in her interviews with journalists about their reporting of sex crimes, she discovered that many had become increasingly less sympathetic towards victims in recent years but was unable to discern why this might be the case. Benedict (1992) concluded that by the 1990s, US journalists had become more insistent that victims had to appear to be 'virginal', 'good' and 'innocent' in order to be represented as 'undeserving' of their fate.

Cuklanz's (1996, 2000) research on the reporting of rape on US television news similarly found that sexual violence was being dramaticized. Moreover, pertinent news stories were typically being structured into individualistic and adversarial patterns. What she means by this is that in television news, journalists tend to view each individual rape case as a unique incident in which it is 'her word against his word'. The way these cases are reported, Cuklanz believes, does not allow news audiences to gain an understanding of the structural explanations for rape. Moreover, she argues, the television news format reinforces traditional models for understanding rape (women are to blame). As such, the presentation of rape stories often leads to a questioning of the honesty of the victim (Is she lying? Is she falsely accusing?) and her sexual history (Is she promiscuous? Was she 'asking for it'?). As Cuklanz (1996: 84) contends, 'In its penchant for case-specific facts, the [televisual] news media seldom discussed the larger social issues or problems, such as relations of power and gender, that created the conditions for verdicts in the respective cases'. Similarly relevant here are Meyers' (1995, 1997) studies of sex crime news in both the US press and television. Like Cuklanz, she maintains that journalists represent incidents of violence against women in ways that are 'socially distorted'. In other words, their reports are rooted in myths and stereotypes about women and men that blame individual pathology for the violence, instead of situating it as the end result of unequal – and gendered – social structures in society.

Research in the UK appears to largely concur with the findings of US studies. For example, Clark's (1992) linguistic examination of the British tabloid newspaper the *Sun* looks at how its use of language in sex crime stories conveys blame. In her analysis, the tabloid's coverage at the time tended to create a false dichotomy between male attackers who were effectively dehumanized (labelled as a 'fiend', 'monster', 'ripper' and 'crazed killer', among other terms) and those whom the paper deemed to be 'normal' (where labels like 'hubby', 'man' and 'daddy' were used). According to Clark, men who fall into the first group are deemed to have done something so terrible that they are no longer 'real men' – discursively speaking, they are no longer human. Those in the second group are less likely to be held culpable for their violence. For the most part, she suggests, victims are blamed for making these men become violent since they are otherwise decent individuals. By dichotomizing men in this way, it follows, the *Sun* fails to adequately represent the continuum of men's violence against women. Moreover, Clark (1992) notes, the newspaper tends to report a higher number of 'stranger attacks' despite the fact that official statistics tell us that women are most likely to be harmed by someone they already know. It is recurrently the case that the everyday incidents of domestic violence some women experience are not deemed to be sufficiently newsworthy by journalists to warrant attention (see Finn 1989–90; Meyers 1995, 1997; Carter et al. 1998).

In seeking to investigate why this is so, Carter's (1995, 1998) research explores the ideological assumptions underpinning news reports. Her findings suggest that there are certain seemingly 'commonsensical' prescriptions of 'normalcy' shaping the narrative structure of these stories. Particularly salient here are the ways in which ideological configurations of 'normalcy' are intertwined with discourses about the 'ideal', 'traditional' family (white, middle-class, nuclear family). Victims who are reported in news accounts as being 'good', family-oriented people tend not to be blamed for experiencing sexual violence. At the same time, however, blame for sexual violence is far more likely to be apportioned to female victims who are constructed as having somehow transgressed the 'normal', 'decent' boundaries of 'acceptable' behaviour (see also Benedict 1992; Meyers 1995, 1997; Allan 1999).

Jermyn's (2001: 348) research reaches similar types of conclusions. Her analysis of British newspaper coverage of the murder of Jill Dando, television presenter on the BBC crime reconstruction programme *Crimewatch*, offers several pertinent insights. Specifically, Jermyn notes how newspapers referred to Dando as 'a nice ordinary girl' whom every parent hoped their son would marry (journalists widely commented on the fact Dando was finally on the verge of fulfilling her lifelong dream to wed, only to be murdered before she could realize it). On the day after her death, the *Daily Mail*'s front page (27 April 1999) simply read:

DEATH OF THE GIRL NEXT DOOR

As a 'nice girl', Dando was discursively constructed as beyond blame for her murder. However, during the trial of Barry George, who was charged in May

Figure 1.2 'Dando suspect: was he driven mad by sexy pose?'
Source: *Daily Star*, 26 May 2000.

2000 and convicted in July 2001 of her murder, the *Daily Star* called Dando's status as a 'nice girl' into question with its front-page headline (26 May 2000):

DANDO SUSPECT: WAS HE DRIVEN MAD BY SEXY POSE?

The accompanying article and photo of Dando in a black leather outfit (Figure 1.2) explains that the murder suspect 'is believed to have been enraged by this picture of her in racy leather gear' (it had originally appeared on the cover of the BBC *Radio Times* television guide in April 1999). Yet nowhere in the *Daily Star* is it explained precisely what is meant by the term 'enraged'. The item then goes on to ask 'Is this the sexy pose which could have driven suspect to kill his 'pure and wholesome' TV favourite?' (Paul and McJannet 2000). What is being implied here, at least in our reading, is that perhaps Dando was partly to blame for her own death. By agreeing to dress in black leather to pose for the *Radio Times* cover, the item is suggesting that she was calling into question her own purity, wholesomeness and need for patriarchal protection. If she was not virginal, then she could be blamed for confusing George, for leading him on and making him think she was one type of woman (virginal, passive, dependent) when in fact she was another (sexual, assertive, independent).

Accordingly, to be regarded as a 'nice girl' and hence qualify as a 'good victim', a woman cannot dress in a way that might be construed as somehow inviting an attack. She cannot be seen to be openly sexual, but rather must be regarded as 'pure and wholesome'. This when the great paradox for women, as we discuss in Chapter 5, is that via media representations – not least through advertising – they are routinely encouraged to believe that their route to self-fulfilment is by being sexually desirable to men. However, as we have seen in this section's discussion, women are much more likely to be blamed for their own victimization, even death, if it is thought that they somehow failed to contain their sexuality within patriarchal limits.

Conclusion

As we have seen in this chapter, the reporting of violence has long been a central feature of western news reporting. Reporters still tend to view violent events, particularly war, as the 'real stuff' of journalism. Many of the great men (and some women) of journalism history have been correspondents who risked their lives to report from the 'front line' (in times of war and social conflict). While to some extent it is true that news audiences are interested in stories about war, crime, social unrest and interpersonal violence, what is apparent is that such tastes have been cultivated over the long period of western journalism history. Moreover, stories about violence are never politically neutral or objective. Journalists like everyone else come from somewhere and have been influenced in various ways by people they have met, things that they have read and experiences they have had in their lives. While most journalists may strive to be fair and balanced in their reporting, media research has clearly shown for many decades now that there are patterned ways violence is covered, in ways that often legitimise the views and actions of those in positions of power in society. As we have seen in this chapter, where less powerful groups are concerned (ethnic minorities, young people and women) coverage tends to reinforce and reproduce their marginalization. As we have tried to demonstrate, reporters tend to construct some groups as inherently violent and therefore as 'threats' to social stability while others are blamed for inciting violence which is then used against them.

In the next chapter, we turn our attention from factual representations of violence to fictional ones. Specifically, we look at film violence and explore the factors behind cinema's increasingly graphic and brutal depictions.

Further reading

Allan, S. (1999) *News Culture*. Buckingham: Open University Press.

Cottle, S. (ed.) (2000) *Ethnic Minorities and the Media*. Buckingham: Open University Press.

Kamalipour, Y.R. and Kampal, K.R. (eds) (2001) *Media, Sex, Violence and Drugs in the Global Village*. Lanham, MD: Rowman and Littlefield.

Meyers, M. (1997) *News Accounts of Violence against Women: Engendering Blame*. Thousand Oaks, CA: Sage.

Zelizer, B. and Allan, S. (2002) *Journalism after September 11*. London: Routledge.

2 | FEARS OF FILM

It's the emotionlessness of so many violent movies that I'm becoming anxious about . . . there's something deeply wrong about anyone's taking for granted the dissociation that this carnage without emotion represents.

(Pauline Kael [1974] 1996a: 178)

I'm always attacked for having an erotic, sexist approach – chopping up women, putting women in peril. I'm making suspense movies! What else is going to happen to them?

(Brian De Palma quoted in Caputi 1988: 91)

Introduction

If there is one medium that has produced the most brutal, macabre, bloody and excessive scenes of violence, and to which controversy about such representations inevitably returns, it is film. In many respects, violence has played a central role in the history of cinema, concerns about the social impacts of film, and the relationship that many of us have developed with the medium. Indeed, it has been said that 'without violence cinema would not have amounted to much at all' (Male 1997: 30), that 'violence is . . . of central importance for the popular appeal of film' (Prince 2000b), and that 'cinema and guns were made for each other' (Jacobs 2000: 9).

In this chapter, we explore the history of violence in Hollywood film from cinema's beginnings to the present day. We identify how social, cultural and economic contexts of film production, as well as trends in filmmaking, have factored in the ongoing development of cinema's violent imagination. We also identify concerns about the effects of film violence on audiences, the **censorship** and regulation of that violence, and attempts to explain viewers' attraction and responses to violence in films. By exploring the history of cinema violence through these perspectives, we illustrate how the controversies that surround film depictions of violence today are in many ways identical to those that have always surrounded cinema's violent representations. Yet, our aim is also to demonstrate how any one film portrayal of violence is intricately bound to the specific social and cultural conditions of its production and reception.

Picturing violence in silent cinema

From the earliest days of cinema in the late nineteenth century, both filmmakers and audiences demonstrated a fascination for portrayals of violence. Indeed, violent imagery was prominent in many films that were significant to the technical and/or stylistic development of the movies. For example, the early kinetescope film *The Execution of Mary Queen of Scots* (1895) demonstrated the 'special effects' potential of stop-motion photography by depicting Mary's beheading. When filming the execution William Heise stopped the camera, substituted a dummy for the actress, and beheaded the stand in (Musser 1990: 86–7). Solomon (1972: 92) suggests that 'original audiences must have been completely bewildered by the head rolling off what they must have thought was an actress'. However, Gunning (1994: 120) argues that this 'aesthetic of astonishment' was actually part of the 'conscious delectation of shocks and thrills' that viewers sought from early cinema, which he defines as the 'cinema of attractions'.

Cinema's first narrative fiction film also overtly acknowledged the emotional thrill that violent imagery could produce for viewers. In 1903 the western and crime genres entered the film medium with Edwin Porter's *The Great Train Robbery*. Exploiting public interest in 'train robberies [that] were being reported in newspapers almost daily' (Jacobs 1939: 42), *The Great Train Robbery* comprised a chase and shoot-out between the outlaw robbers and a posse of lawmakers. The film was by all standards a 'huge' box-office success (Kramer 2001). Yet its most renowned scene comprised a close-up shot of the leader of the outlaw gang looking directly into the camera lens and firing his revolver point-blank at the audience. Included only as a publicity gag (Burch 1978–79: 101) and promoted as providing 'pure sensual and emotional stimulation' (Kramer 2001: 113), the scene has been declared 'Not only . . . perhaps the first great unforgettable moment of screen violence, it is incidentally, also the cinema's first example of truly gratuitous brutality' (French 1996: 5).

During the early years of the twentieth century the enormous popularity of films such as *The Great Train Robbery* caused the middle classes in both the USA and Britain to become concerned about the nature of cinematic entertainment being offered to working-class and juvenile audiences. Complaints were made about the 'vulgarity, gruesomeness and generally unedifying character' (Kuhn 1988: 15) of early movies which were 'held to be dangerous, tending to attract people to vice' (Izod 1988: 12). These fears led to the introduction of censorship regulations in the form of film exhibition licensing requirements in a number of US states and cities (Czitrom 1996; Black 1998; Schaefer 1999). However, the first direct case of US film censorship occurred in 1908 when the Chicago police prevented the exhibition of *The James Boys in Missouri* on the grounds that its depiction of violent lawbreaking 'criminalized' American history (Hoberman 1998: 118). Concerns about film's glorification of crime were equally expressed in Britain where, in 1909, the Metropolitan Police pressured the national Home Office government ministry to introduce the Cinematographic Act. Supposedly intended to ensure that film exhibition premises met fire safety standards, some local authorities used the Act to censor exhibitors who screened films judged 'immoral or indecent in character' (Kuhn 1988: 18) by refusing their exhibition licence (Robertson 1989).

Both the US and British film industries sought to prevent further censorship regulation fearing that it would affect their ability to exploit audiences' readiness to watch, and pay for, its sometimes gruesome and shocking offerings. However, the US industry was also keen to promote itself as socially responsible and so in 1909 created the **National Board of Censorship of Motion Pictures**, which was renamed the **National Board of Review** in 1915. The National Board of Censorship of Motion Pictures was designed to 'insure respectability and good citizenship principles in future films' (Jacobs 1939: 65). Its responsibilities included passing films for exhibition and granting seals of approval to film theatres. A similar self-regulating film industry body, the **British Board of Film Censors** (BBFC), was established in Britain in 1912. Unlike the US body, the BBFC immediately adopted an age-based film certification system – A (adult) or U (Universal) certificate. All films for public exhibition in Britain had to be certified by the BBFC, which could refuse to award an exhibition certificate. Though it experienced difficulties establishing its authority and credibility in its early years (Kuhn 1985; Robertson 1989), the BBFC, which much later, in 1985, became the **British Board of Film Classification**, oversees the British certification of films to this day. In terms of maintaining its role as a censoring body, the US NBR would not enjoy such longevity however.

In many early films, such as D.W. Griffith's *The Lonely Villa* (1909), *The Lonedale Operator* (1911) and *The Girl and her Trust* (1912), narrative suspense was often premised on the threat of a violent and perilous end for a woman at the hands of delinquent male criminals. Thus violence in the movies quickly became gendered, presented as a trait of immoral and often lower-class uneducated males, or as punishment for wayward females. Yet violence was also racialized in early cinema. *The Massacre* (1912) and *The Battle of Elderbush Gulch* (1913) depicted violence as the preoccupation of uncivilized Native American 'savages' (Wiegman 1998). Similarly, cinema's first feature-length narrative fiction film, Griffith's *The Birth of the Nation* (1915), portrayed the emancipated African American male slave as a potential rapist and murderer of white women and consequential threat to white 'civilized' society (Doane 1991). Wiegman (1998: 163) states that as 'a repository for a host of white anger and fear in the aftermath of the civil war, the rapist image was part of a public discourse that "explained" lynching.' Cinema's stereotyping of black males as rapists continues to this day, though now functioning, Giroux (1995: 300) argues, 'to fuel conservative enthusiasm for . . . the death penalty'. *The Birth of the Nation* also glorified the founding of the Ku Klux Klan by portraying its triumphant violent disarming of the marauding blacks as the restoration of social order (Figure 2.1). Protesting that this and the film's racist characterizations promoted hatred and violence toward blacks, the National Association of the Advancement of Colored People (NAACP) succeeded in having the movie banned in 5 states and 19 cities (Wiegman 1998). The US NBR was far less sure of its position on the film. Following the Board's inability to agree on whether *The Birth of the Nation* was racist, and because the film *actually persuaded* the white liberal middle classes of the acceptability of the movies, from 1915 onwards film producers no longer necessarily sought the NBR seal of approval for their films (Izod 1988).

The Birth of the Nation was also at the centre of the 1915 US Supreme Court decision that movies could be subject to censorship (Randall 1976; Kuhn 1985). When the film's producers took the Ohio State censors to court for banning the movie, the case was dismissed on the grounds that as 'a simple commercial product . . . [films] could be regulated through prior censorship and be stopped before reaching their consumers in much the same way dangerous drugs or hazardous chemicals might' (Randall 1976: 433). Denied the rights to **freedom of speech** under the **First Amendment of the US Constitution** and concerned by the possibility of federal censorship intervention, in 1916 the US movie industry established the **National Association of Motion Picture Industries** (NAMPI). NAMPI responded to public complaints about film content and was intended to impose written standards on its members. However, without powers to implement these standards, it proved ineffective (Izod 1988) and in the early 1920s Hollywood was again under critical attack. This followed the release of a cycle of particularly violent movies and a rash of sex hygiene films that social

Figure 2.1 *Birth of a Nation.* Celebrating white supremacy. The 'renegade Negro', Gus, is captured by the Ku Klux Klan in D.W. Griffith's *The Birth of a Nation.*
Source: Kobal/Advertising Archive Online, Picture-desk.com

puritans believed were being viewed out of pornographic interest rather than for their educational message (Kuhn 1988). A series of scandals (including the murder of director William Taylor, comedian 'Fatty' Arbuckle's trial for rape and murder, and the fatal drugs overdose of actor William Reid) also raised questions about Hollywood's moral values (Belton 1996; Schindler 1996; Black 1998; Schaefer 1999). In response to these concerns, and as part of the industry's continued effort to avoid outside control, in 1922 the **Motion Picture Producers and Distributors Association**

(MPPDA) was formed and the Republican reformer Will Hays appointed to its presidency. Hays then created the **Hays Office** that was 'charged with guaranteeing to the public that Hollywood movies would be suitable for family consumption' (Belton 1996: 136).

Exactly what 'suitable for family consumption' means for film representation is always dependent on the cultural politics of any given period. For example, during the First World War spectacular battle scenes, such as those found in Griffith's *Hearts of the World* (1918), were considered acceptable because they functioned as tools of propaganda during the war period (Cook 1985). However, silent cinema's most renowned depiction of military violence is found in the Odessa Steps scene in the Eisenstein's Russian pro-Communist film *Battleship Potemkin* (1925). The scene depicted the Cossack massacre of Russian civilians supporting a sailors' revolt aboard the warship *Potemkin*. Eisenstein's innovative use of montage rather than a graphic exposition of wounding and killing succeeded in creating a sense of intensity, terror and brutality not previously found in the cinema. In Britain the film was banned, ostensibly on the grounds of its violent content, though in reality it was its 'revolutionary tendencies' that most concerned the BBFC censor (Roberston 1989: 29). Quite extraordinarily, the film was not passed for exhibition until 1954 and even then it was given an 'X' certificate.

Meanwhile in the USA in 1927 the Hays Office developed 'The Don'ts and Be Carefuls' guidelines for film production, and began informally reviewing the content of film scripts for the movie studios. However, silent gangster movies such as *Underworld* (1927), *The Racket* (1928) and *The Docks of New York* (1928) soon pushed the boundaries of the socially permissible as a consequence of 'commercial pressures and the knowledge that salacious topics sold tickets' (Izod 1988: 70). It was not so much the fact that these films contained violence that drew criticism, but their romanticizing of underworld criminality and, in the case of *The Racket*, the depiction of 'collusion between gangsters and city politicians' (Maltby 2001: 122). Therefore, a more thorough production code was devised stating that, among other things, 'The technique of murder must be presented in a way that will not inspire imitation . . . Brutal killings are not to be presented in detail . . . Revenge in modern times shall not be justified' (cited in Belton 1996: 139). Additionally, '[a]ttempting to maintain respectable perimeters for screen violence, the Hays Office proscribed on screen bleeding and stipulated that a fire-arm and its victim not be framed together in the same shot' (Hoberman 1998: 119). Broadly the code sought to ensure that 'movies stress proper behaviour, respect for government and "Christian values"' (Springhall 1998: 100). Thus, filmmakers were encouraged to produce narratives that supported, rather than critiqued or challenged, the 'hegemony of the Protestant groups that had imposed their morality and values on American life and culture' (Jowett et al. 1996: 22).

The screams and bangs of sound cinema

The arrival of sound introduced a whole new sensory dimension to the movie-going experience. Sound indices for the occurrence of fear, pain, injury and death were rapidly established across many film genres. In the horror genre, for example, 'female screams, and other sound cues such as creaking doors heightened and transformed the visual effects of the silent era' (Berenstein 1996: 2). Indeed, as Berenstein (1996: 14) points out, 'in the early 1930s . . . horror became a significant American sound phenomenon'. While the film studios' investment in the genre was purely economically motivated (Gomery 1996), it is said that for audiences monster movies such as *Dracula* (1931), *Frankenstein* (1931), *The Mummy* (1932) and *King Kong* (1933) 'offered an instinctive, therapeutic escape' (Skal 1993: 115) from the appalling social and economic circumstances of the depression. These movies all featured violent monsters threatening the lives of individuals and/or whole cities. But a particular target of attack was the ceaselessly screaming woman whose terrorization is as much a part of the early sound movie spectacle as the monster (Williams 1991). Perhaps because they were so fantastical, if misogynist, such films were not considered a danger to viewers or wider society.

The lack of public concern about monster movies contrasts with the fears that circulated around 1930s gangster films, which '[m]any respectable citizens believed . . . led to an increase in juvenile delinquency' (Springhall 1998: 100). Hollywood filmmakers produced gangster movies during this period in an effort to capitalize on intense media and public interest in the activities of gangsters such as Al Capone (Yaquinto 1998). *Little Caesar* (1930), *The Public Enemy* (1931) and *Scarface* (1932) were the early and highly popular classics of this genre. Sound also contributed to these films' appeal. As Rubin (1999: 75) states, the 'screeching of the brakes and roar of automobile engines, the chatter of machine guns, the shattering of glass, and other acoustic outbursts boosted the sensational dimension of gangster films'. Especially popular among young male cinema-goers, the films were blamed for inciting violence and copycat crimes such as instances of armed robbery (Springhall 1998) and juvenile shootings (Hoberman 1998) in exactly the same terms as *Natural Born Killers* (1994) would be over 60 years later.

The **Payne Fund Studies** (PFS) which investigated the effects that film viewing had upon children in the late 1920s and early 1930s added considerable weight to arguments that watching violent films contributed to juvenile crime and violence. Financially supported and administered by reformists who sought to gather 'scientific proof of the potentially harmful influence of the movies' (Jowett et al. 1996: 29), the PFS investigated the 'ways in which motion picture content stimulated children to commit acts of delinquency and crime' (Lowery and DeFleur 1995: 28). They drew on a wide range of research methods – from the content analysis of films, to experiments to test whether movies could encourage behaviour such as teeth brushing, and autobiographical case studies reporting on the influence that films had on male and female juvenile delinquents as well as middle-class college students (Jowett et al. 1996). Out of these various research efforts the PFS concluded that 'motion pictures played a direct role in shaping the delinquent and criminal careers of substantial segments of those studied' (Lowery and DeFleur 1995: 28). However, the means by which the PFS research was commissioned, and the findings obtained and reported, brought the studies into disrepute – especially in terms of their asserting a direct correlation between watching gangster movie violence and violent criminal behaviour. Yet, their conclusions have not been entirely dismissed.

The PFS limited effects findings that 'movies only indirectly encouraged criminal activities by stimulating fantasies and day-dreaming' (Springhall 1998: 111) and, for example, that 'combat fighting and war scenes are imitated in the play of especially young male audiences' (Lowery and DeFleur 1995: 34–5) are generally accepted. Further, one PFS researcher concluded that 'the influence of movies could not be considered outside the context of other popular culture and mass media stimuli or other factors in youngsters' social environments' (Jowett et al. 1996: 91). This finding represented an important milestone in communication research. However, it was downplayed in the reporting of the PFS and went unacknowledged for many decades. This was largely because it suited those groups who sought to impose their standards and values on film content to be able to assert that the movies were a direct cause of crime and violence in society.

One US group that succeeded in wielding considerable power over film content from the 1930s through to the late 1960s was the Catholic Church. Through its **Legion of Decency** the church mounted a campaign to boycott films that used the 'sex and violence formula' and which depicted crime and violence as heroic. The campaign led to the 1934 establishment of the **Production Code Administration** (PCA) empowered by the film industry to ensure that films would not be produced, distributed or exhibited without a MPPDA certificate of approval (Belton 1996; Yaquinto 1998). The US film industry was also forced to concede to the Motion Picture Production Code's regulation of crime films. This 'prohibited any representation of "law-enforcement officers dying at the hands of criminals," "excessive" brutality or gunplay and "action suggestive of wholesale slaughter of human beings, either by criminals, in conflict with police, or as between warring factions of criminals" ' (Maltby 2001: 142). Compliance with the code did not, however, mean an end to Hollywood's growing fascination with violence. Rather than concentrating on the violence of gangsters, films such as *G-Men* (1935), *Special Agent* (1935) and *Bullets or Ballots* (1936) simply kept within the code by glorifying the violence of vicious law enforcers (Yaquinto 1998).

As well as witnessing the rise in popularity of violent police officers and detectives on film, the latter stages of the 1930s and the 1940s also saw the rise of the highly individualized violent male psychopath character. Alloway (1971) links the development of this characterization to the influence of psychoanalysis and existential philosophy on the arts between the wars. He states that this 'turned the prewar action film (basically athletic and cheerful) into the more savage, more pessimistic form of violence with a gallery of extreme situations and desperate heroes' (Alloway 1971: 25). Examples of the psychopath character were found in *This Gun for Hire* (1942), *The Glass Key* (1942) and *The Killers* (1946). The pathologizing of violent characters in film – and indeed across many realms of popular culture – has remained overwhelmingly popular ever since. Indeed it provides the explanatory framework for many violent narratives – especially those in the serial killer genre such as *Psycho* (1960), *Peeping Tom* (1960) and *Silence of the Lambs* (1991) where the male killer's pathology is an outcome of traumatic childhood abuse experienced within the patriarchal nuclear family (Taubin 1991).

The 1940s also saw the popularization of the femme fatale in film narratives. This 'obscurely motivated but physically irresistible' (Alloway 1971: 50) lethal woman was the most evil of characters in films such as *The Maltese Falcon* (1941), *Murder, My Sweet* (1945), *The Killers* (1946), *Out of the Past* (1947) and *Lady from Shanghai* (1948). This characterization of the strong, extremely threatening, and so-called 'castrating' female has been linked to 'male fears about feminism' (Doane 1991: 2) and a backlash against the independence achieved by women during the Second World War when they performed many roles traditionally reserved for men. After the war women were required to give up these positions and 'focus on getting married and raising families ... Rejection of conformity brought harsh punishment' (Yaquinto 1998: 102). Like the male psychopath the femme fatale has remained highly popular with script-writers with more recent notorious incarnations of the stereotype appearing in, for example, *Fatal Attraction* (1987) and *Basic Instinct* (1992).

With the 1950s came an increased emphasis on explicit depictions of violence in film. Influencing this development was Hollywood's need to compete for audiences not only with television (MacCann 1962), but also with the often more daring content of foreign films and a period of extensive suburbanization and booming birth rates that kept viewers from the cinema (Gomery 1996; Black 1998). The increased personal familiarity with both the technologies and extremities of real-life violence experienced during the Second World War also effected changes in movie portrayals of violence. This led to more realistic depictions of death and wounding and, in the western genre, for example, a fascination for guns. *Winchester 73* (1950) and *Colt 45* (1950) emphasized the killing precision of rifles, while *Only the Valiant* (1951) and *Red River* (1954) concentrated on the power of the Gatling guns and *Apache Pass* (1952) the canon (Alloway 1971).

Another factor that contributed to increases in film violence during the 1950s was the landmark 1952 US Supreme Court decision on film censorship. The case involved the New York State Board of Censors' refusal to grant an exhibition permit to Roberto Rossellini's film *The Miracle* on the grounds that it was sacrilegious and blasphemous (Black 1998). Overthrowing the state's decision, the Supreme Court judged that film, 'as an important medium for the communication of ideas' (Jowett 1996: 258), should be constitutionally guaranteed freedom of speech under the First Amendment of the US Constitution (Randall 1976; Black 1998; Schaefer 1999). For the film industry this at last provided the basis to challenge the censorship of its products on the grounds that they were 'harmful', 'immoral' or 'indecent', leaving only 'obscenity' (which is overwhelmingly accepted as a matter relating to the portrayal of sex, and *not* violence), as a reason for their restraint (Randall 1976). This provided filmmakers with much greater freedom in how they depicted mutilation and killing, but maintained constraints in how they could depict sex acts. In Britain too there were changes to film regulation during this period, with the 1951 introduction of the 'X' certificate that permitted the exhibition of adult content to those aged 16 and over (Phelps 1997).

Despite Hollywood's new-found constitutional rights, in the 1950s violence was not generally exploited for its own sake but largely functioned as an expression of social and moral tensions in film narratives. Crime movies depicted violence as part of familiar but morally corrupt cityscapes and underworlds. Fritz Lang's *Big Heat* (1953) and Mickey Spillane's *Kiss Me Deadly* (1955) are particularly associated with the depiction of urban corruption and violence as a justified means of restoring moral order (Alloway 1971). The 'problem film' – represented by movies such as *Blackboard Jungle* (1955) and *Rebel Without a Cause* (1955) – was another

1950s genre that drew on reports of social disintegration but one that certainly did exploit a growing audience appetite for adult themes and portrayals of sex and violence.

Although tame by today's standards, from a 1950s viewer's perspective Barry (1999: 237) remembers that '*Blackboard Jungle* and *Rebel Without a Cause* were deeply alarming in their portrayal of teenagers willing to defy their school teachers and beat up other students.' This response provides an interesting indication of the emotional impact that the films had upon Barry (1999) in that they promoted consideration of the morality and consequences of the students' violent acts. Where violence in film encourages viewers to evaluate the causes, effects and justification of violence, McKinney (1993) argues that the violent portrayal is totally defensible. McKinney (1993: 17) states that as '[s]trong violence, . . . it . . . acts on the mind by refusing glib comfort and immediate emotions'. This compares with what he terms 'weak violence' which requires no emotional investment from the viewer and which 'has only one self-apparent subject: the set piece' (McKinney 1993: 21). Such exploitation of violence for its pure visual display, which McKinney argues is a much less justifiable form of representation, became a defining feature of many films in the late 1980s and 1990s. Yet as we shall now see, this trend in filmmaking had its spectacular birthing in the 1960s and early 1970s.

Slashers and slaughter come to the movies

In 1960 Alfred Hitchcock's *Psycho* played a monumental role in the development of cinema's violent imagination. *Psycho*'s famous shower scene, in which Norman Bates dressed as his mother stabs Marion Crane to death, has been described as 'probably the most horrific incident in any fiction film' (Wood 1984: 146). The audience does not see the knife enter Marion's body. Rather, it is the rapid editing and the camera's point of view that creates the impact. Twitchell (1989) states that this produced

> a far more intense connection with violent action than most of us would even have dreamed of. The director . . . transformed the molester's point of view into our own and in doing so has done what films always have promised. We are forced to respond as if the action were real, as if the action were our own.
>
> (Twitchell 1989: 203–4)

Less enamoured with *Psycho*, feminists have castigated the film for inviting audiences to take pleasure in a woman's violent killing (Burchill 1986;

Haskell 1987; Caputi 1988; Modleski 1988; Williams 1996). Yet while Hitchcock has been accused of introducing a new misogynist aesthetic of violence to the cinema in 1960, Michael Powell's *Peeping Tom*, released in the same year, has been theorized as critiquing this misogynist aesthetic.

Peeping Tom opens with a transvestite serial killer filming his own murder of a prostitute with a knife which is concealed in his camera's tripod. Like *Psycho*, *Peeping Tom* has been condemned as inviting viewers to identify with the killer's terrorization of his victims (Caputi 1988). However, it has also been argued (Silverman 1988; Clover 1992; Williams 1996) that the film investigates the psychodynamics of Hollywood film spectatorship through its examination of a filmmaker's violent abuse of women before the camera. Such self-reflexive filmic examinations of the sadomasochistic nature of film spectatorship are, however, a rare exception in movie making. In the 1960s the predominant trend was to use violence to stylistic and even humorous effect. This trend began with *Dr No* (1962–63) which heralded the arrival of the James Bond spy movies in which 'action and violence (considered unusually strong for its day) [was] mixed with general doses of humor' (Rubin 1999: 128).

However, it was the German-Spanish-Italian co-productions *A Fistful of Dollars* (1964), *For a Few Dollars More* (1966) and *The Good, the Bad and the Ugly* (1967) that first introduced the now predominantly young British and US cinema audience to truly gratuitous tongue-in-cheek brutality. In this trilogy, director Sergio Leone and actor Clint Eastwood coupled ruthless, brutal and cold-blooded violence with a 'more rampant, less romanticised expression of masculine identity' than traditionally depicted in westerns (Gledhill 1985: 71). While the violence in the *Dollars* trilogy 'triggered a storm of protest', the controversy surrounding these 'foreign' films was soon to be superseded by one focused on home-grown productions (Prince 2000b: 9).

A definitive turning point in film violence came in 1967, a year that marks the arrival of a 'fashionable aesthetic of violence for violence's sake – a violence of style as well as content' (Hoberman 1998: 121). Economically this new form of violence reflected cinema's need to 'tell stories which were too big, too sexy, or too violent for television' (Twitchell 1989: 189) to a film-literate audience of young, affluent, baby-boomers seeking movies that were 'visually arresting, thematically challenging, and stylistically individualised by their makers' (Cook 2000: 69). Violent portrayals of the period are also said to have reflected a 'fashionable anti-establishment anger' (Hoberman 1998: 125). It is further claimed that the public unrest at US involvement in the Vietnam War and the assassinations of President John F. Kennedy in 1963, and of Martin Luther King Jr and Robert Kennedy in

1968, produced a 'newly graphic and realist context' for violence and 'a new immediacy to issues of bullet injury' (Jacobs 2000: 10). Yet crucial to film-makers' ability to explore a new stylized aesthetic of violence was the 1966 revision of the PCA 'content injunctions' on film which had been in place since 1934. The 1966 revisions to the code removed specific stipulations on how violence could be depicted and 'merely recommended that filmmakers exercise discretion in showing the taking of human life' (Prince 2000b: 6). This, along with the introduction of the film exhibition classification 'Suggested for Mature Audiences' (SMA) 'significantly expanded the creative license of filmmakers', enabling them 'for the first time to target an adult audience and on that basis take sex and violence much further that in the past when the audience mix included young viewers' (Prince 2000b: 6–7).

Following the changes to film production and exhibition regulation, Arthur Penn's *Bonnie and Clyde* (1967) 'served more than any commercial movie made in America before or since, to redefine the nature of acceptable on-screen violence' (Hoberman 1998: 116). The film followed the exploits of a young bank-robbing outlaw couple in the central Southwest USA in the 1930s. It caused a public outcry by blatantly inviting identification with the couple's crimes against the state, and for portraying their deaths in a hail of police bullets at the film's finale as merciless slaughter, rather than justified law enforcement. Kael wrote of the film at the time of its release:

> The end of the picture, the rag-doll dance of death as the gun blasts keep the bodies of Bonnie and Clyde in motion, is brilliant. It is a horror that seems to go on for eternity, and yet it doesn't last a second beyond what it should. The audience leaving the theatre is the quietest audience imaginable.
>
> (Kael 1996b: 123)

By associating excessive violence with the state, *Bonnie and Clyde* was one of a group of films produced in the late 1960s and early 1970s that 'advanced a revisionist view of the national past that, in effect, argued the centrality of excessive violence to American history' (Hoberman 1998: 133). *The Dirty Dozen* (1967), which challenged dominant representations of the Second World War by depicting a unit of US soldiers as 'composed of murderers, rapists and other violent misfits' (Hoberman 1998: 123), also formed part of this grouping.

After the release of *Bonnie and Clyde* and *The Dirty Dozen* (1967) 'the national debate over film violence reached crisis proportions' (Cook 2000: 7). The **Motion Picture Association of America** (MPAA) was forced to respond and in November 1968 introduced the age-based Code and Rating Administration (CARA) system for the exhibition of films (Black 1998;

Cook 2000). With this the powers of the PCA ended and so too did film censorship, as it was now recognized that adult audiences had a right to view films containing adult themes (Black 1998). Reflecting this, CARA specified four ratings classifications for film exhibition: 'G' (general audience), 'M' (mature audience), 'R' (restricted, persons under 16 not admitted unless accompanied by a parent or guardian) and 'X' (persons under 16 not admitted). The classifications were later revised with the 'R' and 'X' age limit being raised to 17, and the 'M' rating being changed to 'GP', then 'PG' (parental guidance recommended) (Cook 2000: 70). The USA was the last western nation to adopt such an age-based rating system for film exhibition.

The first film to exploit the freedoms provided by the CARA system was Sam Peckinpah's *The Wild Bunch* (1969), which in its final form Cook (2000) believes would have been denied exhibition under the old PCA guidelines. Adding to the revisionist thesis of the USA by overhauling the romantic myths of the western genre, *The Wild Bunch* presented a 'cankered vision of American society made up of religious temperance fanatics, nasty children, lunatic lawmen, unscrupulous, vicious railroad representatives, and an incompetent army' (Carroll 1998: 59). The 'wild bunch' rape and kill women, terrorize townsfolk and, in a notorious scene, engage in a lengthy, chaotic, blood-splattering gun battle (shown in large part in slow motion) in which most of the outlaws, as well as a unit of federal troops and Mexican villagers, are blasted to death. It has been asserted that 'for Peckinpah's heroes violence and death are the only truly glorious ways to fulfilment' (Combs 1981: 1414). During this period, Peckinpah was not alone in proffering such celebrations of violent masculinity.

At the end of the 1960s and into the 1970s revisionist films were joined by a spate of auteur movies that exploited a new audience fascination with graphic violence. In George Romero's *Night of the Living Dead* (1968), Stanley Kubrick's *A Clockwork Orange* (1971), Sam Peckinpah's *Straw Dogs* (1972), Don Siegels's *Dirty Harry* (1971) and Francis Ford Coppola's *The Godfather* (1971), the spectacle of violence was central to the narrative, as it was in many other films of this time. Also central was the association of that violence with male power and either women's subjugation to violence, or their lack of significance to the plot altogether. Feminists saw this as a symbolic backlash against women's liberation. Haskell (1987) argued that:

> The closer women came to claiming their rights and achieving independence in real life, the more loudly and stridently films tell us that it's a man's world. As *Dirty Harry* pummels his victim – a gurgly and girlish psychopath – with a multiple-orgasm splatter of bullets that sends the

audience into groans of ecstasy. As the new Godfather . . . closes the door on his wife and on any further important communication between them. As Susan George, in *Straw Dogs*, struts around like Daisy Mae before the brier-patch yokels, and then gets it once, twice, and again for the little tease she is. The provocative, sex-obsessed bitch is one of the great male-chauvinist (and apparently, territorialist) fantasies, along with the fantasy that she is constantly fantasizing rape.

(Haskell 1987: 363)

A Clockwork Orange and *Straw Dogs* are both especially callous in their rape depictions. At one point in *A Clockwork Orange* a woman is raped to the main character's rendition of 'Singing in the Rain'. Somewhat similarly, Hitchcock's *Frenzy* (1972) contains a lengthy and lurid rape and strangulation after which the sex murderer nonchalantly finishes eating an apple as though the attack was a mere interlude in his snacking. Modleski (1988: 113) describes this as 'infinitely sad, pathetic, among the most disturbing scenes cinema has to offer'.

Since the 1970s explicit depictions of violence against women have been a staple ingredient of cinema. Horror movies of the 1970s and 1980s which 'mutated into an especially vicious brand of filmmaking that offered viewers unsparing graphic violence' were particularly virulent in their sadistic treatment of women (Prince 2000a: 351). *The Texas Chainsaw Massacre* (1974) offers one of the genre's most notorious low-budget examples of the terrorization of a female victim to the 'point where she is literally driven insane' (Sharrett 1984: 266). As a consequence of its highly gratuitous and 'vicious content, the original uncut version of *Texas Chainsaw Massacre* (Figure 2.2) was not granted approval for video release until 2000.' From October 2002, the BBFC also lifted the ban on the video release of *Straw Dogs*, having approved a version different from one submitted to the censors in 1999. The version approved in 2002 was said to have restored original footage that made it clear that the rape victim neither invited nor enjoyed the rape attack (Travis 2002). On these grounds, the film is no longer seen to be harmful to women because it is not perpetrating the myth that women enjoy rape.

A further 1970s film that took violence against women to another extreme was *Snuff* (1976). This low budget exploitation movie, purported to depict the actual murder and mutilation of a woman. This, and a host of other similar films, gave rise to the urban myth of real-life killings taking place on camera for the commercial pornography market (Johnson and Schaefer 1993; Kerekes and Slater 1995). Able to fully exploit the best in gore special effects, big budget films reached quite different heights – though some would say with the identical intent of so-called 'snuff' movies. Brian De Palma's

Figure 2.2 *Texas Chainsaw Massacre*. Depicting the relentless terrorization of a defenceless and screaming young female, Tobe Hooper's low budget horror *Texas Chainsaw Massacre* was never officially labelled a 'video nasty', though the uncut version was banned in the UK for 25 years.
Source: Kobal/Advertising Archive Online, Picture-desk.com

slasher film *Dressed to Kill* (1980), for example, graphically depicts a serial killer's brutal and prolonged murder of a woman with a razor in an elevator and her hopeless struggle to survive. While censors in both the USA and

Britain required minor cuts to the film these 'had nothing to do with the film's misogyny' (Kuhn 1982: 128). Kuhn explains that

> no form of censorship (which in the final instance works only at the level of specific moments in a film) can meet a critique of *Dressed to Kill* which points to a general attitude towards women and female sexuality structuring the film's narrative and cinematic codes. How can patriarchal ideology be censored?
>
> (Kuhn 1982: 128)

Thus, the acceptability of misogynistic violence in films is explained as the consequence of dominant patriarchal social, economic and institutional ideologies of which cinema is a part.

Concerns about cinema's portrayals of violence, and especially sexual violence, reached an all-time peak in the 1980s (Prince 2000a). This was the case in both Britain and in the USA, but a particular British concern was availability of horror films such as *The Exorcist* (1973), *Driller Killer* (1979), *The Evil Dead* (1982) and the rape revenge movie *I Spit on Your Grave* (1978) on video. At this time video was regulated only by the vague laws of obscenity, which meant that films banned from public theatrical exhibition could be released on videotape – along with the uncut versions of other movies censored by the BBFC. Quickly labelled **video nasties** by the British tabloid press, these films were 'blamed for everything from inattentiveness at school to muggings and rape' (Kermode 1997: 157). However, while many video nasties comprised what were considered misogynistic horror films, once again misogyny did not factor in the debates about these film products. Rather, it was children and the 'underclass' who were positioned as potential victims of the films' influence, and it was middle-class society which sought to protect itself and its children from the consequences of that influence (Petley 2001). Consequently, in 1984 the British Conservative government pushed through Parliament the Video Recordings Act (VRA), which required that videos pass BBFC certification approval. In 1994, after *Child's Play 3* was spuriously alleged to have provoked two 10-year-old boys to murder the 2-year-old **James Bulger** in Bootle, near Liverpool in 1993, the VRA regulations were further tightened (Barker 2001).

In the USA the tide of criticism directed at violent film portrayals continued to rise just as it did in Britain. In the USA this period saw increasing support for **neo-conservatism** and the New Right that espoused family values and antagonism toward the purported vices of liberal culture. Culture and the arts became a particular focal point for the ensuing ideological battles that are still to this day waged between the New Right and left-wing liberals in what became termed 'the culture wars' (Lyons 1997). Prince (2000a: 342) explains that 'Hollywood films became a flash point in these battles, which targeted movie content while projecting more substantial and broader visions of what an appropriate American society should look like'. Hollywood thus found itself under attack from diverse and frequently ideologically opposed angles. The New Right accused the industry of eroding traditional social values by promoting the rights of women and gays and exploiting sensationalist depictions of sex, violence and immorality. Anti-pornography feminists argued that films such as *Dressed to Kill* and *Body Double* (1984) promoted violence against women (Lyons 1997). Gay activists argued that films such as *Cruising* (1980) and *American Gigolo* (1980) promoted and reinforced homophobia (Lyons 1997; Prince 2000a). Christian groups, film exhibitors and prominent film critics also attacked Hollywood for exploiting socially undesirable material for profitable gain, or through false notions of 'artistic integrity' (Medved 1992).

Although widespread condemnation of Hollywood's product in the 1980s led to a dwindling popular respect for the industry, box-office attendance did not decline. Indeed, some groups' efforts to encourage the boycotting of films, such as the feminist protests against *Dressed to Kill*, only added to the film's publicity (Lyons 1997). More effective, however, were accusations from theatre exhibitors that the MPAA ratings system lacked integrity and films that should have been rated 'X', such as *Cruising*, were being given the more lenient 'R' rating. In 1984, in an effort to recoup credibility over its ratings system, the MPAA introduced the new 'PG-13' rating category – indicating that parents should give particular guidance to children under 13 attending the film. 'The new category was a direct response to charges that the MPAA was soft on violence and that the content of some PG films was inappropriate for children' (Prince 2000a: 367).

Filmgoers' considerable readiness to watch cinema's increasingly graphic and, in the case of the horror genre, grotesque and gratuitous displays of violence in the 1970s and 1980s, led some film theorists to ask how viewers gained pleasure from this violence. The horror genre was of particular interest given that, as Carroll (1990: 158–9) states, 'there appears to be something paradoxical about the horror genre. It obviously attracts consumers; but it seems to do so by means of the expressively repulsive.' Drawing on **psychoanalytic theory**, Wood (1984: 171, original emphasis) claimed that 'the true subject of the horror genre is the struggle for recognition of all that our civilization *re*presses and *op*presses.' Comprising a conflict between the monster's violent desires and civilized social order, the horror narrative was thus considered a re-enactment of the Freudian Oedipal conflict through which children learn about sexuality and repress into the unconscious socially unacceptable incestuous desires for their mother (Creed 1998a: 78). However, it was argued that these repressed desires still seek satisfaction. The conscious, knowing that the satisfaction of these desires will bring social reprimand, has to ensure that they are expressed only in acceptable ways – such as through watching films symbolically structured around the Oedipal narrative. For example, it is said that violent monsters who capture and violate women, such as Frankenstein and Dracula, represent the symbolic expressions of men's incestuous desires for their mothers. In identifying with the monster the unconscious is able to give vent to its desires, while the conscious ego of the viewer can safely identify with social oppression and destruction of that monster (Evans 1984).

Some feminist psychoanalytic film theorists argue a slightly different perspective on the pleasures of violent horror movies. For them the monster represents male fears of castration. Williams (1996: 20) argues that 'the monster's power is one of sexual difference from the normal male. In this difference he is remarkably like the woman in the eyes of the traumatized male: a biological freak'. The horror of these monsters is said to reside in the fear that their freakish power induces in the viewer, just as the 'castrated' difference of women is said to induce fear in men. This leads Williams (1996: 24) to argue that men gain pleasure from the violent defeat of the monster in horror movies as 'the monster's death is an exorcism of the power of [women's] sexuality'. For Creed (1993), however, the female monster is represented as particularly horrifying because she is in fact *not* castrated, but has the propensity to castrate the male. Examples of this fantasy of the castrating female are found in the horrific and violent devouring monster in *Alien* (1979), the authoritarian mother figure in *Psycho*, and the menstruating killer witch girl in *Carrie* (1976). Such portrayals lead Creed (1993: 7) to argue that '[w]hen woman is represented as monstrous it is almost always in relation to her mothering and reproductive functions.'

The psychoanalytic theorizing of horror and slasher movies dominated critical film theory in the 1970s and 1980s. However, psychoanalytic film theory has been criticized for failing to specifically consider how film content reflects historical, political and cultural issues and attitudes (Creed 1998a). As we shall now discuss, as the 1970s and 1980s progressed, links between Hollywood's blockbuster glorification of excessive violent masculinity, and the growing political dominance of right-wing politics in the USA became impossible to ignore.

Violent masculinity – 'I hurt therefore I am'

There are films that while containing highly graphic violent portrayals are presented by their makers as intended encourage viewers to reflect on the exploitation of violence for the purposes of entertainment. For example, Martin Scorsese, renowned for directing extremely violent films such as *Cape Fear* (1992) and *Casino* (1996), in both *Taxi Driver* (1976) and the biographical boxing film *Raging Bull* (1980), claimed to critique the USA's fascination for violence and violent men.

Taxi Driver follows the development of its central character, Travis, from a position of a New York taxi driver to that of a potential political assassin, and then to media celebrity following his brutal shooting of a 12-year-old prostitute's pimp. Sharrett (1999: 426) states that *Taxi Driver* 'locates the protagonist's identity (significantly shaped by media culture, particularly by media renditions of the American male as regenerative saviour) in a divinely ordained errand or "mission".' Somewhat similarly Mortimer (1997: 31) claims that *Raging Bull*'s depiction of masculinity 'suggests that in the search for an understanding of identity, we must rely on the awareness that "I hurt, therefore I am."' Mortimer additionally argues that in *Raging Bull* violence is both presented and examined as entertainment:

> The elemental level of physical violence, of bodies inflicting damage on bodies – the rawest of experience – becomes the ultimate source of spectacle, consumed as entertainment. The world of boxing, in which fighting is explicitly designed to entertain becomes a metaphor for the uses to which violence has been put in contemporary life.
>
> (Mortimer 1997: 31)

Mortimer's analysis of this film certainly supports Scorsese's claims that he used *Raging Bull* to 'present a didactic outcry against violence to a mass audience' (Tomasulo 1999: 192).

There is, however, the distinct possibility that viewers might not adopt the critical interpretation of violent masculinity that *Taxi Driver* and *Raging Bull* purportedly offer. They might instead read Scorsese's highly crafted and exceedingly bloody scenes in these films as glorification of violence. Prince (2000c) argues that such interpretations would be hardly surprising. In examining Scorsese's claims that *Taxi Driver* critiques violence, alongside Peckinpah's very similar claims about *The Wild Bunch*, Prince argues that:

> Neither Scorsese nor Peckinpah wished to evoke violent fantasies in their viewers. When asked if that was their intention, both passionately denied it. But they could not disengage themselves, as artists, from the

sensuous gratifications of assembling spectacularized violence. While one should not doubt the sincerity of their belief in their own stated intentions, one may still be amazed at their blindness to their own artistic complicity in stimulating the aggressive reactions in viewers.

(Prince 2000c: 199)

Here Prince usefully highlights the contradiction in filmmakers' arguments that their highly stylized violent movies can encourage viewers to enjoy graphic depictions of violence while simultaneously encouraging consideration of the morality of violent acts. Furthermore, it has been said that expressions of sexism, racism and homophobia in both *Taxi Driver* and *Raging Bull* actually lament the 'good old halcyon days when men were men, and women, minorities, and gays were repressed and/or brutalised' (Tomasulo 1999: 192). Thus, Scorsese's films have been seen as calling for a return to the very kind of hyper-masculinity celebrated in action films of the 1970s and 1980s which, featuring muscle-bound stars such as Arnold Schwarzenegger, Sylvester Stallone, Chuck Norris and Jean-Claude van Damme, re-establish the authority of the violent 'indestructible' white male.

In reasserting the legitimacy of masculine power, the 1980s action genre reflects the 'back to basics, get tough' politics espoused by the new US President and ex-Hollywood star Ronald Reagan. In the *Rambo* series (1982, 1985, 1988), Stallone plays a Vietnam War veteran who learned extreme violence in the service of a nation that rejects him upon his return to the USA and upon which he wreaks havoc. By the time of *Rambo III*, however,

Rambo is such a supremely powerful (and superhuman) warrior that he becomes a charged national emblem in the era's cultural discourse, a creature of mythology and symbolism embodying the resolve and strength of no single person but an entire nation.

(Prince 2000a: 316–17)

In the *Rocky* (1976, 1979, 1982, 1985, 1990) films Stallone plays a working-class boxer whose physique brings accolade and acclaim in a life where nothing else is dependable. Twitchell (1989) writes that:

From *Rocky* to *Rambo*, Stallone plays out the same tale, a fable of the inarticulate, the big bodied, small brained, good intentioned vindicator whose only motivation is somehow to make things right, to redress some imbalance. His motivation is the inverse of the stalker-and-slashers, yet his actions are the same. He brutalises people.

(Twitchell 1989: 214)

In political terms Rambo has especially been identified as vindicating right-wing Reaganite 'hawkish foreign policy, a muscular lack of diplomacy' (Tasker 1993: 92). Explaining the genre in terms of male fantasy, Paul Smith (1995: 91) argues that the action movie's **objectification** of the male body – comprising the hero's bodily endurance of extensive violent wounding – functions to reinforce a symbolic 'triumphalist masculinity'. For women action heroes, such symbolic empowerment is far less achievable – despite an increase in their on-screen presence since the late 1970s. For example while the *Alien* (1979, 1986, 1992, 1997) and *Terminator* (1984, 1991) films portray women as capable of heroic violence, they also portray them as vulnerable to either actual or implied rape (Tasker 1993) – a form of violence that men very rarely suffer in film. By definition, male heroes cannot suffer rape given that male penetration is perceived to involve the abdication of power (Wlodarz 2001). Further, as Wlodarz (2001: 72) explains, 'in a patriarchal society, the penetration of a man is generally considered to be a fate worse than (or at least equal to) death.' Yet many films that feature heroines subject these women to this form of attack. *Aliens* (1986), *Thelma and Louise* (1991), *Basic Instinct* (1992), *Blue Steel* (1990) and *Copycat* (1995), which all feature very strong lead women, also have those women, or in the case of *Basic Instinct* a supporting female character, suffer rape attacks. While female viewers might find role models in violent movie heroines, they are then also invited to consider the threat of sexual violence as the price to be paid for pursuing female strength, independence and the ever-elusive symbolic power.

A number of Hollywood films have featured the issue of male violence against women as a central narrative concern. Some have also critiqued those discourses so prevalent in the horror genre, as well as in society generally, that hold women responsible for their sexual attack through their behaviour, manner of dress, and/or suggested promiscuity. In 1989, *The Accused*, trailed as 'reopening the debate on rape in the 80s' (quoted in Cook 1989: 35), directly tackled these issues through the dramatization of a rape victim's attempt to gain legal justice for her gang rape in a suburban bar. However, the film was far from controversial, especially in terms of its marketing emphasis on the inclusion of a lengthy and highly graphic rape portrayal (Weaver 1995). While some (Malcolm 1989) believed that *The Accused* sincerely intended to examine the legal treatment of rape victims, others (Riggs and Willoquet 1989; Faludi 1992) were less convinced of the film's integrity and it was criticized for 'exploiting sex and violence under the guise of condemning them' (Goodman 1989).

Certainly *The Accused* does 'raise the question as to whether the attempt to promote social understandings of rape necessarily required the depiction of the violent act' (Weaver 1995: 94). Indeed, Schlesinger et al.'s (1992) investigation of women's responses to *The Accused* found that women were extremely critical of the explicit nature and length of the rape representation. Interestingly, however, what most concerned women was how men would view the rape scene. A number of the respondents even talked of having watched the film with men who proceeded to blame the rape victim for her attack, or who did not take the film seriously. It was found that:

> There was considerable concern about the appropriateness of a Hollywood film – one essentially premised upon entertainment values as the most suitable vehicle for dealing with this troubling subject . . . The worries were centred upon what 'men' were likely to make of this film. [The gang rape in] *The Accused* evoked extremely powerful feelings and sharp observations about the culture of male solidarity and its negative impact on women. Anxieties about men as viewers were completely consistent with these wider assumptions.
>
> (Schlesinger et al. 1992: 163)

Schlesinger et al.'s (1998) study of men's viewing of screen portrayals of violence, which we discuss at greater length in Chapter 3, lends considerable weight to these concerns. The study found that male viewers frequently demonstrate 'a lack of understanding of or empathy with female characters' (Schlesinger et al. 1998: 50) portrayed as victims of violence in film and television. It also concluded that, in response to the action film *Under Siege* (1992), young male viewers 'revelled in the portrayals of violence, enjoying the many ways in which the hero managed to evade and eliminate the villains' (Schlesinger et al. 1998: 50). The dearth of studies examining how men and women variously engage with film violence means that we lack any detailed understanding of how their interpretations inform, or are informed by, gendered social relationships and ideologies. However, Schlesinger et al.'s (1998) research clearly finds that certainly young, white, heterosexual men are, by and large, far more comfortable with film violence and are less concerned about how it is viewed and interpreted than are women. This is very likely because they can be confident that film violence almost exclusively privileges and condones masculinist discourses and ideologies. Indeed, with the development of the new fashion of 'designer violence' in the movies in the 1990s, these ideologies became even more central to the pleasures afforded to viewers by film depictions of violence.

Serial killers and designer violence

Where the action genre dominated the box office and much of the spectacle of violence in the 1980s, it gave way to the serial killer genre in the 1990s. With this, as well as other genres, also came a new wave of 'designer violence' where highly graphic depictions seemed devoid of meaning beyond the sheer delight of their (intentionally) shocking cinematic spectacle. McKinney (1993) argues that the development of this new fashion for hollow, flamboyant violent portrayals was linked to 'the needs of young earnest filmmakers eager to showcase their formal skills, and who therefore seem worthier of consideration because they're walking the art-house walk' (McKinney 1993: 20).

The rapid rise to fame of writer-director Quentin Tarantino with *Reservoir Dogs* (1992) was unquestionably due to his eroticization of violence to the point where torture is even set to upbeat pop music. Tarantino had a significant involvement in many other violent films of the 1990s, most notably as the director of *True Romance* (1993) and *Pulp Fiction* (1994), and as script-writer for Oliver Stone's *Natural Born Killers* (1994). However, many other films of the period, such as *Henry: A Portrait of a Serial Killer* (1990), *Man Bites Dog* (1991), *Bad Lieutenant* (1992), *Kalifornia* (1993), *Shallow Grave* (1995), *Se7en* (1996) and even novels, such as Brett Easton's notorious *American Psycho* (1991), like Tarantino's works, all 'tend to depict violence as insignificant fact rather than consequential act' (Grant 1999: 33). That is, these largely nihilistic texts offer little, if any, reason as to why characters carry out acts of violence and provide minimal insight into the effects of violence on individuals and society. *Henry: A Portrait of a Serial Killer*, described by Prince (2000a: 302) as 'among the most disturbing pictures ever made', offered the most extreme example of this trend.

Containing a range of graphic and chilling acts of rape and murder, *Henry* can be viewed as a critique of the 'connection between sadism and voyeurism' (Taubin 1991: 17). In one scene Henry and a temporary accomplice, Ottis, videotape their own massacre of a middle-class suburban family and Ottis's rape of the adult female's corpse. Ottis is later seen repeatedly watching the video of the rape – as though achieving the ultimate narcissistic identification with an on-screen violent perpetrator and having the visual evidence to finally, and pathetically, prove 'I hurt therefore I am'. However, there is nothing in the movie that directs the viewer to this reading, aside from the fact that even Henry becomes apparently disgusted by Ottis's narcissistic love of his own violence and when killing Ottis, gouges his eye out.

In the 1990s it was fashionable among US filmmakers to position their graphic flicks as critical and, in some cases, satirical send-ups, of the media exploitation of crime and violence for economic gain (Rich 1992; Prince 2000b; Smith 2000). As well as *Henry*, *Man Bites Dog*, *Natural Born Killers* and David Cronenberg's soft-porn and highly controversial *Crash* (1996) – about a couple who gain sexual gratification from the injuries inflicted by car crashes and which was banned by Westminster City Council in the UK (Creed 1998b) – have all been defended by their makers from this perspective. Others (Grisham 1996; Smith 2000; Springer 2001) consider this defence a superficial pretence through which filmmakers are able 'to have it both ways' and secure the public exhibition of excessively exploitative violent movies. For still others, however, the films – a number of which leave their monstrous killers roaming free at the narrative's end – are reflections of the **postmodern** condition experienced during the latter half of the twentieth century.

In a period when notions of order and causality were said to be terminally undermined, Pinedo (1996: 29) claims that the 'postmodern horror constructs an unstable, open-ended universe in which categories collapse, violence constitutes everyday life, and the irrational prevails'. Indeed, the postmodern horror film is frequently theorized as expressing an apocalyptic denial of dominant ideology's discursive assertions that there are safe places away from pain and cruelty (Sharrett 1984; Crane 1994). As the millennium came to a close, horror's violent representations were further considered antagonistic to dominant ideology as they encouraged a wallowing in an excess of 'body horror' spectacle of special effects and the 'articulat[ion of the] spectacular degradation of everyday life' (Crane 1994: 160).

While this theoretical celebration of cinematic representation at the end of the twentieth century positions that representation as radical, but harmless, some writers (Grisham 1996; Medved 1996) vehemently argued that Hollywood was again provoking young people to commit real-life crimes. For example, in 1995 *Natural Born Killers* was said to have influenced two US teenagers' murdering of a cotton gin manager in Mississippi and a convenience store worker in Louisiana (Grisham 1996). In the same year, *Money Train* (1995) was linked to the sadistic murder of a New York subway worker (Medved 1996). As we have seen, such concerns about the effects of film viewing were regularly expressed throughout the twentieth century. As with previous assertions of this kind, in the 1990s these fears focused on violent movies that many saw as celebrating violence against cherished social institutions such as the family, law enforcement agencies, and even the news media.

Some scholars have however challenged arguments that the 1990s serial killer, horror, and designer violence movies were antagonistic to dominant ideologies and their depictions of violence meaningless. Prince (2000b) argues that these films present violence as a mere object of spectacle for the viewer's consumption, and utterly neglect to reflect on violence 'as a social process' (2000b: 33). Others argue that the violent content of the films is deeply conservative. For example, Simpson (1999: 120) states of *Natural Born Killers*, *Se7en* and *Kalifornia* that the 'values championed in these films are mostly those of a patriarchy that fetishizes reactionary law and order policies'. Tarantino's films have also been critiqued as racist, sexist and homophobic. For example, Guerrero's (2001) analysis of films such *as True Romance*, *Reservoir Dogs* and *Pulp Fiction* concludes that Tarantino

> appears to be deeply disturbed by barely repressed, ambivalent feelings about race in general, black masculinity in particular, and the issues of violence, miscegenation, and sex. Black male delinquents, while hip and alluring in Tarantino's screenplays, wind up eliminated, raped, or murdered, with black male–white female miscegenation always punished. Conversely, black women are the exotic trophies of white male desire.
>
> (Guerrero 2001: 220)

Giroux (1995), who raises similar concerns about Tarantino's representation of black characters, also points to the director's highly misogynistic treatment of women:

> When they [women] do appear in his work, they either act violently, as in Uma Thurman's drug snorting in *Pulp Fiction*, or are violently abused by their pimps, as in the case of Patricia Arquette in *True Romance*. In the end, Tarantino's use of hyper-real violence is propped up by a 'cool' masculinity that simply recycles a patriarchal hatred of women while barely hiding its own homophobic instincts.
>
> (Giroux 1995: 310)

As is the case with the vast majority of cinema's violent offerings, there is no research available to tell us how audiences respond to the violent treatment of black and female characters by filmmakers such as Tarantino.

Hill's (1997) study into the appeal of designer violence movies does suggest, however, that the attraction of these films lies less in their articulation of particular sociocultural or political ideologies, and more in participating in the collective media event that they can become. Hill identifies media hype, peer pressure, and a film's cultural prestige and/or the prestige of directors and actors as influencing viewers to watch violent movies such as *Reservoir Dogs*, *Natural Born Killers* and *Henry*. Her audience research found that the sheer popularity of these created 'cachet in being part of such cultural events, part of a zeitgeist' (Hill 1997: 23) which drove their appeal.

A further finding is that both male and female horror viewers are attracted to violent films as a means of testing various emotional boundaries in relation to violent representations (Hill 1997, 2001). Hill states:

> Certain scenes from specific films produce intense response [*sic*], and part of the process of viewing violence is to anticipate and explore such feelings . . . Evidence suggests participants may expect, even desire, to be shocked or excited, to feel a rush of emotions when viewing fictional violence.
>
> (Hill 1997: 33)

It could then be said that in these terms film violence continues to serve viewers' fascination for 'unbeautiful' and repulsive sights just as much today as Gunning (1994) argues it did over 100 years ago.

When the bodies are real

On September 11 2001 the world witnessed a type of spectacle previously imaginable only in big budget action and disaster movies – the images of passenger airliners slamming into the World Trade Center in New York. One US journalist stated of these images: 'What we saw . . . were the last frames of the disaster movie that never gets made; the unimaginable sequence that occurs when James Bond drops the ball or Harrison Ford loses his grip. This is what it would be like without a happy ending or an action hero' (Hitchens 2001). Perhaps because the movies were the only referent that people had for the September 11 attacks, filmmakers and media commentators suddenly began to reflect on the US nation's use and everyday acceptance of mass carnage in film. For example, Hollywood directors Edward Zwick and Marshall Herskovitz wrote shortly after the attacks:

> Only now do we ask ourselves how can we thrill to an asteroid hitting earth, or watch the White House blown up by aliens, and sit munching our popcorn. Is it because we believed it could never happen? Or were we unwilling to see what these films expressed? Like a child with a toy gun, these images exist in a realm of symbolism. The explosions stand in for what? Perhaps nothing less than our rage at the powerlessness of modern life. Terrorists, the pundits say, harbor a murderously distorted version of the same impulse. Is it possible we are . . . all terrorists in our hearts?
>
> (Zwick and Herskovitz 2001)

After September 11 people in the USA also began to question whether they had become the victim of their nation's own violent imagination – which is, after all, its 'most heavily exported cultural product' (Mitchell 2001).

Immediately following the attacks, Hollywood announced that Arnold Schwarzenegger's *Collateral Damage*, and John Woo's *Windtalkers*, were to be withdrawn from imminent release. Many considered it to be tasteless to exhibit these violent action films in the aftermath of the attacks. At the time, the movie industry was also reported as rethinking its stance on violent entertainment – especially in relation to the depiction of the US military. Within only two months, however, the 'bullish national mood' (Poole 2001) of the USA saw a complete reversal of this position with the release dates of Ridley Scott's *Black Hawk Down* (2001) and Mel Gibson's *We Were Soldiers* (2001) brought forward (Poole 2001). Late 2001 also saw the release of *Collateral Damage*. It was stated that 'Americans want blood and gore at the cinema' and are 'hungry for war films because they reflected the present preoccupation with the dangers US armed forces face in combat abroad' (Poole 2001).

Conclusion

Cinematic depictions of violence cannot be considered simply as entertainment. As we have discussed in this chapter, film representations of violence are intrinsically connected to the social, cultural, economic and institutional ideologies of their production and reception. Where films containing violence do cause controversy and fear, especially with regard to their supposed influence on viewers, it has nearly always been because they depict violent attacks against representatives and/or institutions of the state. 'Everyday representations of violence' – such as violence against women, or the depiction of lesser powerful groups as violent *and* needing to be controlled – have caused comparatively much less general concern. In these terms 'acceptable' film violence performs a social role in communicating who has the legitimate right to be violent and who does not, who should fear violence and who should not. But what is extraordinary about the evident acceptability of so much film violence is that censorship laws deter against the explicit depiction of consenting sex, but permit the screening of explicit and graphic violence. Film regulation practices therefore assume that 'excessive and explicit sex is more offensive and problematic than excessive violence' (Krafka and Linz 1997). Of course the cinema is not alone in having considerable freedom to show graphic depictions of violence that lend legitimacy to certain violent acts and attitudes. As our next chapter outlines, television too participates in condoning certain types of violence.

There is no denying though that cinema has always been able to show violence bigger, bloodier and more expensively than any other medium.

Further reading

Lyons, C. (1997) *The New Censors: Movies and the Culture Wars*. Philadelphia, PA: Temple University Press.

Prince, S. (ed.) (2000) *Screening Violence*. London: Athlone Press.

Sharrett, C. (ed.) (1999) *Mythologies of Violence in Postmodern Media*. Detroit, MI: Wayne State University Press.

Slocum, J.D. (ed.) (2001) *Violence and American Cinema*. London: Routledge.

Tasker, Y. (1993) *Spectacular Bodies: Gender, Genre and the Action Cinema*. London: Routledge.

3 | TELEVISION'S CRIMES AND MISDEMEANOURS

The following show is very scary, with stuff that might give your kids nightmares. You see there are some crybabies out there, religious types mostly, who might be offended. If you are one of them, I advise you to turn off your set now. Come on! I dare ya! . . . Chicken!

(Homer Simpson in *The Simpsons*)

TV is the single most significant factor contributing to violence in America.

(Ted Turner, President, Turner Broadcasting System)

Introduction

The one issue that dominates concerns about violence on television is the ease of access that children have to this medium. Unlike newspapers, engagement with television content does not require reading skills – skills that come only with age. Unlike cinema, until very recently, television viewers could not be restricted from viewing certain programmes according to their age. Indeed, the private, unregulated, domestic viewing context of television provides children with access to all manner of violent content and, consequently, violence on television persists as an issue of much greater controversy than violence in film. Debating this issue, politicians, policy makers, the public, media watchdog groups and researchers have waged a battle around the question of whether images of violence negatively affect young audiences, and whether their viewing of such material should be controlled. This debate is extraordinarily polemic in nature, and is, as Cunningham (1992: 67) describes it, a 'neverending story, one of the hardiest perennials in the thicket of media research and policy'.

Given the overwhelming focus on children in debates about television violence, we devote the first half of this chapter to examining concerns about the effects of violent television programming on young viewers. We focus on why certain programme types have caused concern and how they are said to effect children. We then outline how and why these fears of television's effects are rejected by sociologists who consider them to be expressive of a wider **moral panic** about the nature of childhood. This is followed by an assessment of the findings of research that examines how children engage with television and what meanings they take from it. We end our discussion of children and television violence by outlining television broadcasting policy as it relates to children in a number of western countries. Here we also detail the implementation of the controversial **V-chip** in Canada and the USA which has enabled parents to censor their children's television viewing.

The second half of the chapter investigates issues around violent television content aimed at adults. Here we explore how media researchers theorize the meaning of violence in three television formats: police crime drama, reality crime programmes and sports programming. Our aim is to identify the issues raised by some very different depictions of television violence across factual and fictional programming. Finally, we look at research into how adult viewers make sense of television violence in relation to their lives, experiences and identities. What becomes particularly apparent from this discussion is that adults can be deeply affected, just as much as some people fear children are, by their viewing of television violence and that gender also plays an important part in how they respond.

The problem of children and television violence

In children's studies research, children are categorized as those between the ages of 3 and 11 years old, with those between 12 and 17 years old being defined as 'young people' or 'adolescents'. From the perspective of developmental psychology, it is when we are children that we develop 'behavior patterns, attitudes, and values about social interaction' (Murray 1993: 13). It is claimed that during these formative years, engagement with television violence can create distorted views of society and the acceptability of certain behaviours. Certainly, statistics on how much television violence children encounter in their young lives can appear alarming. For example, it is said that:

> By the time the average American child graduates from elementary school, he or she will have seen about 8,000 murders and about 100,000 other assorted acts of violence (e.g. assaults, rapes) on network television . . . The numbers are higher if the child has access to cable television or a videocassette player, as most do.
>
> (Bushman and Huesmann 2001: 227)

It is by no means as a consequence of watching adult television programmes that children become witness to this quantity of violence. US researchers have found that there are over four times more violent acts committed in children's cartoons than in adult prime-time programming (Gerbner et al. 1995). Translating this into a televisual diet, Fowles (1999: 87) states that the 'young viewer is awash in sequenced drawings of exploding heads, flattened bodies, and jettisoned limbs'. While such animated and often comic material could be considered innocuous, children's cartoons are said to 'provide unacceptable role models for young children since they solve their problems through the use of aggressive and violent behaviour' (Bassett 1991: 73).

Moreover, cartoons have been criticized for letting violence go unpunished, for failing to show it causes pain and injury, for linking violence with heroic acts, and for encouraging children to simply think violence funny (see, for example, UCLA Television Violence Monitoring Report 1995; Levine 1996; National Television Violence Study 1997). Classic cartoons, such as *Bugs Bunny*, *Road Runner*, *Wile E. Coyote*, *The Pink Panther*, *The Flintstones* and *Tom and Jerry* have all been criticized in these terms. More recent cartoon productions such as *Transformers*, *Teenage Mutant Ninja Turtles*, *Sailor Moon*, *The Simpsons*, *Ren and Stimpy*, *South Park*, *X-Men*, *Action Man*, *Biker Mice from Mars* and *Sonic Underground* have been equally berated for their violent content. Of the currently highly popular cartoon *Dragonball Z*, it has even been said 'If there's any message at all, it's "If at first you don't succeed, keep getting the crap beaten out of you until you do"' (Rae 2002: 5). An additional criticism is that some cartoons are associated with toys, such as *Action Man* and *Transformers*, or violent computer games, such as *Sonic Underground*, which further encourage violent play in children.

However, Buckingham et al. (1999) keenly refute assertions that cartoons negatively impact on children. Instead they argue that 'series like *Hey Arnold!*, *South Park* and *The Simpsons* have demonstrated that cartoons can be a vehicle for social commentary, and can tackle children's concerns in ways that are both entertaining and incisive' (Buckingham et al. 1999: 71). Television executives defend their screening of violent cartoons using very similar arguments to these (Kunkel and Wilcox 2001).

While cartoons draw heavily on violent conflict narratives, so too do action programmes aimed at children and youth audiences. In the 1990s *Mighty Morphin Power Rangers* was particularly criticized for encouraging violent play among children. The programme depicts a group of brightly coloured cat suit clad moralistic hero characters who 'preach cooperation and mutual respect, and [who] generally have excellent manners' (Winerip 1995: 77–8), as also using martial arts skills to deadly effect against their enemies. The concern with this type of representation, which shows the 'good guys' using violence to 'good ends', is that it provides little understanding of how conflict can be managed through means other than violence. These arguments can seem especially attractive as explanations for what otherwise appear to be utterly inexplicable behaviours in children. For example, in 1994 *Mighty Morphin Power Rangers* was banned from broadcast in Norway, Denmark and Sweden after it was allegedly linked to the brutal kicking and stoning of a 5-year-old girl by her playmates. When no evidence of links between the show and the children's actions were found, however, the show was subsequently reinstated.

Some media analysts have argued against the assertion that violence in children's television promotes violence in children, and instead suggest that it be considered as a simple and harmless technique for the arousal of excitement in viewers. For example, Sparks (1992) states of action programmes of the 1980s and 1990s such *as Knight Rider*, *Cover Up* and *The A-Team* that:

> The 'violence' is . . . marked as unreal by virtue of its very extravagance and its observation of a stylized choreography, so that it retains its signification of 'excitement' while being freed from any disturbing force. It is thereby established as appropriate for an audience including large numbers of children. In the main it is 'hardware violence', signified through speed of movement, crashing and exploding vehicles and so forth, rather than violence against the body as such.
>
> (Sparks 1992: 137)

Yet as Fiske (1987) has stressed, the violence in action programmes is largely codified as masculine and especially designed to appeal to young male viewers. He theorizes action genre 'hardware violence' as providing a point of fantasy identification for 'young boys whose bodies are not yet strong enough to grant them the power that is their ideological requirement and who also occupy powerless social positions in the family and school' (Fiske 1987: 201). Thus, violent action series are seen as promoting patriarchal ideologies by denying male insecurity while sanctioning male power.

Another television genre that has caused concern in relation to its portrayals of violence and gender representations is music television. Research has found that although this genre is intended for adolescent and young adult audiences, two-thirds of children between the ages of 9 and 11 like to watch it (Signorielli 1991). It has also been found that of all media products, music is the most valued among older children and adolescents (Roberts and Christenson 2001) suggesting that music and music television are important to young people's identities. Consequently, since the 1980s, when explicit song lyrics and music videos containing violent imagery become popular with music artists, music television has been criticized for targeting this at the young 'susceptible' viewer. For example, it is claimed that rock video violence 'taps the most advanced visual and audio techniques to grab the teenager's eye and weaves in sex, morbidity, self-pity, anger, and explicit rebellion against schools, parents and police' (Duff 1993). Yet, research has found that across a range of US music television channels only 14.7 per cent of videos contain 'one or more scenes of overt interpersonal violence' (Rich et al. 1998: 669; see also Smith and Boyson 2002).

What is significant, however, is that when violence does appear in music videos, it is both gendered and raced. Rich et al.'s (1998: 669) study found that in violence music video content, the 'aggressors were 78.1% male' and '[b]lacks were portrayed as aggressors . . . at more than twice the frequency of their 12% representation in the United States population. White females were the single largest race-gender group portrayed as victims.' It is argued that these findings provide cause for concern about how music videos impact on viewers' 'normative expectations about conflict resolution, race, and male–female relationships' (Rich et al. 1998: 669). An additional concern is that in rap music videos, portrayals of adult black characters' recurrent use of violence is often justified and not punished (Smith and Boyson 2002: 79). Such representations, Smith and Boyson (2002: 62) argue, pose the greatest risk to black audiences who are encouraged to view 'the use of violence as a means of social problem solving'. However, other media theorists warn against accepting these concerns.

Buckingham (2000: 123) argues that since the 1980s 'media violence has become implicated in a series of much broader "moral panics" about childhood'. He believes that the 'spectre of the child depraved and brutalized by media violence has come to represent an all-embracing social malaise, a terminal decline in our civilization' (Buckingham 2000: 129). Increases in youth crime rates, horrific acts such as the 1993 murder of 2-year-old James Bulger by two 10-year-olds and the rise of violence in schools, have all prompted fears about what is happening to children. The apparent increase in criminal behaviour among children – behaviour more usually associated with adults – is considered part of a wider breakdown in social and moral order.

Sociologists argue that 'moral panics' about 'the death of childhood', which are found in arguments about the psychological effects of television on young viewers, draw on a discursive construction of children as innocent, vulnerable and in need of protection from the adult world (Gauntlett 1998). Within this discourse, children and adults are constructed in opposition to each other – a construction that Holland (1992, 2001) argues actually works to privilege adult power (see also Davies 1997, 2001). This construction of difference between children and adults is also seen as exerting obligations on those adults 'entrusted' with the care of children – namely parents. Consequentially, allegations about lack of discipline and social morals among the young can be explained as an outcome of 'permissive' parenting (Buckingham 2000: 126).

Ultimately, claims that parents are failing to discipline and teach children appropriate behaviour by restricting their access to the media, lend support to state intervention in children's welfare through, for example, media regulation and censorship. In these terms it can be argued that those who support the censorship of television images of violence are drawing on and using notions of childhood innocence to somewhat wider political ends. This is certainly Buckingham's view when he states that:

> the addition of children to the equation provides a crucial element of rhetorical strength that might otherwise be lacking. While censorship directed at adults could be rejected as authoritarian or as an infringement on individual liberty, the call to protect children is much harder to resist. Particularly in the United States, the notion of childhood has increasingly come to replace the notion of 'national security' as a justification for censorship, not least because of its ability to command political assent.
>
> (Buckingham 2000: 124)

The call to protect children from television violence can then be considered part of neo-conservative political agenda to maintain particular cultural morals, standards and values by preventing the expression of 'undesirable' actions, behaviours and ways of thinking (Barker 2000). By way of contrast, liberal humanists, such as Buckingham (1996, 2000), Barker (2001) and Fowles (1999), defend the rights of both children and adults to engage with a range of moral and 'immoral' ideas. It is also argued the 'frightening image of child*hood*' which constructs children as potentially dangerous, actually serves to silence children' (Holland 2001: 84 original emphasis). Indeed, when children are actually asked about how they engage with violent television content, they reveal a level of complexity of engagement which many media effects theorists seem quite unwilling to even contemplate (Davies 1997, 2001).

Children viewing violence

Just as arguments about the effects of television violence on children are highly polarized, so too are the findings of research into how viewing that violence does indeed impact on children. Consequently these research findings have to be considered in relation to the theoretical and political persuasions of the researchers themselves.

Among media effects theorists it is widely agreed that viewing violence has serious and negative consequences for children in both the short and long term. Paik and Comstock (1994) have reviewed 217 psychological studies, from laboratory experiments through to survey and field research conducted between 1957 and 1990, into the effects of television violence on viewers. From this review they conclude:

> All types of aggressive behaviour, including criminal violence and other illegal activities, have highly significant, albeit, in some cases, small magnitudes of effect size associated with exposure to television violence.
>
> (Paik and Comstock 1994: 538)

They claim that behaviours from aggressive play, to aggressive and violent interpersonal behaviour, through to burglary and criminal violence against other people, are linked to viewing television violence. It is further concluded that the 'effects of TV violence were greatest for the youngest age group' (Bushman and Huesmann 2001).

These findings are explained as tied to children's inability to distinguish fantasy from reality and their imitating even fantasy cartoon depictions of violence, their inability to distinguish between justified and non-justified violence and a susceptibility to identification with violent characters (Bushman and Huesmann 2001). Effects researchers have also found boys to be more prone to the effects of viewing violence than girls because they viewed violence in male characters as socially desirable (Comstock and Paik 1991; Geen 1994). Bushman and Huesmann (2001: 242) suspect that in time girls may well be equally affected by television 'as more aggressive female models have appeared on TV and it has become more socially acceptable for females to behave aggressively'.

The family environment is also seen as a determinant in whether children are negatively affected by television. It is claimed that co-viewing with children reduces the potential for impact, as does parental restriction of the types of programmes watched (Bushman and Huesmann 2001). Clearly, these findings lend support to the censorship of children's television viewing. However, there is an implicit assumption in effects studies of children and television violence that children actively seek out violent entertainment and that this is why they need controlling. Nevertheless, Cantor (1998) has found that children between the ages of 2 and 11 are more likely to watch family sitcoms than programmes containing violence targeted at younger viewers. Where children do demonstrate an eagerness to watch television violence, gender is a prominent factor in that propensity, with boys showing significantly more interest in violent programmes than girls with this interest increasing with age (Cantor 1998). That violent heroes are usually male, and that 'imagining oneself as the aggressor . . . positively correlated with interest in viewing violence [and] . . . empathizing with the victim . . . negatively related to interest in viewing violence' (Cantor 1998: 98) further explains gendered differences in attraction to television violence.

Taking research beyond the question of children's attraction to violent television content and subsequent behaviours, some researchers have investigated what meanings children take from this violence. A particularly interesting study of this type was conducted in Australia by Tulloch and Tulloch (1993). Their research innovatively combined developmental psychology and cultural theory allowing them to consider behaviour as a response to 'institutional, structural and ideological determinants', rather than as an individual response to psychological stimuli – such as images of violence. The study explores the significance of age, class and gender in determining school children's responses to an extract from *Tour of Duty* – the US fiction series featuring the exploits of US soldiers in the Vietnam War. The concern was to investigate how children's understandings of the programme draw on 'everyday explanatory discourses', how they make sense of the violence depicted, levels of tolerance for the violent solutions represented, and an analysis of 'feelings, attitudes and emotions toward heroes, villains and victims of violence' (Tulloch and Tulloch 1993: 213).

Like Cantor (1998), Tulloch and Tulloch (1993) found that children's responses to television violence are gendered; for boys there was an articulated relationship between finding pleasure in the images of violence and assertions of masculinity. In contrast, older girls tended to regard the show as more 'serious' and less entertaining. In response to *Tour of Duty* it was only ever girls who presented an 'anti-macho, anti-US' critique of the programme. In addition, class affected how children interpreted the text. Working-class children, irrespective of gender, were more likely to view the narrative as primarily about violence, whereas middle-class children interpreted it as including a greater range of thematic concerns which helped them to place the violence in a wider explanatory context. Working-class children, both boys and girls, also demonstrated a greater tolerance for physical violence as a solution to problems faced by characters in *Tour of Duty*. Tulloch and Tulloch (1993: 243) argue that such responses reflect the fact that the working classes are 'more subject to societal violence than others'.

Tulloch and Tulloch's (1993: 244, emphasis in the original) research demonstrates how 'children like television itself, are *agents* in the field of TV violence, with complex class, gender and age-influenced agendas of their own. It is these sociocognitive agendas which engage both with violence *and* with "alternatives to its expression".' These findings also demonstrate that children's relationship with television violence needs to be evaluated in very similar – rather than very different terms – as adults' relationships to television violence. However, underlying much of the research into, and concerns about, children and television violence is the assumption that children are indeed very different from adults. This assumption is equally reflected in television broadcasting policy.

Broadcasting policy to protect the innocent

The belief that television violence can have negative effects on viewers, and especially children, determines a great deal of television-broadcasting policy throughout the world (Weaver 1996). In Britain, the USA, Canada, Australia and New Zealand, for example, statutory bodies regulate television content, and receive and adjudicate on viewer complaints about that content. Violence consistently features as one of the primary areas of concern for these bodies, along with sex and issues of taste and decency.

In Britain the Broadcasting Standards Commission (BSC), established under the Broadcasting Act 1996, performs this role, along with the Independent Television Commission. These regulatory bodies have powers to censure broadcasters if content exceeds the bounds of that deemed 'acceptable', and broadcasters are required to comply with specific regulations designed to protect younger audiences. For example in Britain *explicit* sex and violence cannot be broadcast before 9 p.m. (the so-called watershed). In the USA the **Federal Communications Commission** (FCC) 'prohibits indecent programming broadcasts between 6 a.m. and 10 p.m. . . . to curb[ ] the exposure of children to violent programming' (Hamilton 1998: 299).

In an effort to encourage and help parents censor children's viewing, in 1996 the Federal Telecommunications Act (FTA) introduced the legislative requirement that all newly manufactured television sets of 13 inches or larger be installed with a V-chip. The Canadian Radio-Television and Telecommunications Commission similarly introduced such laws in 1999. V-chip software provides the means to block programme television and video reception by either ratings codes or specified age appropriate programming. The age rating system which facilitates the use of the V-chip technology is administered by the broadcasting industry. Programmes are labelled as follows: 'TV-Y' appropriate for all children including those aged 2–6; 'TV-7' for children aged 7 and above; 'TV-PG' parental guidance suggested –

parents may find material unsuitable for younger children; 'TV-14' parents strongly cautioned – contains some material that many parents would find unsuitable for children under 14; 'G' general audience; and 'TV-MA' mature audience only – may be unsuitable for children under 17. Programmes are also rated according to violent (V), sexual (S), coarse/crude/indecent language (L) and suggestive dialogue (D) content. Broadcasters transmit these age and content ratings for 15 seconds at the beginning of all rated programmes, and print them in programme schedules. The V-chip software reads the programme rating and allows, or blocks programme reception based on what it is coded to accept or decline.

The introduction of V-chip technology in the USA was highly controversial, especially in terms of how it might impinge on individual rights to freedom of expression and the rights of a free press under the First Amendment. Fowles (1999) argues that the system could act to dissuade producers from making programmes containing violent imagery fearing that use of the V-chip would cause a decline in ratings and make certain programmes less attractive to advertisers. Legally, it is said that such a 'chilling effect' could be justified as behaviourist psychological research demonstrates that television violence poses a threat to social order, and it is, therefore, in the states' interest to regulate it. Legal scholars diverge in opinion as to whether this constitutes a violation of the First Amendment. Ballard (1995), drawing on the lack of conclusive evidence of links between television violence and anti-social behaviour, argues that the V-chip is an infringement of individual rights. Spitzer (1998: 363) contends that the V-chip system may well be constitutional 'even under strict scrutiny, as supporting parental authority to control children's diet of television'. In Europe, the controversies surrounding the V-chip are not likely to become an issue, as there the introduction of the technology is not favoured. Instead, in European countries the provision of increased information about the content of films and television programmes to assist viewing decisions is preferred (Buckingham 2000).

However, the impact of the V-chip on children's viewing patterns actually appears to be negligible in the USA and Canada. In the USA the V-chip was reported as failing to catch on with the public due to lack of awareness about it, difficulties experienced in using it, and/or because parents simply did not feel the need to use it (Greenman 1999). It would therefore seem that parents are less concerned about the effects of television violence than are media effects theorists, researchers and certain media lobby groups. Yet this may be because, as we shall now turn to explore, for adults television violence is simply an accepted part of everyday media reality and not something to be overly concerned about.

Television violence for adults

Just as we have discussed in relation to the news media in Chapter 1, adult television programmes promote particular understandings of violence and encourage viewers to adopt certain ideological positions in relation to violence, conceiving some types as 'legitimate' and some as 'illegitimate'. Even within single television genres, there are carefully constructed demarcations between legitimate and illegitimate violence. As we illustrate through the discussion of three quite different television genres – police crime drama, reality crime programmes, and television sports programming – these demarcations can be understood only in relation to wider social and cultural structures of power of which television is a part.

Police crime drama

Until the proliferation of reality television in the 1990s, police crime drama was responsible for the greater proportion of the television's violent content. For the most part, until the mid-1970s, this drama portrayed violence as a behavioural characteristic of villains. Thus, a capacity for violence was what marked villains as 'bad', and provided a means of constructing them as 'other'. In Britain this changed with the 1975 arrival of Thames Television's *The Sweeney* and its lead character – the 'tough individualistic freebooting cop' – Jack Regan (Hurd 1981: 61) (Figure 3.1). *The Sweeney* was groundbreaking in its portrayal of a world in which the bureaucracies of the police and legal systems could not be relied upon to deliver justice and protect the innocent (Sparks 1992). Consequentially 'the guarantor of certainty [becomes] the picaresque individual, for whom violence is generally the condition of success' (Sparks 1992: 29). Yet, Hurd argues that in its representation of an anomic world:

> *The Sweeney* marks its violence heavily as method but refuses its substance – the choreographed crazing of shotgun-blasted windscreens, balletic car crashes, iconographic detailing of Lugers, knuckle-dusters and telescopic coshes – in such a way that its presence does no more than confirm our expectations, emptied of its potentially disruptive content. *The Sweeney* is violent but it is not about violence. The nearest Regan gets to philosophizing about the subject is the observation, 'if people carry guns they can end up using them'.
>
> (Hurd 1981: 62)

To an extent the violence in *The Sweeney* is, as Hurd describes it, pure spectacle wrapped in a search and capture narrative. However, *The Sweeney* is

Figure 3.1 *The Sweeney* 'Guns aloft – you're nicked!' It's a man's world. Jack Regan (left) and his partner George Carter are just as violent as the criminals they pursue in the transformational British cop show *The Sweeney*.
Source: FremantleMedia Ltd.

also considered to reflect late capitalist antagonisms between the working-class police officers and the middle-class bureaucrats running the police and legal institutions (Fiske and Hartley 1978; Sparks 1992). Because these institutions are represented as incapacitated and corrupt, the deviant brutality of the policeman 'hero' is represented as a legitimate means of enforcing criminal justice. Thus, as is often the case in crime narratives, 'masculine volatility is harnessed for acceptable purposes' (Cuklanz 2000: 20).

In the USA it was *Hill Street Blues*, first broadcast in 1981, which took US police drama out of what had previously been a good cop/violent villain narrative into a more morally ambiguous and violent police culture. Intentionally pushing broadcasting standards boundaries in its portrayals of sex and violence, the show has been described as the 'first post liberal cop show' to depict the police's 'daily struggle to cope with a violent society' (Gitlin 1994: 310). In *Hill Street Blues* tensions between ethnic groups were at the forefront of the drama *and* its violence. Consequently, while the Hill Street police department includes a small minority of blacks and Hispanics, the programme was criticized for reinforcing stereotypes of these cultures through one-dimensional portrayals of violent ethnic criminal ghettos (Gitlin 1994).

Indeed, Pines (1995) argues that within police crime shows:

> Black characters and black related dramatic situations tend to be constructed within fairly narrow parameters: Black villains are stereotypically linked to drug dealing, violent street crime (for example mugging) and prostitution; while black cop 'heroes' tend to be characterized as noble figures whose mission is to clean up the criminalized black neighborhoods.
>
> (Pines 1995: 74)

To be sure representations of non-whites in crime/police drama have increased in complexity in the 1980s and 1990s with shows such as *NYPD Blue*, *The Bill* and *Law and Order* having more recently introduced audiences to a wider range of 'race relations' narratives (Pines 1995).

Even though racial issues have come to feature more prominently in recent police crime series, Pines (1995: 73) stresses that racial tensions are 'eventually "resolved" or, rather, held in check . . . through exigencies of male bonding'. That is, racial conflicts between police officers ultimately never get in the way of their working together 'as men'. Indeed, police drama often overwhelmingly reinforces the perception of policing as a 'man's world' in which only men are able to stand up to the physical demands of the job of policing a violent and dangerous society. Consequently, viewer identification with this world requires their 'incorporation into the hegemonic masculinity [which] usually precludes any outrage at the exposure to brutality and brutalizing processes which characterize certain aspects of police work' (Eaton 1995: 183).

With the arrival of *Prime Suspect* and *Between the Lines* on British television screens in the early 1990s, television police drama 'presented the viewer with the possibility of concluding that hegemonic masculinity might be a damaging and destructive force' (Eaton 1995: 183). Created after various revelations of police corruption and miscarriages of justice in the UK throughout the 1980s and 1990s, these highly popular series portrayed evidently 'nice blokes' as capable of appallingly violent crimes. They also explored how the male culture of the police force encourages sexist, abusive and even violent behaviour among its officers. *Between the Lines* is especially interesting in this respect: it overtly politicizes law and order and government institutions and claims to 'truth' and calls 'the social positions and values of the central males [in the show] . . . profoundly into question' (Nelson 1997: 188). As Brunsdon (1998) has pointed out though, the programme could do this because it was set in the Complaints Investigation Bureau of the London Metropolitan police, which investigates the conduct of the police rather than the public. The programme consequently provided an innovatively critical view of the police, though one since usurped by the television's new fashion for reality crime shows that have restored the audience's point of identification to the police officer.

Reality crime shows

Since the 1980s reality crime shows have provided viewers with the opportunity to witness actual, rather than fictional, acts of violence. Research suggests that reality-based programmes now exceed all other television genres in the inclusion of depictions of 'extended behavioral violence' (Wilson et al. 1998b: 125). Comprising crime reconstruction programmes such as *Crimewatch UK* and *America's Most Wanted*, and real-life crime shows such as *Cops*, *Night Beat* and *True Stories of the Highway Patrol*, these highly popular formats involve a complex blurring of fact and fiction in their representations: they contain either reconstructions or footage of real-life acts of crime and violence, but draw on narrative and stylistic conventions of crime fiction in (re)presenting those acts to audiences. In these terms it is said that reality crime programming 'blends information and entertainment' and 'exploits the possibilities of crime and punishment as spectacle' (Cavender and Fishman 1998: 12).

While reality crime programmes have proved an extremely popular television genre in the USA, UK, Australia and New Zealand, for example, in Russia they have seemingly reached the heights of a national obsession. Russian viewing schedules comprise a significant number of reality crime shows, such as *Criminal Russia*, *The Accidental Witness* and *The Road Patrol*, with the latter screening four times a day on weekdays, and three times a day at weekends (Figure 3.2). Showing corpses from car crashes, fires and murders, it is said that the pictures included in these Russian programmes 'are so explicit they probably wouldn't be shown on US television' (CNN 1997).

Reality crime programmes have been criticized on a number of levels. It is said that they exploit real-life crime for entertainment purposes (Hebert 1988, 1993; Minogue 1990; Sweeney 1992; Weaver et al. 2000). They have been accused of creating fear of crime, or even capitalizing on that fear

PHOTOGRAPH: ROBERT KING

Ambulance chasing . . . a Road Patrol cameraman films the body of a man who died trying to cross a busy street in Moscow

They prowl the streets of Moscow, filming in close-up the dead victims of fires, crime, and car accidents – and their bulletins make some of the most popular TV in Russia. **Amelia Gentleman** joins the Road Patrol

TV to die for

As dusk settles over Moscow, the Road Patrol team is beginning to get anxious about its failure to find any corpses. The entire day has been spent driving through the city from traffic accident to police station to domestic crisis, and the only success so far has been to catch two crumpled Ladas smashed together in a snowdrift. A slightly injured passenger has already been taken to hospital; instead the cameraman is forced to film a patch of blood-stained snow, before stamping off, muttering: "We're wasting our time. This is rubbish."

So a wave of happy relief sweeps over the team when they receive the final call of the day. A retired engineer has spent the evening lying in bed drinking vodka and smoking, setting himself and his home alight; a raging fire is consuming a central Moscow apartment block.

The team arrives just in time to film the man's burning belongings as they are hurled from a fifth-floor window that is still gushing thick smoke; blackened pages from photograph albums float through the night. Jumping over a tangle of hosepipes, the camera crew runs past the firemen and up the sealed-off stairway to where the dead engineer's widow and daughter are standing speechless over his body.

This moment is recorded for the programme, and supplemented with shots from inside the smouldering flat, lingering on a vast collection of empty vodka bottles. "He looked as though he died in his sleep," the cameraman says. "But we filmed his feet, which had burnt a little."

Outside, a group of children, no older than seven, crowd around - impressed by the team's trademark turquoise jackets. "Wow. Road Patrol," they say.

Broadcast four times a day, seven days a week, Road Patrol is one of Russia's most popular programmes – attracting viewers with its voyeuristic intrusion into the disasters that strike the capital every day. In 15-minute snatches, an assortment of murders, crash deaths and apartment infernos are flashed across the screen. Newly arrested suspects are led out from their police cells and goaded towards on-screen confessions – with a casual approach to the presumption of innocence before guilt is proven. The hysterical grief of victims is recorded. Dead bodies are shown in close-up on primetime television. This is not a show for the squeamish, but its success is immense.

The format was created in the mid-1990s by a group of shrewd television executives who had latched on to the public's growing enthusiasm for televised crime and disaster - subjects glossed over for decades by relentlessly positive Soviet news broadcasts, which were dedicated primarily to the country's agricultural and industrial successes. The show regularly tops the channel's weekly ratings and advertisers compete to have names painted beneath the red lightning arrows on the side of its reporters' cars.

The show's editor, Andrei Chereshnev, is a little defensive about its success, aware that the content is rather strong for western tastes. He insists that this is not entertainment because there is a strong moral message to the show; he claims it is designed to help people – like a horrifyingly graphic public safety warning. "The main purpose is to inform people about the dangers of drinking and driving or of drug abuse. This kind of approach is far more effective than handing out government information leaflets," he says, reclining in a black leather chair. "There is probably a small percentage of people who watch it just for the nasty pictures, but they're a minority because we're quite careful about what we show. We'd only do a close-up on a headless corpse if police wanted help in identifying it."

The reporting teams have managed to persuade themselves that the show makes people feel happy. "We cheer people up. They look at all the terrible things that are happening elsewhere in the city and cross themselves, saying, 'Thank God it wasn't me.' It helps people realise that their own lives are not so bad."

At the end of the evening dispatch, figures for the day's murders, car crashes, drunk drivers and violent attacks are listed. When the programme first appeared, viewers complained that this information heightened people's fear of crime to such an extent that they were afraid to go out. Six years later, the show rarely triggers outrage; mainstream news broadcasts have begun to include equally graphic news footage of dead disaster victims. "People aren't shocked by our programme – it takes a lot to shock people here, but we realise it could never be shown in Europe or America because tastes are very different," Chereshnev says. Dozens of viewers telephone every day to tip off the programme about the location of developing catastrophes. Moscow police also ring in, happy to be filmed for the show.

No one likes to admit that Road Patrol may simply be satisfying the public's appetite for violent disaster. But in a quiet moment, the cameraman points out that the reporting teams are under immense pressure to provide an ample supply of bleeding flesh. "Sometimes people ring up complaining that there hasn't been enough blood. Ratings drop," he said. There is a lucrative market for bootleg greatest-hits videos that bring together the worst moments ever filmed.

The reporters charged with scouring the city for disaster have developed a refined brand of morgue humour to help them cope with their work. They have sinister euphemisms for the mutilated corpses they come across. A murder victim whose arms and legs have been chopped off is called a "samovar" (a reference to the torso-shaped Russian kettle); those who have simply been chopped up are referred to as "Lego"; people who have thrown themselves from the roofs of buildings are "parachutists"; those who have drowned themselves are "divers"; the travelling morgue van, with its cold-storage facilities, is called "Baskin Robbins" (after the US ice-cream company). To the uninitiated, conversation with the team is extremely bemusing.

Beneath the bleak humour, they claim to work to a strict ethical code. "We may be cynical but we have our limits. We don't like filming dead children. Yesterday we found a baby that someone had thrown into a rubbish bin in the street. We didn't film that," the presenter says. Instead the team made up their quota of material when they came across two teenage heroin addicts hanging from the ceiling of an apartment block stairway. "They'd run out of money for drugs so they killed themselves," the reporter says. Later there was an elderly woman who had slipped on the ice and fallen under a tram, so they were able to use that too, filming her greying body lying by the road, covered in a thin layer of snow. In a sombre voiceover, the presenter reported that the tram line was out of action for half an hour after the incident.

Aside from the unsatisfactory road accidents, today's most successful report is the interview with a young boy accused of stealing a leather jacket from a man in an apartment-block lift. Police remove him from the police station cage to be interviewed. After a few minutes of aggressive questioning, the reporter asks him if his mother knows he is in jail, and the boy turns his face to the wall and begins to weep. The cameraman (who would rather be filming wildlife documentaries) lingers on the boy's shuddering back before spending several minutes trying to film sunshine through the police station's barred window. Satisfied, the reporter confides later: "It looks good when they cry." A few hours later the boy's humiliation is broadcast to millions.

This is a wearying job. "I've stopped having nightmares, but I can never bring myself to watch the programme," the cameraman says. "I still can't cope with the sight of bits of brain on the pavement, or dismembered hands or feet. I hate the sound of people crying in pain, begging for help. But it's my job to film it; my brain has learned to wash away the memories."

Figure 3.2 'To Die for' Russian Road Patrol. Amelia Gentleman. The Russian reality programme *The Road Patrol* attracted widespread media attention and critiques for its explicit and graphic content which, it is claimed, works as a warning of the dangers of the roads.
Source: © *Guardian*, 20 March 2001.

(Hebert 1993; Moore 1993; Osborne 1995) and research indicates that they especially induce fear of violent crime among women viewers (BBC Broadcasting Research 1988; Wober and Gunter 1990; Schlesinger et al. 1992; C.K. Weaver 1998). Programmes have been described as voyeuristic (Cavender 1998; Culf 1993; Hebert 1993) in that they invite viewers into the private world of crime victims and, on occasion, crime perpetrators. Moreover, they are criticized for emphasizing the reporting of particular types of sensationalist crime in an effort to attract viewers (Schlesinger and Tumber 1994). For example, Schlesinger et al. (1991: 408) state of *Crimewatch UK* that 'the programme team select their crime stories from the popular end of the market, with murder, armed robbery with violence and sexual crime as the staple items of coverage'.

While fears about the impact of television violence on viewers predominantly focus on whether it will induce violence in viewers, criticisms of crime reality shows conversely focus on the programmes' promotion of right wing 'get tough' law and order politics. For example, Osborne (1995) states that:

> The selectivity of these programmes, the agenda they adopt and set, the kinds of media messages they generate all point towards an analysis which suggests that they are creating a popular culture of cynicism and despair, mixed with a neo-fascistic longing for order and retribution.
>
> (Osborne 1995: 39)

Cavender (1998) argues that reality crime shows also encourage discursive identification with law and order crime control through the 'othering' of crime perpetrators. Perpetrators are codified as having different ideological values from the audience and as carrying identifiable physical markers such as tattoos and other deviant symbols. 'This "them vs. us" dichotomy speaks to a perceived cohesive social order which the criminal threatens' (Cavender 1998: 86).

It is also argued that reality crime television's focus on the capture of individual offenders displaces any focus on the structural causes of crime such as racism, sexism, poverty and unemployment (Anderson 1995; Doyle 1998). Indeed, Anderson explains that reality police shows usually end with

> an image of the cops pushing the head of the suspect – hands cuffed behind his back – as he bends awkwardly into the back seat of a police car. This resolution is presented as the resolution to crime, the answer endlessly promoted by political and media discourse: Get the criminal (suspect?) off the streets and into prison.
>
> (Anderson 1995: 195)

What particularly worries many critics of reality crime programmes is how the mutually beneficial and dependent relationship which television companies and the police have developed in broadcasting these programmes has eroded media independence in relation to the police. Anderson (1995: 181) argues that this 'has had a profound impact on media representations of crime and the general discussion of those issues within the public sphere'. While some fiction police dramas have portrayed issues of law and order in complex ways and examined tensions around violence, racism and sexism *within* our law and order institutions, shows like *Cops* and *Night Beat* re-establish the legitimacy of (male) police violence as necessary to combat 'illegitimate' criminal violence.

Violent sports programming

Televised sports depend on carefully marked distinctions between 'legitimate' and 'illegitimate' violence. Yet, because violent contact sports such as boxing, World Wrestling Federation wrestling, American football and rugby union, which are highly popular with television audiences, all celebrate violent masculinity they raise concerns about the discursive messages that they communicate to viewers.

For violence in sport to be sanctioned a number of criteria must be fulfilled. First, violence must fall within the accepted rules of play (McLaughlin 1999). Second, the violence must be performed within a determined space (a pitch or ring), and involve a referee or judge and consenting participants. However, most importantly, only men are able to give their consent to this participation. This is because the 'legitimacy of violence in sport . . . balances upon the axis of power in the gender order, where physical combat, blood and bruises are considered "natural" for men, and alien to women' (Boyle and Haynes 2000: 137).

With violent sports such as boxing and rugby receiving prime-time television coverage, as well as big money prizes and pay cheques, sports programming contributes to the discursive marking of violent masculinity as hegemonically valued. Yet the financial incentive to participate in violent sport is not only reserved for athletes. Television broadcasters make enormous profits in advertising revenue by screening high-rating sports shows such as the Superbowl, hence their willingness to pay vast sums of money demanded by sports bodies for the broadcast rights to these games. Violent sports programming can even play a crucial role attracting audiences to new systems of television delivery. As Schlesinger et al. (1998: 51) detail, 'In March 1996, the world title fight between Frank Bruno and Mike Tyson heralded the introduction of pay-per-view (ppv) television in the UK, with 660,000 willing customers'.

Mike Tyson is perhaps the most notoriously violent of sports stars, attracting labels such as 'the killing machine', 'the man-beast machine' and 'evil incarnate' (Sloop 1997). He is known not only as a fearless sportsman, but also as one who goes well beyond what his sport deems 'legitimate' violence. For example, in a 1997 bout, Tyson bit a chunk from his opponent Evander Holyfield's ear. Consequently his boxing licence was temporarily revoked. Tyson is also known for his violence outside the ring. In 1992 he was convicted of rape for which he served three years in prison. In 2001 he got into a highly publicized brawl with Lennox Lewis at a pre-match press conference that was widely broadcast on television. Again this cost him his licence to box.

Tyson is not alone among sports stars for having an association with acts of violence outside of the sporting arena. Other stars, most recently the former American footballer OJ Simpson (who was arrested for killing his ex-wife and her companion 1994) and figure skater Tonya Harding (who in 1994 conspired to injure her US Olympic team-mate and rival Nancy Kerrigan), have attracted considerable media reporting for their (in Simpson's case alleged) acts of criminal violence. Yet what is especially significant in relation to Tyson is how the media construct his violence as the trait of a sex-obsessed, uneducated, socially inept, African American (Sloop 1997). OJ Simpson's alleged murder was also popularly constructed by the media in these terms with its 'themes of . . . murder and sexual jealousy, reviv[ing] the associations of predatory black male sexuality linked to brutal violence' (Burstyn 1999: 209).

In the cases of both OJ Simpson and Mike Tyson, their violence outside of the sports arena has not been popularly explored as potentially linked to western culture's cherishing of violent masculinity. Rather, media reporting constructs their actions in racist terms as the traits of the 'uncontrollable black savage'. This is the same discursive construction of blacks featured in the film *The Birth of the Nation* that we discussed in Chapter 2, which functions to condone white racism and the violent oppression of blacks. Within this racism there is no consideration of how black athletes are 'exploited for violence within the "rules of the game", then despised when that violence spills over into real life' (Burstyn 1999: 164). What is also rarely considered is not only how sports stars' immersion in a violent sport might impact on their everyday personal behaviour, but also how violent sports culture 'spills over' into the home where audiences watch violent sport on television.

In light of the value that television places on violent male sports, feminist sports scholars 'have been concerned about the potential linkages among sports, masculinity, and men's violence' (Sabo and Jansen 1998: 207). Especially troubling to these scholars are the dramatic increases in the number of telephone calls made to battered women's help-lines when events like the Superbowl are broadcast (McBride 1995). It is *not* claimed that watching the Superbowl has the 'effect' of causing men to be violent. Rather, it is said that:

> Mediated sports appear[ ] to function for these battering men as a cultural site in which a confluence occur[s] between psychosocial pro- cesses (e.g., boyhood and adult identification with sports and aggres- sion and interpersonal dynamics in family relationships) and the adoption of cultural scripts that equate manhood to violence proneness and domination over women.
>
> (Sabo and Jansen 1998: 209)

Interestingly, in light of publicity about connections between the Superbowl and violence against women, the National Football League has sponsored pre-game television public service announcements promoting telephone help- line numbers to victims of male battery (McBride 1995). However, neither the National Football League nor broadcasters of the Superbowl will concede to associations between American football and men's battering of women (McBride 1995). To do so would be to suggest that women's rights to be free from violence are greater than the rights of sporting bodies and media con- glomerates to make money from violent sports, and audiences' right to the entertainment those sports provide. It is in this context that Whannel (1992: 192) is led to assert that 'television must be seen as one of the bastions of patriarchy'. Certainly recent research into men's and women's engagement with television violence lends some support to this claim.

Adults viewing television violence

In the 1990s, dissatisfied with both effects and text-based arguments about how television violence impacts on viewers, a number of sociology, media and cultural studies researchers turned to examine how adults actually engage with violent television content. Often examining how factors such as class, race, age and sexuality affected response, these studies have provided significant insights into how audiences relate to and make sense of television violence.

In investigating how viewers related to violence in television fiction, Docherty (1990) found that they are more concerned by violent portrayals in realistic drama than in escapist genres. Escapist material, although con- taining great quantities of violence and blood, was considered to be largely innocuous among his research respondents. In these terms Docherty theo- rized escapist drama as providing for pleasures associated with 'shallow play', which he defined as 'leav[ing] most people untroubled. Culturally, and socially, there is little or nothing at stake in shallow play' (Docherty 1990: 10).

Whether the television images of the September 11 World Trade Center attacks will have changed this type of evaluation of, and response to, so-called 'escapist' images of violence remains to be seen. A prominent feature of responses to those images, as discussed in Chapter 2, was their initial association with fantastical screen entertainment. Thus while those images fitted viewers' expectations of what Docherty defines as 'shallow play', the fact that they were real takes them into the realms of what he defines as 'deep play'. Docherty states that 'deep play'

> may occur when . . . viewers feel that a fiction is an indictment on . . . life, or if a drama contains violence which viewers can see on our streets. Such entertainment may trigger anxious concern about the possible effects of the images or resentment at the inaccurate depiction of society.
>
> (Docherty 1990: 10)

Docherty found, however, that such responses were as much related to the types of *issues* dealt within a programme as they were to actual images of violence. For example, in relation to *The Firm*, a BBC play about football hooliganism, Docherty found that:

> To approve of the play, for many people, was to approve of the actions – despite the play's more or less explicit rejection of the violence which it examined. People who were committed to the play explained their pleasure not in terms of the drama, but in terms of its import – its contribution to understanding and therefore resolving a major problem.
>
> (Docherty 1990: 31)

These findings provide interesting insight into the complex means by which viewers respond to and evaluate violent representations. They also lend support to McKinney's (1993) assertions, discussed in Chapter 2, that what he defines as 'strong violence' (which Docherty defines as 'deep play'), can be socially valuable in promoting thinking about violence, its causes, effects, and consequences.

Like Docherty, Schlesinger et al. (1992) explore how viewers attribute meaning to television portrayals of violence across different programme genres. However, they specifically confine their British-based study to examining women's responses to portrayals of violence against women. The programmes investigated comprise an edition of *Crimewatch UK* featuring the reconstruction concerning a young woman's sexual assault and murder, a portrayal of domestic violence in the soap opera *EastEnders*, and domestic violence and police violence in the one-off television drama *Closing Ranks*. The research examines how representations of violence 'are actually received and how the impact of televised violence upon women's conceptions of themselves – their gender identities – might be variously described' (Schlesinger et al. 1992: 3). Women from different class, regional and ethnic backgrounds participated in the study. Half of the respondents had also experienced actual physical violence committed against them by men. This allowed the researchers to consider how women's social, cultural and material experiences affected their interpretations of violence.

Schlesinger et al. (1992) found subtle differences in how different women engaged with the representations of violence. Class, ethnicity and women's experience or non-experience of male violence all influenced response. Women were often not greatly concerned by television's actual depiction of violence. Rather, a feature of their interpretation was the significance of the violent act in relation to their own lives and behaviours. For example, for many Asian women the *Crimewatch* reconstruction confirmed culturally inscribed beliefs that women who ventured out alone were putting themselves in grave danger. This produced a lack of sympathy among some Asian women toward female victims of male violence and – as was also a case for many African Caribbean respondents, a lack of identification with especially white female victims of violent attack.

Experience of violence, or lack of it, also played a significant part in structuring interpretations. Women with experience of violence reported that watching television violence increased their levels of anxiety, fear and upset. These women also tended to be more sympathetic toward victims of attack and less likely to blame the victims and provide excuses for the perpetrators, than were the women with no experience of violence. In these terms, the study highlights how viewers' experiential backgrounds affect the interpretation of television violence, and how women who have not experienced violence themselves were apt to adopt patriarchal explanations of why women become victims of male attack. Interestingly, the research found little support among respondents for censoring depictions of violence against women. Respondents predominantly felt that as long as depictions were of 'relevance' and 'educational' use value, they were acceptable.

There are some incongruities in Schlesinger et al.'s (1992) findings of how women interpret portrayals of violence. For example, while many interviewees argued that violence against women should not be portrayed for entertainment's sake, all the texts featuring in the research can be regarded as produced for exactly that purpose. There is also a need to consider how audio-visual texts promote certain social and cultural assumptions about why women are vulnerable to male attack and in what contexts. In the continued exploration of the data collected by Schlesinger et al. (1992), Weaver (1995, 1998; Weaver et al. 2000) explored these issues and re-examined how the women respondents were interpreting the texts used in the research as 'educational'. Weaver concludes that the programmes were actually educating women to believe that it is 'their individual responsibility to restrict and censure their activities so as to avoid becoming the victim of [male attack]' (C.K. Weaver 1998: 262). In these terms, Weaver argues that images of violence against women frequently function to support patriarchal hegemonic privilege and women's symbolic oppression.

Schlesinger et al.'s (1998) research into men's interpretations of television portrayals of violence lends some support to Weaver's conclusions. Their investigation examines the responses of British male viewers of differing ages, sexual preferences and ethnic, class and regional backgrounds, to a range of factual and fictional screen media depictions of male violence committed against both men and women. The study revealed that, unlike women, men did not have an everyday fear of violence, and screen violence had little impact upon their levels of fear or anxiety.

In relation to men's interpretations of screen images of violence, Schlesinger et al. (1998: iv) found that violence in factual television 'rooted as it was in reality, had the greatest impact whether the men were watching sport or documentary programming'. Additionally, the 'more "real" the representation of violence the greater the respondents' engagement with a particular programme became' (Schlesinger et al. 1998: 30). All the men in Schlesinger et al.'s (1998: iv) study 'identified sport as a masculine pursuit that they acknowledged as being linked with aggression and sometimes violence'. Violence depicted in more fantastical fiction genres had less impact upon the men as it is 'seen as less socially consequential than violence operating within a realistic mode of representation' (Schlesinger et al. 1998: 63).

Perhaps the most significant of Schlesinger et al.'s (1998) findings is how men's reactions to violent portrayals, and their interpretations of these, reflected a largely very masculine view of violence. They state that the research 'highlighted a key limit in the capacity for men to imagine themselves outside of the world of masculinity' (Schlesinger et al. 1998: 67). This resulted in infrequent sympathy toward women victims of violence, and frequent victim blaming. Gay men were, however, more likely to sympathize with female victims of violence and were less likely than heterosexual men to gain pleasure from watching realistic violence. Heterosexual men, and especially young working-class men, were more inclined to enjoy violent representations. This reflects the fact that such men's identities are more dependent on the association of masculinity with violence as power. The working-class men's enjoyment of violent portrayals also bears considerable similarity to Tulloch and Tulloch's (1993) finding (discussed earlier) that working-class boys are more likely to enjoy violence than middle-class boys.

Increasingly evident from the developing research inquiry into the meaning of violence for viewers is the significance of gender to audiences' interpretations of television violence and the pleasure they take from watching violence. This is further confirmed by Morrison et al. (1999), who examined how both men and women define and relate to screen violence. Their study found that '[a]lthough quite a few of our female respondents enjoyed scenes of violence, absolute enjoyment was more a male preserve' (Morrison et al. 1999: 131).

Conclusion

Television presents images of violence in an enormous variety of contexts and formats. Through some of these genres, violence is presented as a legitimate action – for example, when it is part of a defined 'rules of the game' or when it serves to enforce criminal justice when other systems of justice have failed. As this chapter has illustrated, gender is an important structuring factor in how television represents violence, and how viewers interpret that violence; masculinity provides the conduit for the representation of legitimate violence, and the basis for much of the enjoyment of such representation. In this context, concerns about children's viewing of television violence are somewhat misguided in seeking to reconfigure television content as this content comprises the expression of an entire ideological infrastructure which celebrates violence, and specifically masculine violence. Changing television content will be meaningful only when violent masculinity is no longer culturally cherished.

As our next chapter explores, pornography has also raised significant concerns in terms of whether it has negative effects for both its audiences and social perceptions of women. However, pornography allows us to investigate how violence and explicit sex are articulated together in the media, which raises a whole new set of issues for the definition of violence and questions of its effects.

Further reading

Burstyn, V. (1999) *The Rites of Men: Manhood, Politics, and the Culture of Sport.* Toronto: University of Toronto Press.

Fishman, M. and Cavender, G. (eds) (1998) *Entertaining Crime: Television Reality Programs*. New York: Aldine de Gruyter.

Gunter, B. and McAleer, J. (1997) *Children and Television*, 4th edn. London: Routledge.

Schlesinger, P., Dobash, R.E., Dobash, R. and Weaver, C.K. (1992) *Women Viewing Violence*. London: British Film Institute.

Schlesinger, P., Haynes, R., Boyle, R. et al. (1998) *Men Viewing Violence*. London: Broadcasting Standards Commission.

4

PORNOFURY

Some have said that pornography is a superficial target . . . The premises of
pornography are controlling in every rape and every rape case, whenever a
woman is battered or prostituted, in incest . . . and in murder – murders of
women by husbands, lovers, and serial killers. If this is superficial, what's deep?

(Andrea Dworkin 1997: 99–100)

The battle against pornography . . . is the battle against public and private
violence, against unequal pay structures, against a lack of opportunities, for
girls and women. Films and publications which glorify non-sexual violence
probably do far more damage than 'Page Three' and *Hustler*.

(Gillian Rodgerson and Elizabeth Wilson 1991: 75)

Introduction

There are few subjects in media and cultural studies that have elicited such
fierce debate as pornography. It is this issue that probably best epitomizes
the intransigence of binaristic debates around media violence. Some view
pornography as a type of free speech. As such, it ought to be protected by
law. Others regard it as a form of violence against women (and children).
Accordingly, it should be legally censored.

Despite the long and wide-ranging nature of discussions around pornography, what has not yet been addressed in sufficient depth in our view is the
extent to which the articulation of sex and violence cultivates, over time, a
collective taken-for-grantedness of its presence – arguably leading, in turn,
to its eventual 'normalization'. Before we engage with this and related issues,
we want to make a very direct point. To understand the significance of
pornography in western cultures, it is helpful to deconstruct certain basic
cultural assumptions about gender.

Prevailing views about 'natural' differences between men and women and their 'proper' sex roles construct and maintain unequal power relations. This has had real material effects on people's lives – on their chances for further and higher education, affordable housing, well paid employment, and so on. For instance, in the USA, a greater proportion of women than men now live in poverty (hooks 2000a). The same holds true for the UK, where the fastest growing group living below the poverty line is women (particularly those who are lone parents) (Walter 1999; Office for National Statistics 2000).

The apparent normalization of a link between sex and violence is dangerous. It has enormous potential to further harm women's material position in society by exacerbating social, economic, and political inequalities between them and men. As such, finding a way forward in this debate now demands looking afresh at familiar arguments. To begin this long overdue task, it is useful to understand conclusions from past research in this area. This first step is important, since it throws into sharp relief where gaps in the arguments and research exist. It also enables us to identify new points of intervention to potentially allow the pornography debates to go beyond the limitations of the free speech versus censorship positions of the past.

This chapter is organized to take the reader through several of the main debates around pornography and violence over the past few decades – a period in which the influence of feminism, **civil libertarian** and conservative arguments have all been significant. We begin by examining various definitions of pornography and some of the ideological assumptions underpinning these definitions. From there we briefly trace libertarian views of pornography. Proponents of this approach tend to view pornography as a form of free speech to be protected from censorship (Rodgerson and Wilson 1991; R. Dworkin 1998; Gracyk 1998). Against this we examine conservative perspectives on pornography that regard it as corrupting of family values and a dangerous incitement to violence against women (Bork 1998; LaHaye 1998; Parker 1998).

From there we look at some of the arguments of certain anti-pornography radical feminists. Most of them regard pornography both as a form of violence against women and as a tool that men can use in real life to inflict pain, suffering and humiliation upon them (Caputi 1988; Itzin 1992; A. Dworkin 2000; MacKinnon 2000a, 2000b; Russell 2000). We end with an overview of selected cultural studies approaches that regard certain types of pornography to be potentially empowering. Some argue that women's involvement as both producers and consumers of pornography may provide spaces for the articulation of desire hitherto closed to them (Williams 1989; Rodgerson and Wilson 1991; Juffer 1998; hooks 2000a, 2000b).

Defining pornography

It is now something of a truism to say that it is difficult, if not impossible, to define exactly what constitutes pornography. As the old saying goes, one person's pornography is another person's erotica. We can find pornographic magazines in our corner shop on the top shelf. Soft-core pornography is also available in video shops in the 'adult' section and on late night cable television. 'Hard-core' pornography (sexually explicit, showing an erect penis and accompanying acts of penetration) can be found in almost every major town and city, albeit primarily in licensed 'sex shops' that restrict admittance to those over 18 years of age.

Various attempts have been made by a wide array of groups and concerned individuals to delimit the meaning of 'pornography' in line with their particular agenda or interests. US radical feminist Russell (2000), for example, defines pornography as 'material that combines sex and/or the exposure of genitals with abuse or degradation in a manner that appears to endorse, condone, or encourage such behaviour'. In contrast, in her view, erotica refers to 'sexually suggestive or arousing material that is free of sexism, racism, and homophobia and is respectful of all human beings and animals portrayed' (Russell 2000: 48).

US feminist Steinem (1998) makes the distinction between pornography and erotica in a different way. She notes that pornography's etymological root 'porno' means 'prostitution' or 'female captives', suggesting 'not mutual love, or love at all, but domination and violence against women'. The word 'graphos' which is the root of the second part of the word means 'writing about' or 'description of', implying that there is a 'distance between subject and object, and replaces a spontaneous yearning for closeness with objectification and voyeurism'. Conversely, the word 'erotica' is rooted in 'eros' or passionate love. Here, Steinem (1998: 91) contends, there is an idea of 'positive choice, free will, the yearning for a particular person'.

British legal scholar Easton (1994) maintains that the Canadian legal decision *R*. v. *Butler* (1992) offers up a potentially useful definition of pornography. It makes an important distinction between different types of materials featuring sex:

- explicit sex with violence
- explicit sex without violence but which subjects people to treatment that is degrading and dehumanizing
- explicit sex without violence which is neither degrading nor dehumanizing.

Using this distinction, argues Easton (1994), one could easily campaign for the prohibition of the first two categories without including the third.

US civil libertarian Gracyk (1998) has a similar view to Easton's. While he concedes that most pornography is indefensible because it degrades and defames women, he challenges certain attempts to legislate as a response. Most notable here is his critique of radical feminists Andrea Dworkin and Catherine MacKinnon's well-known efforts to provide a statutory definition of pornography in an amendment to the 'Human Rights Ordinance of the City of Minneapolis' in 1983. The amendment, he claims, used 'unacceptable criteria' to define what is pornography. Specifically, Dworkin and MacKinnon defined pornography as being 'graphic sexually explicit materials that subordinate women through pictures or words', a definition which revolves around the following points:

(i) women are presented dehumanized as sexual objects, things, or commodities; or (ii) women are presented as sexual objects who enjoy pain or humiliation; or (iii) women are presented as sexual objects who experience sexual pleasure at being raped; or (iv) women are presented as sexual objects tied up or cut up or mutilated or bruised or physically hurt; or (v) women are presented in postures or positions of sexual submission, servility, or display; or (vi) women's body parts – including but not limited to vaginas, breasts or buttocks – are exhibited such that women are reduced to those parts; or (vii) women are presented as whores by nature; or (viii) women are presented as being penetrated by objects or animals; or (ix) women are presented in scenarios of degradation, injury, torture, shown as filthy or inferior, bleeding, bruised, or hurt in a context that makes these conditions sexual.

(cited in Cornell 2000b: 4–5)

Gracyk suggests that less effort should be expended trying to define pornography and the corresponding subordination of women so as to place a greater emphasis on trying to understand what he and others have called the 'pornographic attitude'. In his view, the pornographic attitude is the 'real locus of the defamation argument against pornography' (Gracyk 1998: 156). To elaborate on the core of his libertarian position, Gracyk explains:

Sexually explicit materials are just one forum for degrading women in images. A degrading attitude can and does occur in representations which are not sexually explicit (e.g., in advertisements and some popular novels). The pornographic attitude does not accompany only sexually explicit representations, just as many sexually explicit representations that are commonly labeled 'pornographic' (e.g., sexually explicit films of homosexual or lesbian lovemaking) need not express the pornographic attitude. The real goal, then, is to distinguish objectionable pornography from the sexually explicit *per se* (to distinguish the pornographic from, say, the erotic) while providing for restriction of the former but not the latter.

(Gracyk 1998: 168–9)

This is an argument supported by Canadian professor of philosophy Christensen (1998) who also makes a distinction between representations of sexually explicit material and their supposed causal link to sexually violent behaviour. In the case of the former, experimental research is cited that appears to show that any increase in aggressiveness induced by exposure to sexually explicit material is 'nothing more than the excitement they produce. It is not a feeling of contempt for women, or a special moral nastiness, or anything of the sort; it is just a general state of heightened physiological activity' (Christenson 1998: 270). Here the claim is made that higher levels of aggression are only short lived (a few minutes), dissipating as excitement levels drop. At the same time, however, Christensen maintains that there is sufficient research evidence to support the view that there is a general human tendency to do what others are doing – modelling one's behaviour around what is considered to be normal and acceptable, particularly among children (Christensen 1998: 271). However, more worrying than short-term exposure to sexual violence is the potential for much more subtle, often imperceptible long-term influences on people's attitudes. As Christensen argues:

It is certain that the level of aggression in a given society is largely determined by socialization; though violence is a human universal, some groups have far less of it than others. Given that fact, and given that the media are such a pervasive force in our own society, it is difficult to believe all the violence they portray does not have a significant impact.

(Christensen 1998: 272–3)

If images of sexual violence do have a negative influence on our attitudes and behaviour, does this mean that they should be censored? As we shall see in the next section of this chapter, civil libertarians believe the answer is 'no'.

Keep it free

Civil libertarian thought is based on arguments drawn from classical liberal theory. In the eighteenth and nineteenth centuries, British philosophers like James Mill and John Stuart Mill as well as thinkers like Thomas Jefferson in the USA set out several of the organizing tenets of this theory. Briefly, they believed that no human expression should be suppressed unless it can be proved that it will result in harming someone. Only in a 'free marketplace of ideas' will truth emerge and human society advance democratically. In this free marketplace the circulation of good, true ideas will eventually override bad, harmful or untrue ones. Given that no one has 'infallible knowledge' about themselves, it followed that there should be no censorship (see also Assister 1989).

Liberal theory has fundamentally shaped the political, legal and philo-sophical structures of many nation states around the world. In the USA, the Constitution written by the 'founding fathers' of the new nation in the eight-eenth century formally guaranteed individuals the right to free speech (First Amendment) as a fundamental element in the creation and preservation of a free, open and democratic society. Civil libertarians in the USA view the constitutional right to free speech as more important than the potential offence of certain forms of speech (including pornography), even when the majority of people believe that it should be censored. At the heart of the libertarian defence of pornography, then, is an insistence that 'the con-sumption of pornography falls squarely within the self-regarding sphere, in which the individual is sovereign' (Easton 1994: x). As a rational subject, each individual has the unalienable right to enjoy freedom of thought, speech and publication 'to allow for the possibility of learning through errors and experience' (Easton 1994: x). These freedoms form the essential building blocks of democratic society and as such must be protected (within certain society-wide agreed limits). As libertarian and professor of law at both Oxford and New York Universities Ronald Dworkin (1998) explains:

> Pornography is often grotesquely offensive; it is insulting, not only to women but to men as well. But we cannot consider that a sufficient reason for banning it without destroying the principle that the speech we hate is as much entitled to protection as any other. The essence of negative liberty is freedom to offend, and that applies to the tawdry as well as the heroic.
>
> (R. Dworkin 1998: 206–7)

While largely agreeing with this view, various critics nevertheless suggest that certain forms of pornography are so offensive that they should be cen-sored because they may cause harm, particularly where children and young people are concerned. Taking exception with libertarian arguments about free speech, British journalist David Aaronovitch (2000) argues that the main problem with pornography is that it may teach young people who are already predisposed to see sexual violence as 'normal' that it is okay to emu-late what they might see (Figure 4.1). Aaronovitch further elaborates upon this point, saying that:

Pornography is a danger to children

Toby Melville/PA

DAVID AARONOVITCH

'The third law of parenting is: you must assume that children will find everything, from pills to Christmas presents'

CENSORSHIP IS easy to ridicule. No job is as absurd as that of the person who earns a living snipping the willies out of *Raunchy Cowboys III*. Many of us – having accidentally tuned in to the hotel adult movie in our conference bedrooms late at night – wonder at the care taken to excise the ruder details. Lascivious downward pans end inexplicably at the navel, jump cuts plunge the viewer from busty foreplay straight into strenuous coitus – presumably because this is the one circumstance in a porn pic in which the genitals are, mmn, covered. The effect is disconcerting: like walking fully clothed through the door of a swimming pool and into the water; the mind simultaneously absorbing both the intention of the pornographer and the strategy of the censor.

The nation's chief censor, chairman of the British Board of Film Classification, is – of course – our own Andreas Whittam Smith, who, the day before yesterday, invited readers to comment on the latest court case involving his board. As he reminded us (and as I cannot resist repeating), the videos at the heart of the judgment included *Nympho Nurse Nancy*, *Horny Catdale* and *Office Tart*.

For some time now, even videos sold at licensed sex shops, depicting what you might call "strip, fiddle and sex" (violent sex and sex involving children or animals being banned by law), have been subject to restrictions. As Andreas put it, "Erections may be shown, but there must be no clear sight of penetration or of masturbation or of ejaculation." So adults have not been able to purchase films showing sexual activities that rank among the most common available.

Then the manufacturers of *Catbabes* and *Horny Tarts*, as was their right, appealed against the ruling of the BBFC, on the grounds of masturbation and ejaculation. Were I to find out that one of them had been to Jonny's place and watched a mucky movie, that would be the last time they would set foot in that house. I cannot think of a responsible parent who would willingly allow their child to be exposed to hard-core pornography.

Ah yes, but is that restrictive impulse justified? Would such exposure really (asks the siren voice of ultra-liberalism) be so bad? Am I attempting to realise an ideal of childish innocence, a construct at odds with the facts? Isn't the truth that I am frightened by my own children's sexuality? After all, they are need not to ac-

The board took the case to court and lost. Mr Justice Hooper ruled that the appeals committee had struck the right balance between freedom of expression, on the one hand, and the possible harm that might be done to children, on the other.

The board's counsel had argued that, since so many children had access to video players, there was a danger that some of them would get to see the masturbating nurses and penetrated cat-tarts, and – as a result – be damaged. This view would have been, by witnessing an erection or two. The appeal committee's brief, for his part, contended that certification could be refused only if "it was shown that there is devastating damage to a significant proportion of children", and went on to argue that such a case had not been made. The judge agreed.

It seems to me that there are three issues here. First, is it the case that more children will actually see more frenzied ejaculations as a result of this ruling? Second, if they do, will they be harmed in any way? And third, even if the answer to the first two questions were to be "yes", would prohibition be the most effective method of dealing with the problem?

The third law of parenthood is that you must assume that children will find everything, from attractive-looking pills to their Christmas presents. If the videos are sold, some children will discover them where they have been secreted in cupboards, desk drawers or under beds, and will watch them, and show them to their friends. In the pre-video age we sneaked into horror movies, or exchanged books with nudes in them. It hasn't changed.

So what about damage? "Visceral clutch" (I can't remember who invented the term), perfectly describes my own reaction to the possibility of my children being exposed to this kind of stuff.

that, then I have a shock for you. All the above is more or less what paedophiles argue. They need to believe that children are not damaged by non-enforced sexual encounters, and that such encounters constitute a form of teaching. The *modus operandi* of many paedophiles involves the exposure of their targets to pornography, presumably because this "normalises" adult genital sex for the child.

But there's no proof. One of the things that drives me crazy about some anti-censorship liberals as a liberal myself is that they refuse to accept the cost of their liberalism. For years they have been trying to convince us that you can churn out increasingly attractive violence on screen, but never in any way add to the amount of violence in society. This completely counter-intuitive proposition (one which no aid agency would credit for five seconds) is bolstered by the lack of hard evidence that those who watch violent movies go on to offend themselves.

Yet, what you can say as Professor Kevin Browne of Birmingham University has discovered, is that those youngsters predisposed towards violence, are stimulated by screen mayhem. So it isn't too far fetched to suggest that films indicating the normality of certain kinds of sexual encounters, are likely to "permit" some children to emulate them. If so, then that's damaging enough, because we certainly do have research which indicates that early sex results in increased incidence of STDs, teen pregnancies, low self-esteem and unsatisfactory sexual encounters.

Even so, there is still a need to ac-
cept this chain, you might agree that we should invoke the famous precautionary principle – that "devastating damage to a significant proportion of children" is far too high a threshold. At the moment I am not at liberty, for instance, to plant my garden with GM oil-seed rape, for fear of contaminating my neighbour's garden. But I am (as of now) allowed to decorate my in-

ternal garden with oil, seed and rape. And the risk to my neighbour is thought too negligible for the state to demand that I stop.

So, yes and yes and on, briefly, to the third question. It is hardly likely that a government that issues advice on the inherent dangers of musical chairs is going to sit by and allow sticky videos to be sold openly. Soon Mr Straw will emerge clutching a Bill aimed at preventing an avalanche of filth from engulfing us. But, like GM seeds, the problem is that this stuff is already out there and widely tolerated. On the Net you can indulge any perversion you like providing (a) you can pay the phone bill, and (b) you know what it's called. There are ways of screening out the most obvious dangers, but they can all be got round with a little ingenuity – ingenuity that can be shared in the playground.

Which leaves us with the only defence that really works: good parents. Which is another story.

David.Aaronovitch@btinternet.com

No responsible parent would willingly permit their children to watch any of the products of the pornography industry

Figure 4.1 'Pornography is a danger to children'. David Aaronovitch.
Source: *Independent*, 24 May 2000.

One of the things that drives me crazy about some anti-censorship liberals (as a liberal myself) is that they refuse to accept the cost of their liberalism. For years they have been trying to convince us that you can churn out increasingly attractive violence on screen, but never in any way add to the amount of violence in society. This completely counter-intuitive proposition (one which no ad agency would credit for five seconds) is bolstered by the lack of hard evidence that those who watch violent movies go on to offend themselves.

Yet, what you can say . . . is that those youngsters predisposed towards violence are stimulated by screen mayhem. So it isn't too far fetched to suggest that filmings indicating the normality of certain kinds of sexual encounters, are likely to 'permit' some children to emulate them.

(Aaronovitch 2000: 5)

Ronald Dworkin (1998) counters this position, insisting that although there is some evidence that pornography sometimes makes people less critical of sexual violence, there is nevertheless no substantive proof to support the view that it leads to a greater number of sexual assaults than would otherwise occur without exposure to it. Pertinent here are those research studies that have claimed to find that pornography tends to be used as part of a sexual offender's sexual orientation rather than being the direct cause or catalyst of sexual violence. From this perspective, it does not seem possible to separate out sexually violent representations available in pornography from those much more widely found in the mainstream media. Due to their daily repetition and cultural pervasiveness, it could be argued that mainstream representations have a far greater potential to influence the everyday construction of cultural attitudes around the articulation of sex and violence than pornography, even when it depicts violence (R. Dworkin 1998: 207).

Concurring with this line of argument, British feminists Rodgerson and Wilson (1991) contend that representations of sexual violence must be contextualized within a wider system of gender inequality, rather than singling them out as the main or only cause of women's oppression. It would be wrong to think that the censorship of pornography could improve the position of women in society. Instead, what needs to be done is to 'challenge the central assumptions about sexuality which determine sexual ideology in our culture . . . It [is] also necessary to consider the many other factors which create danger for women in sexual and other relationships' (Rodgerson and Wilson 1991: 12).

Defence of free speech has been less vociferous in Britain than in the USA.

For example, going back to 1979, the British government's Williams Committee's *Report on Obscenity and Film Censorship* maintained that the law must protect free speech unless it can be proved that it results in some direct harm. The report's main conclusion was that some would claim that it is absurd to apply this philosophical principle to pornography since most of it was 'totally empty' (not serious works of art or writing with intellectual content) and could not be considered, therefore, to be speech. The **Williams report** noted in this context that on several occasions, including the 1970 US Presidential Commission on Obscenity and Pornography, that the US Supreme Court had clearly upheld First Amendment rights to freedom of speech. In so doing, however, members of the Supreme Court conceded that protection of free speech did not extend to hard core pornography, namely because 'such pornography is not, in a constitutional sense, "speech": the idea being that it lacks communicative content' (cited in Assister 1989: 3).

In the next section of this chapter, we retain an emphasis on free speech, this time exploring how conservative thinkers have sought to uphold the concept while simultaneously arguing for the censorship of most forms of pornography.

Protecting 'family values'

While it may seem strange that a libertarian view on pornography might concur with one held by a conservative, the conservative US legal scholar and former US Supreme Court nominee Bork (1998) notes that:

> The original meaning of the speech clause [in the US Constitution] was the protection of ideas and the circulation of ideas, not the protection of self-gratification through pornography and other stuff. In fact, in the early cases, the pornographers, when they were prosecuted, didn't even raise the First Amendment, because nobody thought it was relevant. I think that's a big cultural shift the Court has worked on us.
>
> (cited in Cromartie 1998: 73)

The cultural shift to which Bork is referring highlights, in turn, the extent to which there has been agreement among a number of decision makers (courts, police, politicians, cultural commentators) defending free speech that certain forms of cultural expression are seen to be sufficiently serious and intellectual (high culture) so as to invite protection. The cultural shift, then, presumably took place at a time when popular culture began to be taken seriously both intellectually (within the academy with the rise of media and cultural studies) and commercially (as popular culture began to sell to wider, more prosperous audiences in the post-war period). The shift also coincided with the 'sexual revolution' and the development and widespread availability of the birth control pill.

Accordingly, a longstanding conservative argument is that the liberalization of western societies that began in earnest after the Second World War undermined legal judgments about the status of pornography in relation to the rights of its makers' free expression. It is often the case that conservative thinkers link the 'sexual revolution' of the post-war period with liberal values, sexual permissiveness, radical political rights groups (women's liberation, civil rights, gay liberation) and a 'decline' in the 'sanctity' of the patriarchal nuclear family. Thus in contrast with those who have welcomed the cultural shift to a more open and tolerant society in which a wider range of cultural expression is possible, conservatives have tended to regard liberalization and greater cultural diversity as threats to religious, moral and patriarchal control.

Conservative journalist Will (1998) is particularly concerned about what he sees as the 'mainstreaming' of sexually violent lyrics in popular music, such as 2 Live Crew's 'Me so Horny'. He argues that songs such as this one contribute to a 'coarsening of a community' and thus a 'desensitizing of a society' which will have 'behaviour consequences' (Will 1998: 257). Most journalists have a tendency, according to Will, to refer to sexually violent lyrics like those of the **gangsta rap** group 2 Live Crew, or more recently that of white rapper Eminem, as 'explicit', 'controversial' or 'provocative'. They often do so, he argues, without actually reprinting them for audiences so they can judge for themselves. As such, it is impossible for any sustained and informed public debate to take place. Here, then, and with our apologies for its offensiveness, is an excerpt from the lyrics from 'Me so Horny':

> To have her walk funny we try to abuse it
> A big stinking pussy can't do it all
> So we try real hard just to bust the walls [of the vagina]
> [. . .]
> I'll break ya down and dick ya long
> Bust your pussy then break your backbone
>
> (cited in Will 1998: 257)

In 2 Live Crew's lyrics and those of other groups (some forms of gangsta rap music, in particular, have long been criticized for the extreme nature of their violence and sexism) women are often called 'bitches' and are forced to engage in sexually violent acts. Will (1998) argues that such music promotes the idea that sexual violence against women is fun (for men). He places the blame for this situation squarely on entertainment corporations and liberals who support their businesses. In Will's view, both have the 'morals of the marketplace'.

Corporations, he argues, 'sell civil pollution for profit; liberals rationalize it as virtuous tolerance in "the marketplace of ideas"' (Will 1998: 257). What galls Will the most, however, is how certain issues, such as smoking or toxic waste, are seen to be intolerable in US society, while sexual violence against women is greeted with indifference, if not praise. Will (1998: 258) concludes that, 'we legislate against smoking in restaurants; singing "Me so Horny" is a constitutional right. Secondary smoke is carcinogenic; celebration of torn vaginas is "mere words".'

Similar lines of criticism are advanced in more explicitly religious terms by conservative Christians. In placing an emphasis on the importance of traditional family values as a 'defence' against both sexual and violent imagery from mainstream culture, they support arguments for outright censorship. Christian conservatives typically find in their faith the basis for a well-ordered, divinely inspired plan for human conduct. Sex – which should transpire only between husband and wife – is regarded as important and pleasurable, but only within the context of long-term commitment to family life. In the family, men are meant to be gentle and temperate but also in control of the household, while women are to be supportive, loving and understanding of their husbands. This model of relations between the sexes is sometimes referred to as one of 'complementarity'. This is where the man and the woman accept their divinely ordained place within the family and act accordingly (the man is the head of the household and the woman, while also important, is nevertheless subservient to him). Such a 'wholesome' attitude to sexuality is seen to be threatened by the 'sexual perversity' or 'abnormality' of pornographic representations. Once it is assumed that pornography damages the commitment and intimacy of marriage and family life, the reasons for censorship are made that much clearer.

A case in point are the views of Parker (1998), director of psychology at 'The Family Workshop' who insists that contemporary pornography encourages men to be violent with women and children. In his opinion, pornography 'is a treason against the American family and a treason against our society'. 'Treason', he adds, 'has no First Amendment rights' (Parker 1998: 228). Concurring with this view, Christian conservative LaHaye (1998) maintains that pornography fuels sexual violence. In LaHaye's view:

Many of the most shocking crimes today are inspired when morally sick words and living-color pictures are transmitted, through the printing press, into an equally sick mind, arousing the individual to horrifying action. We will not halt this sordid, sex-crazed crime rate until we rid our nation of pornography in magazines, X-rated and 'adult' movies, and particularly 'kiddie porn' . . . I am confident that pornographic literature and movies would be declared the prime causes of today's sex crimes.

(LaHaye 1998: 215–16)

At the heart of LaHaye's argument is the idea that pornography is harmful to the Christian family. Use of pornography within marriage, in particular, leads to 'unnatural expectations' that leave a partner who does not like pornography to feel 'inadequate, dirty and used' (LaHaye 1998: 216). Pornography is a 'mental poison' that destroys familial relationships, that causes men, in particular, to have a less respectful view of women that they would hold otherwise.

In our view, however, it is precisely the insistence upon the 'divinely inspired' notion of 'complementarity' between husbands and wives, based as it is on unequal power relations, that lies at the heart of the 'pornographic imagination'. Such hierarchical dynamics actually support one of the dominant themes of pornography – the separation of procreative sex from erotic pleasure, and the construction of eroticism within the context of female submission. As Mary Jo Weaver (1998) explains:

> The doctrine of complementarity – a form of sex-role discrimination that relegates men and women to specific roles on the basis of their supposed divinely assigned natures – continues to tell Christian women that God designed them for subservient roles . . . It is not far-fetched to say that pornography is an intensification of the gender differences in traditional Christianity. 'Good Christian businessmen' who spend their lunch hours in 'adult' bookstores live not in two worlds but in one, single universe in which men dominate women. Pornography, therefore, does not grow at the expense of traditional Christianity but as a further distortion of the already distorted social roles embodied in its own religious vision.
>
> (M.J. Weaver 1998: 238)

In the next section of this chapter, attention turns to radical feminist views on pornography. As we shall see, these views have made a substantial and important contribution to debates around pornography for several decades now.

Pornography, misogyny and power

Given that some conservative and certain radical feminist anti-pornography arguments share a commitment to the censorship of pornography, various critics have suggested that there is really very little difference between them. However, as M.J. Weaver (1998) argues:

> A pact between [radical feminist] Andrea Dworkin and [Christian fundamentalist] Jerry Falwell is impossible because of their profound disagreements about the nature of pornography itself ... Her [Dworkin's] work has helped to change the terms of the debate so that pornography is now an issue of power rather than an index of purity. And since her arguments are political rather than moral, her work makes some clear definitional distinctions between anti-pornography feminists and anti-pornography religious conservatives.
>
> (M.J. Weaver 1998: 229–32)

Although there is no one, unified radical feminist view on pornography and what, if anything should be done about it, there is nevertheless general agreement that mainstream, heterosexual (patriarchal) pornographic representations should be a cause for concern (A. Dworkin 1981, 1998; Griffin 1981; Kappeller 1988; Caputi 1992; Russell 1993, 1998; Dines 1997; Dyson 2000). Western culture is inherently misogynistic, it is frequently asserted, and pornographic representations reflect this form of hatred. All forms of pornography, particularly those constructed by men, reveal the pervasiveness of this ideology. As such, it is argued that pornography itself is a form of violence against women. It tells women and men that women are second-class citizens, mere sexual objects there for men's sexual use. Pornography is said to reinforce the western cultural view that men naturally dominate, a view that is often portrayed in the media in violent ways (humiliation, sadomasochism, rape, beating, murder and so on). What makes the situation even worse is that pornography often depicts women enjoying this domination, humiliation and pain. Not only are women shown to 'deserve' such treatment, but also they are represented as finding it pleasurable. This, radical feminists argue, is the pernicious and dangerous lie of pornography.

In pornography, argues MacKinnon (2000b), women's sexual desires are constructed from a male point of view. On patriarchal terms, women are depicted as enjoying 'dispossession and cruelty'. Moreover, MacKinnon (2000b: 171) states, 'Men, permitted to put words (and other things) in women's mouths, create scenes in which women desperately want to be bound, battered, tortured, humiliated, and killed. Or merely taken and used.

This is erotic to the male point of view'. Underlying such representations is a sexual objectification of women which depersonalizes them (they are objectified and identified by their body parts). As such, they are not represented as rational, thinking and productive human subjects and thus not deemed worthy of equality with men.

What most infuriates some radical feminists is that western cultures persist in identifying pornography as a form of 'speech' and as such deserving of legal protection. Dworkin (1997), for example, argues that in protecting the 'free speech' of pornographers, libertarians have been 'gutless wonders'. In her view, they have failed to support women's rights to equality with men and their rights to human dignity. Thus, libertarians have therefore 'accepted the dehumanization, humiliation and injury of women in the sex industry as entertainment' (Dworkin 1997: 194). In questioning how free speech is currently defined, and what and whom exactly is being protected, Dworkin outlines an alternative approach:

> The challenges to the civil rights law have been abstract arguments about speech, as if women's lives are abstract, as if the harms are abstract, conceded but not real. The women trapped in the picture continue to be perceived as the free speech of the pimps who exploit them. No judge seems willing to look such a woman, three-dimensional and breathing, in the face and tell her that the pimp's use of her is his constitutionally protected right of speech; that he has a right to express himself by violating her. The women on whom the pornography is used in assault remain invisible and speechless in these court cases. No judge has had to try to sleep at night having heard a real woman's voice describing what happened to her, the incest, the rape, the gang rape, the battery, the forced prostitution. Keeping these women silent in courts of law is the main strategy of the free speech lawyers who defend the pornography industry . . . If some women get hurt, that's the price we pay for freedom. Who are the 'we'? What is the 'freedom'? These speech-loving lawyers keep the women from speaking in courts so that no judge will actually be able to listen to them.
>
> (Dworkin 1997: 93)

Not all feminists share Dworkin's views, of course. Rather than seeing pornography as being, by definition, always degrading to women, some claim that it can serve as a resource for women's sexual liberation. It is this line of argument which we examine in the next section of this chapter.

Rethinking the erotic

Some feminists believe that campaigns against pornography have typically failed to draw public attention to other ways in which the media reinforce sexist assumptions about women (Gibson and Gibson 1993; Cameron and Frazer 2000). As British 'Feminists Against Censorship' group members Rodgerson and Wilson (1991: 38) argue, for example, the emphasis among anti-pornography feminists has been on depictions of sex and the suggestion that there is a clear and direct link between pornography and violence against women. One effect of this position is that other sources of women's oppression in society have been less vigorously critiqued (see also Burstyn 1985). A further effect is the widespread misconception that all feminists oppose pornography in every form.

Views of women as passive victims of pornography have arguably played into the hands of right-wing conservative ideas about femininity (see also Segal 1993). As Rodgerson and Wilson (1991) write:

> They [anti-pornography radical feminists] offer no remedies save more censorship at the margins of the mass media, leaving untouched and uncriticized the much more pervasive daily diet of sexist, but not explicitly sexual, images. All that the campaign has achieved is to give undeserved respectability to the beliefs of the moral right and the fundamentalist lobby.
>
> (Rodgerson and Wilson 1991: 39)

Rather than attacking the surface content of pornography, US legal and women's studies scholar Cornell (2000a: 565) argues that feminist energies would be better directed at considering the unconscious appeal of mainstream heterosexual pornography. She maintains that psychoanalytic theorist Jacques Lacan's work is particularly useful in theorizing how men's sexual imagination is formed from infancy through to adulthood. The argument is that in a man's sexual fantasy is the desire to control that which frightens him most – the all-powerful mother figure who had ultimate control over him when he was a baby. As Cornell (2000a: 559) writes, 'the ever-erect prick we see in pornography is the imagined prick of the father who can control the terrifying figure of the Phallic [all powerful] Mother'. The main focus of heterosexual pornography is the all-powerful penis. The penis represents sexual agency, power and control over the dismembered woman's body (in pornography women are often reduced to their breasts, vagina, mouth, and so on). Even though some heterosexual pornography shows women in a dominating position where they are seen to be objectifying and enacting violence on male bodies, in Cornell's view, this is not enough to undermine the position of the penis/phallus as the figure of sexual agency and power. Instead, it is simply an inversion of the fantasy rather than something that is drawing attention to the fantasy in order to disrupt it.

Cornell sees the violence of this fantasy as a problem that needs to be resolved. Because this violent fantasy is one that is deeply embedded in our unconscious (both men and women), she argues, it cannot be simply undermined through changes in the law. In fact, censoring pornography could make it even more appealing. The 'dirtier' and more violent pornography is, the better – the forbidden is made more compelling. What is needed to challenge the violent fantasy, it follows, are sustained challenges to the rigidity and sexual reductiveness of the contemporary pornographic imagination. Instead of more censorship, women need to explore pornography and represent different visions of sexual desire. As Cornell maintains:

> Thus, the challenge from within by women pornographers may ultimately be more unsettling to the mainstream pornography industry than any outside legal challenge to it: just one more reason why we should focus pornography regulation not on constraining men and their fantasies, but on protecting the breathing space of the feminine imaginary.
>
> (Cornell 2000a: 565)

More speech, feminist speech, is one way of getting at the violence of the pornographic imaginary and one which may, in the long run, provide the most powerful challenge to it (Segal and McIntosh 1992; hooks 1993; Kipnis 1996; Huntley 1998; Royalle 2000).

Perhaps more controversially, a number of feminists have claimed that sexual free speech need not always portray mutuality and equality in order to be politically progressive. According to US feminist Rubin (1993) for example, feminist representations of SM may provide some women with the opportunity to undermine traditional gender roles which assign to men greater cultural power. Defending her view against claims that SM necessarily or always represents a harmful type of pornography, Rubin argues that:

> Sadomasochism is not a form of violence, but is rather a type of ritual and contractual sex play whose aficionados go to great lengths in order to do it and to ensure the safety and enjoyment of one another. SM fantasy does involve images of coercion and sexual activities that may appear violent to outsiders. SM erotic materials can be shocking to those unfamiliar with the highly negotiated nature of most SM encounters.
>
> (Rubin 1993: 22)

Representations of SM can be upsetting to those not part of the 'in-group' audience who know the rules and codes for their interpretation. Assister and Carol (1993) concur with this point, suggesting that most hard-core pornography

> principally shows equal relationships in which no one particularly dominates anyone, and the SM porn manages to show a far higher proportion of stories in which females are dominant. Given the number of porn films and magazines in which men perform as objects, or as virtual sexual slaves to women, it is hard to believe anyone could get the message of male dominance from modern porn.
>
> (Assister and Carol 1993: 15–16)

In Rubin's (1993) view, pornography is not necessarily more violent and/or sexist than the mainstream media. There are more images and descriptions of violence against women in the mainstream media (TV, movies, fiction), she insists, than in pornography. 'Gender inequality and contemptuous attitudes toward women are endemic to this society', she writes, 'and are consequently reflected in virtually all our media, including advertising and pornography'. Moreover, she adds, they 'do not originate in pornography and migrate from there into the rest of popular culture' (Rubin 1993: 24–5).

Other feminists have similarly sought to challenge the view that only men enjoy pornography or that pornographic representation is, by definition, consistent with the subordination of women. Many women, they point out, enjoy watching or reading pornography, finding it to be a sexual turn on (see A. Smith 1995; Juffer 1998; Mourão 1999). Evidently, various studies have shown that women spend almost as much money as men on pornography of different types. By the mid-1990s, women made up 40 per cent of the pornographic video rental market in the USA, for example (see O'Toole 1998: 356). Many women regularly watch or read hard-core pornography, while even some romance novels ('bodice rippers') resemble elements of SM fiction. Not surprisingly, then, some women take strong exception to the claim that pornography is offensive or dangerous (see Juffer 1998).

There are also feminists who have sought to use the Internet to rewrite violent narratives so as to empower women both sexually and socially. One of the most influential and controversial commentators in this area has been US lesbian feminist and SM pornographer Pat Califia. When interviewed for the *Techno-Dyke Headquarters* website, she argued that the Internet makes it possible to have access to a realm of fantasy unknown just a decade previously (Figure 4.2). She regards this development as 'mostly a positive thing'. To clarify, Califia says that: 'Being isolated is quite stressful, and reinforces a sense that there must be something wrong with what you like, if you

The Gathering Place for the Web Savvy Dyke!

[Feature Archive] [Write for Us!]

Join the Mailing List:
your email

Pat Califia - A Three Part Interview
- By Shosho

Part 1 - Women's Movement, Trans communities and Leather/Queer Online | **Part 2** - Transitioning, Fatherhood & Partnership | **Part 3** - Little Sisters legal battle & Pat's Books

Other Interviews:
* Amy Ray
* Kate Clinton
* Melissa Ferrick
* Doria Roberts
* Rebekah Radisch
* Teresa Trull
* Terry Wolverton

Part I: Larger Picture: Gay Communities, The Women's Movement and Transgender Communities

TechnoDyke.Com: What do you see happening to the gay community's attitudes toward sexuality on the Internet?

Pat: Well, I think a lot of queers are using the internet to hook up with potential partners and tricks. Gay men of course are more successful at this than any other group of people. So the Internet is just, for those folks, a much quicker way of getting a personal ad to work. Like takeout for blowjobs. Less often do you see any consciousness about on-line censorship, but that's growing. The recent threat to boycott AOL over their homophobic terms of service was great activism. AOL has been getting away with antigay crap for years and years now, and should be held more accountable by their queer subscribers.

TechnoDyke.Com: What is the lesbian communities' response to the use of the concept of 'queer' - in particular online?

Pat: I think there is a big split in the lesbian community both online and offline about sexual values, and one of the ways you can take that temperature is to see how any particular woman reacts to the term "queer." I think there are always going to be some cultural feminists who think that women are good and men are bad; that you can't change your gender; that it's wrong to sleep with men; bisexual can't be trusted; porn is evil and sexist and causes violence against women; etc. But there are a growing number of younger women who have been involved in AIDS activism and expanded their political horizons. They take the existence of lesbian porn and women-only sex parties for granted. They are able to see that they have some political causes in common with other queer people, and they don't want to live in a separatist culture. To be really honest, I see these young women as my spiritual grandchildren, and I'm so happy and proud of them. You can be a dyke and be out and proud, you can be a feminist, without being a bigot who hates people whose notions of pleasure or whose presentation of their gender differs from

Figure 4.2 Pat Califia – A Three Part Interview.
Source: Techno-Dyke Headquarters website.

are the only person you know who wants to be tied up or spanked, or put tit clamps on your girlfriend. It's now possible to get printed information and live advice about safe S/M play' (cited in Schlolar 2002). It is the Internet's ability to create virtual spaces for gender fluidity that she regards as a progressive development in breaking down gender hierarchies and the dominance of patriarchy. Says Califia: 'This fluid play with all the colors of the rainbow of pleasure puts us in touch with what we all have in common as human beings.' However, Califia does worry that there is sometimes a failure among people engaged in SM play on the Internet to distinguish it from play in the 'real world'. On this point she notes:

> I get concerned when people substitute the illusion of instant intimacy that you get in a chat room for the effort that goes into building a face-to-face S/M relationship that actually works. Many on-line S/M interactions escalate way beyond what would be necessary or feasible in person, because when you are fantasizing you tend to think of more and more extreme acts in order to build the excitement. The sensation is missing, and that's an invaluable reality check for real S/M play. I am concerned about the possibility that some people may expect themselves to be able to do the same things in a real session that they like to hear about on-line. Somebody once said, 'Fantasies are hungrier than bodies,' and this is a wise precept to keep in mind.
>
> (cited in Schlolar 2002)

As Califia suggests, despite such potential dangers, efforts to give voice to women's sexual desires must continue to be supported. Concurring with this stance, Cornell (2000a) argues that anti-pornography censorship, whether it comes from those on the conservative right or from radical feminists, may do more to actually prop up existing unequal and sometimes violent relations between men and women than to tear them down. By falling back into the binaristic and essentialist trap that all men have an inherently violent nature and women a passive one which requires 'protection' (by the law, the church, the state) serves only to reify this specific gender construction. Instead of increasing censorship of pornography, some cultural studies feminists insist that there is now a greater necessity to challenge the terms of production in the mainstream heterosexual porn industry. Cornell (2000a: 551, original emphasis) writes: 'Political action, not legal action, should be the main mode of intervention in the *production* of pornography'.

Conclusion

We would like to conclude this chapter with the caution that the arguments made here are most pertinent to societies where it is possible to openly challenge the often oppressively patriarchal (and sometimes violent) heterosexism of media representations of women and sexuality, including those found in pornography. What such arguments have sometimes failed to consider are the social, cultural, racist, religious and economic barriers to free, open, exploratory and non-sexist sexual (and non-sexual) expression that many women face around the world. At a very basic level, these barriers often impede their general contribution to the progressive reshaping of the societies in which they live. To then expect that it can be straightforward or indeed politically acceptable to use the arguments outlined in this chapter to progressively rearticulate sexuality everywhere in the world would be mistaken. The punishments that many women face, both in poor and rich countries, for transgressing normative forms of sexuality are very real. They can range from social sanction (being called a 'slut', 'whore' or 'slag'), to social exclusion, mental and physical punishment, and even death.

To address the very real social problem of sexual violence against women and girls, we need to interrogate what our societies deem to be 'normal' sexuality. Each society must develop locally derived solutions if there is to be any hope of progressive change. It is possible to be critical of pornography without either having to accept it 'as is' or to reject it outright as proponents within the binaristic debates of the past have insisted. Feminists and other political progressives have to continue to encourage the creation of alternative sexual representations that advance sexual openness and diversity. The recent preoccupation in western countries with whether or not violent pornography causes sexual violence represents a 'retreat' from a radical sexual politics that shaped early activism in this area. As O'Toole (1998: 57) remarks, 'a sexually repressive culture is also traditionally one where women are less likely to be able to speak about sexual abuse'.

Turning from our discussion of pornography and sexual violence, in the next chapter we shall take a look at research that has investigated the ways on which western advertising has used violence to sell goods and lifestyles. For it is in mainstream culture, as several commentators noted in our discussion of pornography in this chapter, that the need to understand media violence is most pressing.

Further reading

Baird, R.M. and Rosenbaum, S.E. (eds) (1998) *Pornography: Private Right or Public Menace?* New York: Prometheus.

Cornell, D. (ed.) (2000) *Feminism and Pornography.* Oxford: Oxford University Press.

Dworkin, A. (1997) *Life and Death: Unapologetic Writings on the Continuing War against Women.* London: Virago.

Juffer, J. (1998) *At Home with Pornography: Women, Sex, and Everyday Life.* New York: New York University Press.

O'Toole, L. (1998) *Pornocopia: Porn, Sex, Technology and Desire.* London: Serpent's Tail.

5

ADVERTISING BODY PARTS

[I]n a world inundated with media messages . . . advertisers have been forced to invent new strategies in order to identify their products and arrest viewer attention. Arguably, one such strategy has been the appropriation and exploitation of violence.

(Andrew Grainger and Steven Jackson 1999: 515)

Visualize your opponent as your worst enemy. The person you absolutely despise the most.

(Nike 1994 'Just do it' television commercial)

Introduction

Advertising is frequently neglected in discussions of media violence. However, recently media critics and theorists have come to see advertising as significantly involved in the media's normalization of violence, and especially violence against women. We begin this chapter with a brief exploration of how commercial television's need to deliver audiences to advertisers encourages the screening of programmes containing violence, and how this viewing environment might impact on how audiences engage with advertisements. Turning to the content of television advertisements themselves, we examine the extent to which these actually contain violent imagery. However, even where advertising does not contain specific images of violence, its dominant constructions of masculinity and femininity have been linked to the social acceptance of male violence toward women.

Advertising has been predominately theorized as normalizing violence in relation to gender representations, and the larger part of this chapter is devoted to exploring how and why this is the case. Of course, advertising communication is used to many different ends, and while criticized for promoting ideological power relations that support violence, it is also used in efforts to reduce violence. We follow our consideration of gender and violence in advertising with a discussion of advertising campaigns aimed at combating violence against women, exploring how these encourage audiences to understand such violence.

The final part of the chapter outlines the recent controversy surrounding the advertising and marketing industries' promotion of violent films, computer games, and music products containing explicit lyrics to children. In the USA fears about the effects of these promotion practices on young people led to a **Federal Trade Commission** (FTC) investigation into the marketing of violent entertainment to children. Concluding its investigation, the FTC criticized the marketing and entertainment industries for placing the pursuit of corporate profits above the interests of young people who were being encouraged to seek out violent entertainment. Yet the drive for corporate profit underpins all of the advertising strategies that we examine in this chapter, even some of those used in campaigns designed to prevent violence.

Sponsored violence

It is well understood that the primary purpose of the commercial media is to 'sell audiences to advertisers' (Kilbourne 1995: 34). In the case of commercial television this means that broadcasters need to schedule programmes to attract specific types of viewers in sufficiently large numbers so that advertisers will want to purchase advertising 'spots' in those programmes. Hamilton (1998: 3) explains that in this context, '[e]conomics determines the supply and demand of violent images . . . The portrayal of violence is used as a competitive tool in both entertainment and news shows to attract particular audiences'. Television broadcasters use violent programme content in this way because they believe it increases the sensational and dramatic appeal of programmes and levels of excitement that they produce for viewers – certainly for those viewers sought by advertisers (Prasad and Smith 1994). As Hamilton (1998: 3) details, the 'top consumers of television violence are males aged 18–34, followed by females 18–34'. With a higher than average disposable income '[a]dvertisers are willing to pay a premium for these viewers, which means that some programmers will face incentives to offer violent shows' (Hamilton 1998: 3).

However, violent content not only is included in television programming in an effort to appeal to domestic viewers, but also helps to sell television products to other countries. As Gerbner (1995: 293) states, 'In the international marketplace of television, violent programming needs no translation, is image driven, and "speaks action" in any language and in any culture'.

In the USA as well as in other countries, the media industries (including advertising) have been heavily criticized by public and government representatives alike for exploiting violence in order to sell programmes and advertising slots within these programmes (Prasad and Smith 1994; Gerbner 1995; Weaver 1996; Shen and Prinsen 1999). Consequently, as Prasad and Smith outline:

> In the late 1970s and early 1980s, the public mood against television violence was so intense that some large national advertisers such as Eastman Kodak, Sears, GM's Chevrolet Division, and Procter and Gamble announced antiviolence advertising policies and or/shifted time purchases away from television programmes they considered to be excessively violent.
>
> (Prasad and Smith 1994: 340)

Many media watchdog and advocacy groups in the USA and in other countries (Weaver 1996) continue to lobby advertisers to adopt these policies. However, recent research has found that while violent programme content can deliver audiences to advertisers, it might not actually help sell the products advertised.

Prasad and Smith (1994) have examined how violent programme content impacts on children's responses to commercials and found that this viewing context can reduce favourable attitudes toward the advertised brand and learning about the brand. They explain these findings as related to 'mood transfer effect' where the violent programme content produces a negative mood in the viewer that is transferred to their viewing of the advertisement. The authors suggest that this

> points to potential pitfalls in advertisers' choice of violent television programmes as media vehicles. It cautions advertisers to examine carefully whether, in reaching for high audience ratings and cost efficiency through violent television programme vehicles, they may be potentially sacrificing communication effectiveness of their brand advertising.
>
> (Prasad and Smith 1994: 349)

Further research does lend some support to these claims. For example Shen and Prinsen's (1999) study of adult responses to advertisements screened within violent contexts finds that while that context 'had no significant effect on brand recall, ad copy recognition, and brand attitudes', it 'significantly reduced subject's purchase intention scores for . . . products' (Shen and Prinsen 1999: 104–5). Again the researchers explain this as a consequence of negative mood transferring from the violent programme to the advertised product. Interestingly, however, Shen and Prinsen's use of the film *Natural Born Killers* to create the violent programming context in their study is not discussed in terms of how it might impact on the research findings. They do not consider, for example, how that film's nihilistic content and supposed critique of commercial media systems may have influenced research participant's responses.

Indeed, no researchers have investigated how the interpreted *meaning* taken from programmes containing violence might influence viewers' interpretation of and responses to advertisements. Nevertheless, Shen and Prinsen's (1999: 105) point that 'advertisers and media buyers should consider the possible impact of the violence in their media planning' is a salient one. What this might also suggest is that advertisers themselves ought to be cautious in how they use violent imagery, or associations with violence, to promote products – as companies such as Nike, Nissan, Dell Computers, Reebok and even Wallis Clothing, to name just a few, are now doing. However, there is no doubt that when advertisers do use violence in their own communications, they do so in ways that they believe enhance the social and psychological appeal of the promoted product because certain types of violent expression are regarded as socially legitimate.

Selling violence/violent selling

The paucity of research into the quantity of media advertisements that contain images of violence makes it difficult to generalize about the advertising and marketing industries' appropriation of violence as an advertising strategy. What research there is in this area has found that television advertisements actually contain images of violence in relatively few cases.

Maguire et al.'s (2000) US-based study found that of 1699 television commercials screened during selected periods in 1996 and 1997, 'only 49 (2.8%) contained violent content . . . Twenty-six of the 49 ads depicted physical harm. About half of these commercials featured "legal" violence. Examples included individuals participating in hockey, wrestling, and boxing' (Maguire et al. 2000: 131–2). The other half of the advertisements containing violence comprised those defined as showing ' "illegal" human bodily harm', those displaying 'property destruction' and those containing 'threatened violence'. Within all of these commercials Maguire et al. (2000: 132) found that 'the type of violence shown is generally tame'. They concluded that the 'commercials that would likely be most upsetting to viewers are those coded in the "illegal" human bodily harm category', providing an example of a 'Slim Jim ad in which a wrestler crashes through a store ceiling resulting in the store manager being thrown to the floor' (Maguire et al. 2000: 131).

Certainly, violent content of this kind can be considered innocuous. However, as is discussed further below in relation to gender and violence in advertising, print advertising, which was not included in Maguire et al.'s (2000) study, provides examples of more alarming violent imagery. This suggests that advertisers may be more careful about how they promote products on television than in other media. Yet there are signs this might be changing. Maguire et al. (2000) found a 100 per cent increase in violent content in television advertisements in 1997 compared to 1996. Though the researchers rightly caution against generalizing from this very limited sample period, others (Katz 1995; Goldman and Papson 1996; Caputi 1999; Grainger and Jackson 1999; Kilbourne 1999) have also identified an increased use of violent imagery within advertisements. We discuss the concerns raised by this phenomenon further below. But we note that while a number of advertisers are clearly turning to violence as a means of attracting the attention of media audiences, the need to associate products with pleasant activities and distance them from forms of negative connotation (Maguire et al. 2000) and controversy (Hamilton 1998), *might* prevent a very broad move in this direction. Further, at least in theory, advertising standards should function to impede the growth of such communication strategies.

In countries such as the USA, Canada, UK, Australia and New Zealand voluntary advertising standards codes expressively state that violence should not be exploited in advertising. It was through the application of such codes that, for example, a Nike 'Just do it' television commercial was withdrawn from screening in New Zealand in 1994. The advertisement depicted a rugby coach psyching up his team of men with the words 'Visualize your opponent as your worst enemy. The person you absolutely despise the most . . . the absolute most' followed by images of the players attacking their imagined enemies, including a traffic warden, the English cricketer Ian Botham and a New Zealand rugby player (Grainger and Jackson 1999: 513). In response to public complaints, the New Zealand Advertising Standards Complaints Board

> was firmly of the view that the representation of people being tackled, the majority of whom were not rugby players, was violent. They were of the opinion that a combination of inciting phrases coupled with tackling was offensive. Furthermore, they argued that there was a general public concern with violence on and off the sports field and that this added to the inappropriateness of the commercial.
>
> (Grainger and Jackson 1999: 513)

The specific cultural context of this decision is clearly significant to the outcome – especially given that the Nike commercial was not censored in any other country apart from New Zealand. As Grainger and Jackson (1999) argue, this illustrates how local context can factor in the success or failure of advertisers' use of explicit violence for strategic promotional purposes, and in providing the climate for the acceptance, or rejection, of the increased prevalence of violence in advertising. However, while explicit violent content in advertising can attract the attention of censoring bodies, advertising's gender representations, which some media critics regard as normalizing male violence against women, are far less likely to be the subject of sanction.

Constructing gender with violence

Even a cursory examination of advertising content across the media reveals that '[a]dvertising, in a commodity-driven consumer culture, is an omnipresent and rich source of gender ideology' (Katz 1995: 135). Indeed, as Jhally (1987: 135) states, in 'modern advertising, gender is probably the social resource that is used most by advertisers. Thousands of images surround us every day of our lives that address us along gender lines. Advertising seems to be obsessed with gender and sexuality'. In terms of *how* it represents gender, advertising constructs men and women very differently; men are predominately portrayed as active, independent, self-centred, autonomous subjects, whereas women are largely depicted as passive objects of male desire. Thus, advertising draws on and reinforces cultural prescriptions of ideal 'masculinity' and 'femininity'.

The impacts of these gendered portrayals have concerned feminists since 'the late 1960s, [when] the women's movement . . . singled out advertising as one of society's most disturbing cultural products' (van Zoonen 1994: 67). During that period advertising was largely criticized for representing women in a limited range of stereotypical roles and locations. These representations were considered to 'serve a political purpose in maintaining the male domination of all the major sectors of society and an economic one in maintaining a corps of reliable consumers and an unpaid work force in the home (as well as a low paid one elsewhere)' (Millum 1975: 179). However, feminist researchers have also extended the critique of advertising to argue that its **sexualization** of gender power relations and objectification of women contributes to, and upholds, social structures that support violence against women.

The objectification of women involves their representation as objects of men's desires and fantasies, rather than as subjects of their own individual desires and fantasies. It is this aspect of advertising's construction of women – which positions them as finding ultimate pleasure, and indeed power, in catering to men's desires – which feminist media theorists have most heavily criticized. They have also identified how advertising constantly **fetishizes** women by reducing them to bodies and body parts such as lips, legs, breasts, hair and finger nails. Women are encouraged to believe that the adornment of these body parts will make them more sexually attractive.

But it is not only feminist theorists who critique advertising in this way. Male sociologists Goldman and Papson (1996: 98) agree that 'decades of consumer goods ads targeted at women have been predicated on the narrative assumption that self-fetishization provides a route to social power'. Wolf (1990) argues that this encourages women to have cosmetic surgery to enhance their looks, and to develop eating disorders in the quest for 'the perfect body', which she views as socially sanctioned self-inflicted violence. From a slightly different perspective, Torrens (1998: 28) argues that advertising 'aimed at focusing women's attention and energies on their bodies' participates in the violent social control of women:

> This form of social control is violent because what occurs is the disembodiment and disempowerment of a large portion of the population. It is violent because people are separated blatantly from their rights to self-government and control. It is violent also because of its insidious, symbolic nature; advertising as a productive cultural force perpetuates attitudes and actions that support the disempowerment of women.
>
> (Torrens 1998: 28)

Other writers have argued that the objectification of women creates an environment that facilitates men's violence toward women. For example, Kilbourne argues that:

> Ads don't directly cause violence of course. But the violent images contribute to the state of terror . . . Turning a human being into a thing, an object, is almost always the first step toward justifying violence against that person . . . This step is already taken with women. The violence, the abuse, is partly the chilling but logical result of the objectification.
>
> (Kilbourne 1999: 278)

Feminist theorists have also noted the similarities between the objectification of women in advertising representation and in pornographic texts (Coward 1982; Caputi 1988, 1999; van Zoonen 1994; Kilbourne 1999). In both advertising and pornography women's bodies are dismembered, cut up into parts – such as buttocks, thighs, legs, breasts, facial skin – which are fetishized.

Advertising's dominant constructions of desirable femininity have also been criticized as contributing to men's violence against women. Analyses of advertising texts identify the archetypal 'desirable woman' as young, white, and dressed in a provocative manner to attract the gaze of men (Williamson 1978; Wolf 1990; Goldman 1992; Torrens 1998; Kilbourne 1999). Further, in terms of bodily make-up, women in advertisements frequently have adolescent and even androgynous bodies – not the typical body of a fully developed mature woman. Indeed, advertising generally depicts women as childish in their mannerisms and behaviour, and needing and enjoying the paternal protection of men (Goffman 1976; Jhally 1987; Hawkins and Nakayama 1992). On the one hand this is considered a 'hyper-ritualization' of social gender relations (Goffman 1976; Jhally 1987: 135) through which the structures of those relations are communicated and learnt. On the other hand, it is considered more insidiously as promoting sexism and the sexual harassment and violation of women. From the latter perspective it is argued that '[s]exist advertising reinforces notions about women and perpetuates male dominance by encouraging both men and women to expect women to be submissive and dependent' (Woodruff 1996: 332).

Supermodels, 'women with an iconic status as ideals of (hetero)sexual desirability' (Lewis and Rolley 1997: 300), provide good examples of this ideal 'submissive and dependent' look. Kate Moss, for example, who has featured as the 'face' of Calvin Klein, is especially thin and has the appearance of a vulnerable teenager. It is perhaps extraordinary that part of Moss's appeal is based on the fact that she 'look[s] vulnerable, abused, and exploited' (Kilbourne 1999: 283). While this childish dependency is promoted as the feminine ideal, it is also eroticized through both the words and imagery of advertising. The child-woman is likely to be photographed in few clothes, or at least dressed provocatively (Williamson 1978; Kilbourne 1999). As Walkerdine (1997: 172) has argued in her analysis of girls in advertising, the representation of the child as woman and, equally, we would argue, the representation of woman as child, articulates two contradictory characteristics 'in which the eroticized child-woman is a position presented publicly for the little girl to enter, but is simultaneously treated as a position which removes childhood innocence, allows entry of the whore and makes the girl vulnerable to abuse'.

While the image of the provocative child-woman is the staple of a vast range of mainstream media advertisements, it is especially concerning in relation to products such as alcohol where the promise of sex is used to encourage male consumption. Examples of this promotional strategy have been critiqued for many years. In the 1970s Williamson's (1978) seminal **semiotic analysis** of advertising identified Bacardi's use of sexual connotation in the 'Get into Bacardi shorts' campaign as linking the consumption of rum with men's 'getting into' women's shorts. More recently Woodruff (1996: 333) has critiqued advertisers' promotion of the idea that 'getting a beer' involves getting the woman who serves it 'suggest[ing] that women and beer are commodities that are equal in value'. She concludes that the 'cumulative effect of sexist alcohol ads is to foster an environment in which women are less likely to be taken seriously and alcohol is seen to grant permission for a range of abusive behaviours' (Woodruff 1996: 333).

Yet it is not only alcohol advertising that encourages men to consider that with product purchase comes sex with women. Advertising for many other products, including cologne, equally uses this strategy. For example, Pacorabanne's 'Stop Thinking' advertisement shows a man in mid-close-up staring at the reader through a 'crotch shot' of a woman. In a typical example of the fetishizing of a woman's body only the legs are shown – starting at the hips and ending just below the knees, which are naked apart from a small pair of knickers. Wills (2001) has argued that the 'crotch shot' depicts the crotch as the 'apex of femininity'. Indeed, the composition of the advertisement presents the woman's crotch as the central point of interest for the man and, by impli-cation, the reader. The advertisement's strap-line 'Stop Thinking', printed left-of-centre between the woman's legs and at the man's chest height, obviously then implies that, when wearing Pacorabanne, men need not think about how they can 'get what they want', or even ask for it, but just 'go for it'. In short, the advertisement explicitly promotes *thoughtless* sexual behaviour.

In 1994, van Zoonen took the analysis of product promotion and sex further by considering the representation of black women in advertising. Her discussion draws on a print advertisement for Safari Liquor depicting an African woman in a strapless zebra print dress holding a young tiger and looking at a large foregrounded bottle of liquor. In the background a herd of zebra gallop across a plain at sunset; van Zoonen (1994: 82) states that the representation involves the 'articulation of gender and ethnicity' where 'African femininity is constructed as wild and close to nature'. Indeed, the 'construction of . . . black female sexuality that is made synonymous with wild animalistic lust' (hooks 1992: 67) is a highly popular racist cultural stereotype – itself a product of the violent domination of blacks by whites. As hooks (1992: 69) argues, 'the wild woman pornographic myth of black female sexuality [was] created by men in a white supremacist patriarchy'. In perpetuating this mythical stereotype advertising connotatively associates blackness with danger. While such danger is represented as sexually desir-able – the white male is encouraged to view the black sexualized woman as 'savage, wild and exciting' – it simultaneously justifies white supremacist control of the black 'savage' through racist social structures. These structures impact on both black men and women, but for women they have particular consequences when they become the victims of male sexual violence – violence which men are encouraged through highly sexualized representations of black women to see as invited.

A particularly insidious outcome of such representation is that when black women bring charges of sexual violence against men, they are required to defend themselves against the 'all-too-common stereotypes of black women as oversexed Jezebels and Sapphires' (Steiner 1999: 229). White women's sex lives are also interrogated in court cases of alleged sexual violence, again as a consequence of the discursive construction of women as provocatively soliciting male desire. Yet for black women the intersection of racist and sexist stereotyping in white-patriarchy makes it all the more likely that they will face allegations of provocation, and find justice for violence committed against them all the more elusive.

While we have argued that the advertising stereotype of the provocative woman has particular negative consequences for women, stereotyped representations of men also play into these consequences. Kilbourne (1999: 272) asserts that 'Male violence is subtly encouraged by ads that encourage men to be forceful and dominant, and to value sexual intimacy more than emotional intimacy'. She further states that advertising encourages men to believe that 'the way to get beautiful women is to ignore them, perhaps mistreat them' (Kilbourne 1999: 272).

> Indeed the very worst kind of man for a woman to be in an intimate relationship with, often a truly dangerous man, is the one considered most sexy and desirable in the popular culture. And the men capable of real intimacy . . . constantly have their very masculinity impugned. Advertising often encourages women to be attracted to hostile and indifferent men while encouraging boys to become these men.
>
> (Kilbourne 1999: 273)

What Kilbourne is alluding to is the fact that advertising idealizes violent masculinity. Katz explains that:

> Historically, use of gender in advertising has stressed difference, implicitly and even explicitly reaffirming the 'natural' dissimilarity of males and females . . . Stressing gender difference in the context means defining masculinity in opposition to femininity. This requires constantly asserting what is masculine and what is feminine. One of the ways this is accomplished in the image system, is to equate masculinity with violence (and femininity with passivity).
>
> (Katz 1995: 135)

As Katz outlines, muscularity, heroic masculinity, and even overt male violence are used to promote anything from running shoes, to beer, cologne, food products, cars and even computers, to male consumers. What is more, advertising's glamorization of the male potential for violence actually encourages both men and women to value that violence.

Some advertisements also glamorize men's domination of women, and even the ultimate in passivity, women's death (Coward 1982; Faludi 1992; Caputi 1999; Kilbourne 1999). Faludi (1992: 244) has argued that this pushing of the 'idealization of weak and yielding women to its logical extreme' represents a marketing backlash against feminism. She cites 1980s Opium and Floral perfume advertisements featuring female corpses as typical examples of the trend. Opium continues to cause controversy in using this type of advertising strategy. In 2000–01, an Yves St Laurent Opium Perfume billboard advertising campaign featuring the model Sophie Dahl entirely naked aside from a pair of stiletto heels caused considerable public consternation in the UK. In the advertisement the model lies on her back, apparently in the throes of ecstasy, with her legs splayed apart as she cups one of her breasts in her hand. The British Advertising Standards Authority banned the advertisement following over 700 public complaints that it was offensive, degrading to women and, as little more than soft-porn, was inappropriately displayed in settings where children and those who preferred not to engage with pornographic material were forced to view it.

Opium's billboard advertisement does not depict an actual violent act against a woman (although some have argued that Dahl's position, the whiteness of her skin and bright red lips make her look like an embalmed cadaver). However, Kilbourne (1999) identifies many examples of advertisements that do depict such violence. For example, Bitch skateboards promotion showed a male stick figure pointing a gun to the head of a female stick character. A jeans advertisement depicted three men attacking a woman with the words 'Wear it out and make it scream'. A Baby-G watch advertisement on the side of a bus depicted a naked woman tied up with giant watches. 'Most of us become numb' to these images, Kilbourne argues, 'just as we become numb to the daily litany on the news of women being raped, battered and killed' (Kilbourne 1999: 277). She views these images as contributing to the cultural normalization of violence against women, as do many other feminist writers (Benedict 1992; Meyers 1997; Carter 1998; Weaver et al. 2000). Caputi (1999: 76) takes this claim further, asserting that 'misogynistic, objectifying, and racist imagery . . . is itself a form of violence' because it constitutes the 'emotional/psychological abuse' of women through their 'belittlement', 'humiliation' and 'degradation'.

It could be argued that men are now, like women, similarly, and increasingly, objectified in advertising, and that they feature in these texts as victims of violence in the same manner as women. However, the effects of this development are, arguably, not the same because men are not, and have not historically been, the subjects of systematic and oppression. Kilbourne (1999: 279) states: 'When men objectify women, they do so in a cultural context in which women are constantly objectified and in which there are consequences – from economic discrimination to violence – to that objectification'. Interestingly though, as advertisers attempt to market products in a cultural context in which women are enjoying greater social and economic autonomy and independence from men, advertising campaigns have attempted to appeal to women by symbolically associating them with assertiveness, self-assurance, power and even acts of violence.

From a post-feminist perspective, Winship (2000: 47) argues that advertisements which associate women with power 'offer a scopic regime different from that of earlier ads, and incite fantasies that play on psychic and social tensions pertinent to women in the 1990s'. Using Wallis Clothing's 'Dressed to Kill' and Nissan's 'Ask before you borrow it' print campaigns, Winship (2000) demonstrates how some advertisers now draw on sexual discourses which centrally foreground and play upon tensions between women and the **male gaze**. An example of this is provided in the Wallis 'Crash' advertisement where, as a result of a male driver distractedly looking at a woman who leans over a street railing gazing out over the horizon, he has crashed his Porsche sports car. The 'Barber' advertisement from the same campaign depicts a barber coming inadvertently close to slashing his male client's throat with a cutthroat razor as he is distracted by a Wallis-clothed woman walking past his shop window. In these examples the male gaze is depicted as having dangerous consequences for men. This is not to deny, however, that the texts continue to draw on stereotypical representations of femininity and female fashion, which are constructed for that gaze.

By deploying images of both assertive and sexually desirable femininity, recent advertising promotes what Goldman (1992: 149) defines as 'commodity feminism' in which '[f]emininity and feminism become presented as interchangeable alternatives'. This strategy is equally evident in the Return to Castle Wolfenstein computer game print advertisement that we found in a popular young men's magazine in the UK (Figure 5.1). Depicting a leather-clad female 'elite guard' complete with Nazi memorabilia accessories and a large phallic gun, the advertisement portrays the woman as independent, assertive and aggressive. The game itself is fairly typical of a genre of games that revolves around fighting the bad guys (Nazis) to win the war for the good guys (the gamer). Interestingly, however, of all the opponents in this game the silent all female elite guards are the most ruthless and deadly and, constructed in these terms, bear obvious similarities to cinema's violent femme fatale character that we discussed in Chapter 2.

In the advertisement for Return to Castle Wolfenstein the female figure poses a provocative sexual invitation expressed through the advertisement's 'Want Some?' strap line. This invitation is underscored by the fact that the zip of the woman's tight leather jacket is opened to expose the bulge of her breast. Thus, the reader is challenged to think about sex with her (if they dare!) and if they dare it is suggested it will involve sadomasochism. Texts such as this codify women as independent, in control and not necessarily interested in the male gaze. Ironically, though, the power of the promotional message is dependent on a woman adorning herself in a fashion that tells the gamer she is bad, dangerous and enjoys violence. Those who know the computer game will also know that the ultimate aim of the game is to kill this woman and all of those like her. Thus, the advertisement links women's sexual attractiveness with their abuse in an effort to construct this game as entertaining to the male audience at whom the advertisement is pitched. One could also wonder whether the advertisement is intended to eroticize fascism and the violent white supremacy associated with that political movement?

In the Nissan campaign examined by Winship (2000), women threaten actual violence toward men in revenge for their male partners having used their car without first asking permission. One advertisement shows a tabloid newspaper clipping featuring the real-life 'Bobbitt' case in which a woman cut off her unfaithful partner's penis, while another shows the torso of a man holding his hands to his groin as if to protect his genitals from being kicked. Winship (2000: 40) argues that these advertisements position the independent woman who seeks control over her life as 'dangerous and uncontrollable'. While such symbolic representations of women could be considered, from a feminist perspective, culturally regressive, Winship (2000) views them as

> evidence of shifting and contested relations between men and women. Representationally, the ads refigure the tensions and anxieties involved through the construction of a fantastical and pleasurable feminine identity which is organized less around sexual desire/desirability than around autonomy/dependency.
>
> (Winship 2000: 43)

Winship's analysis of representations of women in advertising is particularly useful. It addresses why representations of the kind that feminists traditionally heavily criticize are seemingly popular with women audiences – certainly to the extent that the advertisements evidently sell products. This

Figure 5.1 Wolfenstein 'Want Some?' Lusty and better dead. Activision Inc.'s Return to Castle Wolfenstein advertisement invites male computer gamers to eliminate this sexually provocative female elite guard.
Source: *id software.*

question has been a problem for feminist analyses of advertising, a point that Jhally (1987) makes in stating:

> the reason why the feminist critiques concerning regressive represen-
> tations in advertising have not been very successful [is because] they
> have not recognized the basis of its *attraction*. If the critique does not
> recognize this attraction then the attack on advertising becomes an
> attack on people. People thus feel guilty about being attracted to the
> images of advertising, while being told that they should not find it
> attractive.
>
> (Jhally 1987: 137, emphasis in the original)

Feminist critiques of advertising have tended to depend on a Marxist concept of false consciousness, where patriarchal capitalist ideology, through
processes of alienation and objectification, manipulates women to identify
with forms of femininity that benefit patriarchal capitalism, but not
women's own physical and mental well-being. This approach tends to deny
women any free will or agency in the construction of their own identities, as
well as any ability to critique advertising's gendered representations.

However, while false consciousness arguments construct women as victims of patriarchal ideology, an alternative argument that women are free
agents who choose to identify with destructive idealized femininities equally
constructs women as victims, although of their own agency. While the
apparent impasse of these positions causes difficulties in attempting to make
assertions about direct effects of advertising on audiences, the theoretical
deadlock is circumnavigated by considering advertising as participating in
'condition[ing] and delimit[ing] the field of discourse within which our
public and private conversations take place' (Goldman 1992: 2). Thus we
can understand how advertising contributes to ideologically structured
gender and racial power relations and how those power relations factor in
the normalization of relations of violence.

Promoting the anti-violence message

While advertising contributes to the normalization of violence against
women, it has also been used in efforts to stop such violence. Advertising
thus needs to be understood as promoting competing and often highly contradictory discourses about gender and gender power relations.

Advertising campaigns promoting anti-violence messages are found in
many countries throughout the world. In the UK the 'Zero Tolerance of
Violence against Women' campaign, first launched in Edinburgh in 1992,

has since been funded and promoted by a number of councils in other major cities. Since the early 1990s, the Young Women's Christian Association (YWCA) has run an annual campaign in a number of states in the USA entitled 'Imagine life without violence' (YWCA 1996). The YWCA campaign aims to educate audiences about a range of types of violence – from domestic violence and child abuse, violence among men, racist violence and hate crimes, to violence in the workplace. In Australia in 1997 the New South Wales Police had the Saatchi and Saatchi advertising agency produce a media campaign aimed at reducing domestic violence, and between 1994 and 1997 the New Zealand Police ran an extensive advertising and media campaign entitled 'Family Violence is a Crime'. New Zealand has also been the site of a government agency funded television advertising campaign 'Stop the Cycle of Violence' aimed at preventing child abuse. In the UK too, Barnardo's, the children's charity organization, launched in 2001 what became a controversial advertising campaign to stop the neglect and abuse of children. In depicting the consequences of violence, including sexual abuse and domestic violence, the advertisements were considered by some to be shocking and distressing.

A number of advertising and promotional campaigns intended to help prevent violence have been designed and supported by the corporate sector. In the USA both the clothing retailer Liz Claiborne and cigarette manufacturer Philip Morris have committed themselves to highlighting and reducing violence against women. Media conglomerates such as Time Warner have also sponsored anti-violence campaigns (Gerbner 1995). It is public relations ambitions to attain the image of a socially responsible and caring organization that motivate the corporate sponsors' involvement in these campaigns. For example, Liz Claiborne's decision to promote awareness of domestic violence was motivated by the company's need to 'enhance corporate reputation and ultimately drive profitability' (Pringle and Thompson 1999: 229). The Philip Morris promotion of anti-violence messages is similarly intended to improve the company's corporate reputation that was critiqued as trading on the lives of consumers by encouraging them to smoke. However, this campaign can also be considered in the light of women currently comprising the fastest growing group of smokers. Philip Morris may be attempting to win women's support for the company and their allegiance to its cigarette products.

Corporate support for anti-violence campaigns may significantly limit the extent to which campaigns are able to target and identify the social causes of violence, as well as the freedom to explicitly identify and criticize those who commit acts of violence. For example, in the UK in 2001, although British Airways had initially offered to sponsor billboard-advertising space for a 'Save the Children' anti-war campaign, immediately after the September 11 attacks on the USA, it withdrew that support. The advertisement had featured a Muslim girl and a white girl with the words 'Save the Children' in English under the Muslim girl and in Arabic under the white girl. In the context of the US retaliation against Afghanistan for the attacks, the advertisement's message – that retaliation would cause the deaths of innocent children – was considered too controversial for British Airways to support.

The New Zealand Police 'Family Violence is a Crime' campaign was also funded by corporate sponsorship. It neither explicitly identified men as the primary perpetrators of family violence, nor acknowledged any link between family violence and sexual abuse. Feminists have long argued for the need to explicitly identify cherished cultural prescriptions of violent masculinity as the root cause of violence against women. Yet the New Zealand campaign producers explained that to identify family violence as male violence would have been too controversial for the sponsors given that men would find the message objectionable (Weaver and Michelle 1999). Controversy is often considered potentially damaging to profits. Consequently, campaigns not dependent on corporate financing have been able to be harder hitting in their approach. For example, the Edinburgh 'Zero Tolerance' campaign (Figure 5.2) is considered radical and feminist in that it set out to

> challenge existing power relations and effect far reaching social change; it is feminist in the way it links sexual violence, domestic violence and child sexual abuse as part of the 'continuum of violence'; it names emotional and psychological abuse as forms of violence. The campaign uses feminist analysis of violence as a male abuse of power, and it challenges men to take responsibility for their violence.
>
> (MacKay 1996: 210)

While this approach could be considered controversial, and was avoided by the New Zealand Police campaign, it had widespread public and organizational support (Kitzinger and Hunt 1993; Hunt and Kitzinger 1996) and resulted in a 'marked increase of women seeking help' (MacKay 1996: 212).

Very few anti-violence campaigns explicitly identify media constructions of masculinity and femininity as contributing to the prevalence of violence against women. However, some encourage audiences to consider how the media might more broadly create acceptance of violence and violent culture. For example, the US YWCA campaign literature encourages audiences to think more critically about media representations of violence, and suggests that to help reduce violence in society 'we can stop exposing ourselves and our children to relentless messages glamorizing violence, dishonesty and

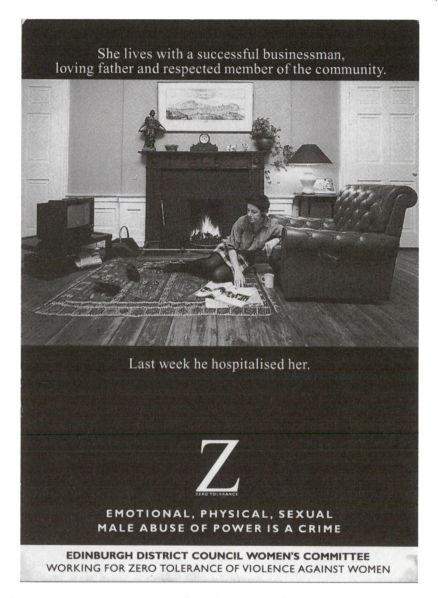

Figure 5.2 Zero Tolerance. Violence knows no class boundaries. A poster from Edinburgh's acclaimed radical feminist 'Zero Tolerance' of violence against women campaign.
Source: Zero Tolerance campaign.

materialism' (YWCA 1996: 2). The degree to which anti-violence campaigns are likely to achieve their goals has to be considered in relation to the sheer quantity and longevity of media representations that contribute to the normalization of violence. Clearly vast profits can be made from media representations of violence, whether they be factual representations, fictional, or promotional. However, in the USA the extent to which these profits are pursued to the utter neglect of concern for individual and social welfare has very recently resulted in grave concerns within the walls of government.

Peddling violence to children

As is often the case after incidents of seemingly extraordinary acts of violence committed by young people, following the 1999 **Columbine High School shootings** in Colorado, it was suggested that 'the motivations for the . . . incident revolved around the killers' immersion in entertainment media' (Grier 2001: 123). The teenage killers' engagement with violent media content, and especially computer and video games, was considered to have influenced their crime, and questions were asked about the extent to which the entertainment and marketing industries actually promoted that engagement. Consequently, in the direct aftermath of the shootings, then President Bill Clinton and members of the US Congress called for a FTC and Department of Justice investigation into the marketing practices of the entertainment industries.

The FTC review focused on two questions: 'Do the industries promote products they themselves acknowledge warrant parental caution in venues where children make up a substantial percentage of the audience? And are these advertisements intended to attract children and teenagers' (Federal Trade Commission 2000). The 15-month review concluded that the answers to both questions was an overwhelming 'Yes': 80 per cent of 'R' (restricted: under 17 requires accompanying parent or adult guardian) rated movies, 100 per cent of 'explicit-content' labelled music, and 70 per cent of M (mature) rated games were being promoted to children under 17 years old (Grier 2001). Grier outlines that

> one studio was found to have conducted research on 10- and 11-year-olds to devise a marketing strategy for an R-rated film. Furthermore, companies promoted their products using television programmes, Internet sites, magazines, and teen hangouts (e.g., game rooms, sports apparel stores) that were most popular with the under-17 age group.
>
> (Grier 2001: 126)

In effect, the FTC findings made a mockery of the film industry's age rating system for film exhibition that we outlined in Chapter 2, as well as the music and video industries' voluntary labelling systems for their products. As Sack (2000) reported, the FTC revealed that 'all three industries have used marketing strategies to entice young consumers to buy products that the industries themselves deem inappropriate.'

No legislative action followed the FTC findings and, as Grier (2001: 128) explains, 'because of First Amendment concerns, the most likely scenario is continuing political heat on the industries to enhance their self regulation rather than direct government intervention'. For their part, a number of industry executives reported that their companies would stop marketing violent media content to children (Rosenbaum 2000). Others argued that the Democrat government was simply using the media violence issue as an electioneering platform and was scapegoating the media as the cause of violence in society (Lyman 2000). Film executive Gale Anne Hurd asserted that 'Hollywood is an easy target. And since guns are apparently sacrosanct, it's very easy to say, no, teenage violence is caused by the media' (cited in Lyman 2000). Access to guns is of course an important factor in the perpetration of much violence in the USA. Yet, it cannot be denied that the media play a part in shaping American social and cultural values, and attitudes toward and understandings of violence. As we have identified in the preceding discussions of violence in the print media, film, television and advertising, the media make a significant contribution to promoting and upholding social power structures that underpin the perpetration of violence. Indeed, in that media content the potential for violence is imagined as seductive, exciting and desirable.

Conclusion

The task of the promotion industries is to make us consume by whatever means possible. In encouraging us to consume, advertisers and their clients promote ideological subject positions as positions of power that they hope we will literally buy into. Advertising encourages women to believe that their greatest power resides in enhancing their feminine looks and sex appeal (but they are not warned that with this comes the prospect of being blamed when they are sexually harassed or attacked by a man). At the same time, men are told that their power lies in their independence, control and ability to be aggressive and violent (and if they are not they have not yet purchased the right product and adopted the right 'brand attitude'). Meanwhile television executives who need to sell advertising space in their programmes schedule popular violent films, crime and actions series, and violent male contact sports during peak viewing hours to maximize audiences. Patriarchal capitalism talks to us as consumers, but never quite speaks of the true costs of our consumption.

There are, as we have discussed, glimpses of advertising campaign content that encourage reflection on the effects of violence on individuals. But these messages, like the occasional official questioning of the marketing of violent entertainment, are rare in relation to the sheer quantity of messages that condone our absorption in violence and the subjectivities that support acts of violence. As we discuss in the following chapter, developments in the computer technologies of cyberspace have even brought us a word where we are able to act out our violent fantasies, subjectivities and desires in increasingly violent contexts.

Further reading

Goldman, R. and Papson, S. (1996) *Sign Wars: The Cluttered Landscape of Advertising*. New York: Guilford Press.
Hamilton, J.T. (1998) *Channeling Violence: The Economic Market for Violent Television*. Princeton, NJ: Princeton University Press.
Kilbourne, J. (1999) *Deadly Persuasion: Why Women and Girls Must Fight the Addictive Power of Advertising*. New York: Free Press.

Videos

Media Education Foundation (1999) *Tough Guise: Violence, Media and the Crisis in Masculinity*. Northampton, MA: Media Education Foundation.
Media Education Foundation (2000) *Killing Us Softly 3: Advertising's Image of Women*. Northampton, MA: Media Education Foundation.

6 | THE DARK SIDE OF CYBERSPACE

A . . . fear that haunts cyberspace's imaginary . . . is that all the various powers that individuals gain in cyberspace can be used for evil purposes.

(Tim Jordan 1999: 203)

Many users of the Internet moved into cyberspace because it seemed less threatening than the world beyond the computer room . . . But now it seems that putting oneself on the Internet leaves one more exposed than ever before.

(Andrew Calcutt 1999: 112)

Introduction

This chapter examines emerging debates linking violence and cyberspace. There is now a relatively small yet growing body of scholarly research and media commentary addressing what some have referred to as the 'dark side' of the Internet (Brophy et al. 1999; Oswell 1999; Jones and Adeniji-Adele 2001; Owen 2001).

As Beck (1992, 1999) and Giddens (1992) argue, people in western societies are increasingly experiencing the world as a place that is shaped by hazards, fears and risks. The golden promises of modernity (for progressively better health, security and wealth) have proven to have grave human consequences. Such 'progress' has translated not only into greater wealth for more people in certain countries, but also into greater poverty in others – as well as environmental degradation and increased levels of crime. Growing global anxieties and uncertainties about the future have resulted in an increased reliance on relations of trust – particularly in 'experts' who claim to have come up with ideas for dealing with the problems indicative of what Beck (1992) refers to as our 'Risk Society'. As Giddens (1992: 88) similarly argues, 'Trust in systems takes the form of faceless commitments, in which faith is sustained in the workings of knowledge of which the lay person is largely ignorant'.

Such trust certainly accompanied the initial development of what would become known as the 'information superhighway'. When Internet technology passed from the US military to the academy in the late 1960s and then to the public in the late 1970s to early 1980s there was a strong belief that it would eventually provide a way of connecting people to a benignly interdependent global village. Canadian cultural theorist Marshall McLuhan (1964) coined the term 'global village' to describe his utopian vision for the future, one in which the world's peoples would be interconnected by new communications technologies for the good of all. Whereas newspapers, radio and to some extent television had helped to create temporal and spatial social boundaries between people, new media would collapse divisions of time and space by drawing them together in an interdependent and cooperative global community. In recent times, some have questioned this utopian narrative. Various scares around the security and safety of cyberspace have shaken many people's faith and trust in such a positive stance. Commenting on this, Branscombe (1997: 452), a US communications lawyer, notes: 'Now that "cyberporn", hate messages, and inflammatory content are beginning to creep out into the real world, the "cybercops" are coming into these lawless frontiers of cyberspace and attempting to tame the natives'.

To explore the ways in which violence is portrayed in cyberspace, in the first section of this chapter we critically survey research that looks at what has been said about violent cybergames and the ways in which they allegedly extend and intensify the violence of earlier video games. This area of study represents a response to one of the earliest public concerns around computer-mediated violence going back to the 1970s. This is followed by a discussion of cybersexploitation, where we offer a general survey of feminist media and cultural studies research on women's sometimes frightening experiences of the Internet. While some scholars champion its potential to reshape gender identities and power relations, others warn that the 'macho culture' of the Internet oftentimes inhibits, if not scares, many women from exploring its radical, democratic potential.

Attention then turns to the ways in which the Internet is allegedly implicated in encouraging violence against children through the exchange of child pornography. Because so many children are active users of the Internet, particularly in western, industrialized countries, some critics suggest that paedophiles have an extremely powerful tool that provides them with easy access to victims. From there we explore the presence of racist groups on the Internet and assess the current state of research on 'hate websites'. We consider how some groups may have used the Internet to attract like-minded individuals to racist arguments and political action. Concluding on a more general note, we turn to the subject of regulation and censorship. Here we consider debates around efforts to regulate – as well as censor – violent Internet content.

Cybergames

As it is now widely known, the Internet was developed in the 1960s by the US military to facilitate strategic communication between military person-nel in the event of war (an aim was to create a communication system that would be able to survive a nuclear attack). Given this heritage, it is hardly surprising that computerized games were, from a very early stage, militaris-tic in their orientation. A wide range of communications technologies, including the Internet, developed in and through the construction of what US cyberfeminist Donna Haraway (2000) sees as a 'militarized imagination'. On this point, she comments that:

> The culture of video games is heavily orientated to individual com-petition and extraterrestrial warfare, destruction of the planet and a sci-ence fiction escape from its consequences. More than our imaginations is militarized; and the other realities of electronic and nuclear warfare are inescapable.
>
> (Haraway 2000: 306)

Before the development of both stand-alone and web-based computer games was, of course, the video game. The 1970s saw the very first video game, called 'Odyssey and Pong'. Many would now find the game to be laughably simple and perhaps boring (it featured a ball and paddle – a glorified digital translation of Ping-Pong). However, at the time it was extremely popular (Parratt and Wadham 1999: 11). On the strength of its financial success came a steady stream of increasingly sophisticated and violent video games. Two of the most favoured ones in the 1970s and 1980s were *PacMan* (a round-headed creature who gobbled up opponents in its path) and *Space Invaders* (consisting of a team of space ships whose mission it was to destroy those of the opposing team).

By the early 1980s, at a time that saw the widespread purchase of what had become relatively inexpensive video recorder-players, US consumers were spending more on home and arcade video games ($11 billion) than they were on movies and music put together (Parratt and Wadham 1999: 2). It may be surprising to discover, therefore, that only a few years later, by the mid-1980s, the market for video games had more or less collapsed (falling to annual sales of a mere $100 million in the USA). Media commentators have suggested this was because the public had grown bored with the limited range and lack of sophistication exhibited by most games (Parratt and Wadham 1999: 2).

Then, in 1987, the Japanese toy firm Nintendo introduced a new game called 'Famicon', as well as a range of other fast-action (more 'realistic' and violent) games with more advanced graphics, thereby stimulating new interest in the marketplace. By the end of the 1980s, at the point when the Internet was first coming into its own, the market for computer games had bounced back to $3 billion. By the early 1990s, 20 per cent of all US households owned a Nintendo computer games set (cited in Parratt and Wadham 1999: 2). It was around that time that the computer games company, Sega, came under fire for some of its interactive video games. One such game that incorporated both sex and violence, *Night Trap*, featured photographic images of women, rather than cartoon characters, in provocative sexual poses and engaged in violent action. Trying to defend the game, Sega Vice-President Jeff McCarthy suggested that as gamers aged, they were demanding more realistic sex and violence (Parratt and Wadham 1999: 4). Trends in technology also need to be related to recent trends in the growth of game sales. In 2002, console-based games such as those played on Sony PlayStation, Sega and Nintendo systems now account for the bulk of the game software market, now estimated at annual sales of over £5.6 billion in the USA and Canada, £2.8 billion in Japan (ANANOVA 2002) and £1.6 billion in the UK (ELSPA 2002).

Various commentators have pointed out that the incessant drive for profits has sometimes meant that companies have failed to consider the possible impact of increasingly realistic violence on people who have bought their games. Bringing this concern to the fore, the British broadsheet newspaper the *Daily Telegraph* reported in 1993 on research claiming there was a link between children's use of violent video games and violent behaviour.

CHILDREN 'ACT OUT VIDEO VIOLENCE'
Children who regularly play video games admit they can be addictive and lead to them acting out the violent scenes that are an intrinsic part of many games, according to a survey by researchers at Aston University. Many described violent scenes 'with relish', they found. Almost 60 per cent had witnessed other children mimicking violent games.
(*Daily Telegraph*, 25 October 1993, cited in Craig and Petley 2001: 187)

Growing public concerns around the increasingly violent names of computer games grew in the 1990s, arguably culminating in 1999 when a number of journalists writing about the high school massacre at Columbine

High School in Littleton, Colorado noted how one of the shooters, Eric Harris, 'reconfigured a violent computer game called Doom, possibly as a dry run for the deadly shootings' (Hubbard 1999). According to US journalist Hubbard (1999), Harris changed the game 'from a shooting competition into a massacre' and had some dying characters crying 'Lord, why is this happening to me?' In Canada, Rose Dyson, Chair of Canadians Concerned About Violence in Entertainment (CCAVE), writes that: 'Clearly, trends in the technology underscore the growing urgency for government action as virtual reality games now offer enhanced opportunities to participate in the experience of actually *killing* someone' (Dyson 2000: 94, original emphasis).

Another important development since the early 1990s has been the response of computer software companies to public demands to tone down violence or at least to issue rating guides to assist parents in their choice of games for their children. During the 1990s, several software regulatory bodies were established in response to growing public concern over game violence. In 1994, for example, an independent self-regulatory organization called the Entertainment Software Rating Board (ESRB) was set up in the USA by a number of people worried about children and young people's access to violent computer games. The ESRB provides a voluntary rating system not only for software but also for online websites for the gaming industry (see www.esrb.org).

In the following year, Bethesda Softworks, a computer software company, created its own filtering software called *Childguard* that enables parents to control the level of violence in their children's computer games. Another development in 1995 was the establishment of the World Wide Web Consortium (W3C) Platform for Internet Content Selection (PICS) which set about to define a web infrastructure that would encourage web content providers to voluntarily rate their sites. Shortly after this, Microsoft (2000) introduced a feature in Internet Explorer called the 'Content Advisor' through which parents could rate the appropriateness of web content and control the websites their children could visit (see www.microsoft.com/windows2000/techinfo).

Aside from ratings boards and filtering software, some computer games manufacturers have also introduced controls which parents can use to restrict the child's exposure to explicit language, sex and violence. For example, in 1997, computer games company Acclaim embedded control features in its game *Turok* – the main one being an ability to eliminate the portrayal of blood. Sceptical of these initiatives, former games developer Howard Schwartz, Chief Executive of Heynetwork.com, a family Internet site, claims that such codes will not stop hackers from trying to get around them. Writes Schwartz, 'If people can put macro-viruses into Microsoft Word, I think there will be a crack in this' (cited in King 1999).

After the attacks on the USA on September 11 2001, some computer games manufacturers decided to remove certain scenes of violence thought to be too close to the reality of what happened that day. For example, Microsoft delayed the release of a new version of *Flight Simulator* in order to make it impossible to purposely crash planes into the World Trade Center. Public concerns around the reality of game violence have become even more pronounced since the attacks, possibly due in part to the fact that many people in the USA were staying closer to home for their entertainment. Retailers reported that the sales of videotapes, televisions and computer games increased substantially after the attacks. At the same time, some news reporters have highlighted parents' fears that some of the games their children are playing have exploited 11 September and its aftermath. Shortly after the attacks, for example, a new game appeared that could be downloaded from the Internet allowing gamers to take virtual shots at a cartoon figure of Osama bin Laden (ABCNEWS.com 2002).

Children's use of violent and aggressive computer games (boys in particular) since 11 September, US psychologist Karen Binder-Brynes suggests, may have become more pronounced because they were feeling a loss of control over their lives. Binder-Brynes notes, 'It does give them a temporary sense of some type of control but probably does not help children to "vent their fear and anger". Instead, such games can often make them feel worse. Control over a game is not the same thing as feeling a sense of control over something that actually happened' (cited in ABCNEWS.com 2002).

Yet is such public concern about violent games misplaced? Is it reasonable to single them out as being among the worst media forms for encouraging violent behaviour? Alloway and Gilbert (1998) argue that computer game narratives and gaming culture cannot be extracted from the broader culture in which violence is discursively constructed (see also Craig and Petley 2001). The authors go on to suggest that:

> Violence is not just a feature of video game culture. Violence is . . . everywhere. You can't avoid it. We can plug into violence on television, popular film, the Internet, radio, advertisements, brochures, magazines, newspapers, novels, theatre, MTV . . . The video game site is but one site within a complex set of sites.
>
> (Alloway and Gilbert 1998: 96–7)

It is with this counter-argument in mind that the next section of this chapter turns to examine cyberculture more broadly. Here we review what some media and cultural studies commentators have had to say about issues such as cybersexual harassment, flaming and cyberstalking and how women have fought to maintain and extend their web presence despite such forms of intimidation.

Cybersexploitation

Internet user efforts to exclude, threaten and harass others in cyberspace are often (although not exclusively) directed at women. In the mid-1990s, a female *Washington Post* reporter suggested that 'If you are a woman, sometimes cyberspace can get ugly . . . There have been recent reports of sexual harassment – and worse' (cited in the *Los Angeles Times* 1994). Sexual harassment on the Net can consist of emails that are used to make unsolicited sexual advances, the distribution of unwanted pornography, unwelcome website postings of a sexual nature, promises of career advancement in return for sexual favours, and so on. While some feminist researchers have optimistically claimed the Internet to be a potentially liberatory space for women (Plant 1996; Burke 1999; Haraway 2000), others have suggested that this claim is rather utopian (Herring 1999; Chalaby 2000). For example, van Zoonen (2001) argues that:

> Although there are few systematic analyses of the representations and constructions of gender on the Internet, there is enough evidence about (child) pornography, right wing extremism, sexual harassment, flaming and other unpleasantness to disclaim any utopian vision of the Internet as an unproblematic feminine environment.
>
> (van Zoonen 2001: 68)

Before directly engaging with what is happening today with regard to this issue, it is helpful to look back to the beginning of the Internet in the 1970s to see how women's relationship to it has developed since then. This will provide a context with which to better understand contemporary feminist claims about cybersexploitation.

Reid (1999) contends that after the Internet passed from the control of the US military to the public in the 1970s, the ideal of complete freedom of expression quickly eroded. By the middle of the 1980s new Internet communities had already begun to collapse 'under the onslaught of messages, often obscene, posted by the first generation of adolescent school children [mostly boys] with personal computers and modems' (Reid 1999: 5). What happened next was that computer system administrators began to monitor and censor 'inappropriate' messages (see Stone 1991). Without such interception, it was felt that **MUDs** (originally multi-user dungeons) and other types of online gaming communities where users take on alter-identities/genders, would disintegrate into chaos. Looking at how mechanisms for social control have been developed on MUDs, Reid (1999) suggests that the intimacy and disinhibition fostered by such groups had another, hostile side. Because MUD users feel relatively safe, some use the forum to express negative, sometimes even violent feelings. Since identity in cyberspace games is virtual and anonymous, there is a sense in which players tend to feel that they will not be directly punished for such behaviour (see Turkle 1999). Says Reid (1999):

> The supposed safety of the medium causes the sanction of physical violence to appear irrelevant to virtual actions . . . The safety of anonymous expression of hostilities and obscenities that would usually incur social sanctions – or a punch in the nose – in a face-to-face encounter encourages some people to use MUDs as a forum for airing their resentment of individuals or groups in a blatantly uninhibited manner.
>
> (Reid 1999: 115)

By the early 1990s, feminist researchers were becoming increasingly interested in women's relationship to the Internet. Around that time, Kramarae and Taylor (1993) undertook a pioneering study on women's use of this new medium of communication. One of their conclusions was that men tended to monopolize web chat and news groups. At the time, men greatly outnumbered women on the Internet, taking up more e-space than women and therefore largely calling the shots. For many women, men's numerical superiority either was seen to be threatening or, at the very least, made the Internet seem less welcoming.

Aside from men's numerical advantage on the Net, Spender (1995) points out that the tactic of flaming anyone perceived to be in violation of masculine-defined **netiquette** (rules of etiquette for the Internet) has tended to dissuade many women from active participation. For example, informal netiquette rules state that capital letters (which signify shouting) should be used only in rare cases where yelling at someone is absolutely necessary. However, many women new to the Internet found that those who had been using the technology for some time already (primarily men) were shouting at them with great regularity (being rather impatient with Net 'newbies'). Some commentators have gone so far as to argue that the rules of netiquette have contributed to the creation of a macho culture which can make it feel like a threatening place for women (Herman 1999: 202). As the female *Washington Post* journalist we heard from earlier concludes: 'Although verbal muggings, or "flames," are relatively rare, they give newcomers pause. Getting mugged in the real world doesn't happen that often, but knowing it happens at all makes us think twice before going out after midnight' (cited in the *Los Angeles Times* 1994).

By the mid-1990s, many more people were coming online as computer hardware, software and Internet links became more widely available, affordable and user friendly. At this time, there was a growing perception and fairly widespread enthusiasm for cyberspace (particularly in the affluent west) as an 'electronic playground where anything goes and everything is safe' (Calcutt 1999: 108). However, not everyone shared this sentiment. Some viewed the Internet as anything but safe, and were worried about an increasing number of reports regarding the growing numbers of cybervictims and cyberpredators. Attempting to contextualize this rather sharp shift in perceptions, Calcutt (1999) explains:

> Naïve enthusiasm for life in cyberspace is often an expression of pessimism about pre-existing society. Cyberbabble usually represents a yearning to escape from the apparently intractable problems of the offline world into the virgin territory of digital communications, untainted by the 'geek-flesh' of human beings. Likewise, cynicism about cyberspace is a symptom of the excessive problematization of already existing society. Such a low opinion of a new and as yet largely unexplored terrain can only have been formed by negative perceptions of the offline world which we already know and love to hate. Both strands, cyberbabble and Net-lash [backlash against the Internet], are predicated on an extremely negative view of humanity and an intensely apprehensive attitude towards society.
>
> (Calcutt 1999: 109)

With this point in mind, in the next section of our discussion on cybersexploitation, we turn our attention upon the phenomenon of cyberstalking. This is an issue that has recently received a great deal of attention and has been widely reported both in the USA and UK as a growing source of public anxiety. While demands for state intervention have increased, so too have the activities of 'cybervigilante' groups like *cyberangels* and *online guardians*, both of whom work closely with the FBI in the USA and MI5 in the UK (Whittle 2002: 4).

Cyberstalking

Stalking has been described as a set of behaviours comprising of 'repeated and persistent attempts to impose on another person unwanted communication and/or contact' (Mullen et al. 1999: 244). Meloy and Gothard (1995: 258) define stalking as the 'willful, malicious, and repeated following and harassing of another person that threatens his or her safety'. With the development of new communication technologies, stalking now occurs via email and the Internet. The technology of the Internet and its relative low cost allows cyberstalkers to potentially reach large numbers of victims (Ogilvie 2000). It is possible for a single cyberstalker to send the same harassing file to hundreds if not thousands of people in a mere fraction of the time that it would take to telephone or write to them.

There are three principal ways in which cyberstalking occurs. First, unsolicited email is often associated with cyberstalking, especially where it includes 'hate, obscene or threatening mail' (Ogilvie 2000: 2). Victims are also sometimes the targets of computer viruses or spamming (sending large volumes of junk email messages). Deliberately sending viruses or spamming does not constitute stalking in and by itself, but can become so if such email is 'repetitively sent in a manner which is designed to intimidate' (Ogilvie 2000: 2).

In the first case of its kind brought to court in Australia, a cyberstalker was convicted for sending a woman death threats. Email correspondence started off in a friendly manner, but turned ugly after she tried to break off contact. The cyberstalker threatened to 'have [her] pack-raped, videotaped and uploaded on the Internet' (Ogilvie 2000: 2). Because email cyberstalking closely resembles its postal variant, stalkers can often be traced through their email addresses. As such, prosecutions for this type of activity are more common than for other types of cyberstalking. However, the growing availability and cheapness of anonymizers (anonymous emailers that hide the identity of the sender) increasingly mean that cyberstalkers' identity can be concealed.

A second type of cyberstalking occurs on the Internet, moving from the more private world of email to that of a more public forum of the World Wide Web, where the identity of the cyberstalker is better hidden than through email. Examples include instances where cyberstalkers have used chat rooms and websites to harass and threaten their victims. In 2000, movie actress Kate Winslet confirmed that she had received a number of email death threats that had been sent to her fan website. According to the British tabloid newspaper the *Mirror*, the stalker was female and claimed that she would visit London to 'rape', 'kill' and 'hit' the then pregnant Winslet (cited in the *Coventry Evening Telegraph*, 22 June 2000). Internet stalking has often led to other forms of stalking, including use of the telephone, post, acts of vandalism and physical attacks (Laughren 2000). While most instances of Internet violence do not turn into physical violence, the fear and apprehensions they cause victims are very real and emotionally distressing.

The third type of cyberstalking is 'computer stalking'. In this instance, the offender uses the Internet and the Windows operating system to link his or her computer directly to someone else's in order to control it. At the moment, to undertake this kind of connection requires fairly sophisticated computer skills. Nevertheless, instructions on how to do this are now becoming more widely available on the Internet and increasingly easier for novices to understand. Computer stalking radically reduces the virtual and physical distance between victim and stalker typical of email and Internet cyberstalking. As Ogilvie (2000: 4) notes, the analogy here is 'like discovering that anytime you pick up the phone, a stalker is on-line and in control of your phone'. The only defence in such instances is to disconnect the telephone line and take up a new one. With a computer, a victim has to give up their Internet address and select another. One rather startling case of this in the USA involved a cyberstalker who sent a message to a woman through her computer. The cyberstalker threatened to 'get' the victim and proceeded to open the CD-ROM drive to demonstrate the level of control over her computer (Karp 2000).

While flaming, sexual harassment and cyberstalking may seem to be rather abstract because they are 'virtual' rather than 'physical' attacks, their effects on women's (and men's) relationship to the Internet are real enough. Studies have shown, for example, how women tend to be less enthusiastic about the radical potential of the Internet (Spender 1995; van Zoonen 2001). However, it would be wrong to assume that as a result all women feel intimidated by their experiences on the Internet and therefore less inclined to explore its liberatory possibilities. Scott et al. (1999) claim that while women are sometimes the victims of Internet violence and that this violence can constrain their participation, it does not tell us the whole story of women's relationships to the Net. The authors argue that:

> [M]ost net-users *do* have some means to control or avoid intimidation and violence. Helpless victimization is not the experience of most women, in cyberspace or elsewhere. This version of 'women and the internet' can be counter-productive for feminists; if cyberspace is so dangerous, women might well come to believe that their daughters would be safer spending their time somewhere else.
>
> (Scott et al. 1999: 549, original emphasis)

Clearly, many women have actively embraced new communications technologies as a space for self-expression, information gathering and the establishment of online communities. 'To be sure,' argues a *Washington Post* journalist, 'lots of women have no trouble holding their own in cyberspace, cheerfully lambasting the bozos. Still others welcome the more intriguing advances and use their modems to indulge in a libidinous escape' (cited in

The Guerrilla Girls, established in 1985 and still going strong in the 21st
century, are a group of women artists, writers, performers and film makers
who fight discrimination. Dubbing ourselves the conscience of culture, we
declare ourselves feminist counterparts to the mostly male tradition of
anonymous do-gooders like Robin Hood, Batman, and the Lone Ranger. We
wear gorilla masks to focus on the issues rather than our personalities. We
use humor to convey information, provoke discussion, and show that
feminists can be funny. In 17 years we have produced over 80 posters,
printed projects, and actions that expose sexism and racism in politics, the
art world and the culture at large. Our work has been passed around the
world by kindred spirits who we are proud to have as supporters. The
mystery surrounding our identities has attracted attention. We could be
anyone; we are everywhere.

Figure 6.1 Guerrilla Girls.
Source: website contents copyright © 1985–2002 by Guerrilla Girls, Inc.

the *Los Angeles Times* 1994). Plant (1996) is perhaps one of the more optimistic voices of cyberspace's opportunities for the empowerment of women. In her view, 'The Internet promises women a network of lines on which to chatter, natter, work and play; virtuality brings a fluidity to identities which once had to be fixed' (Plant 1996: 324).

One of the responses women and girls have made to the hostility and intimidation faced on the Internet has been to develop woman and girl only spaces whose aim it is to provide safe, flame-free places to explore cyberspace. The cyberfeminist activist group *Guerrilla Girls* is a good example of this (Figure 6.1). Established in 1985 by women artists, writers, performers and filmmakers, its purpose was and still is to use the power of the Internet to operate anonymously in the name of fighting sex discrimination (Guerrilla Girls 2002). Since 1985, the collective has 'produced over 70 posters, printed projects, and actions that expose sexism and racism in politics, the art world and the culture at large' (www.guerrillagirls.com). *Cybergrrl* ('voices of women') is another website that offers women support to fight sexism. One of their site pages, 'Cybergrrl Safety Net', features a range of links to information about domestic violence (Figure 6.2). Women are invited to share their stories of domestic abuse with others, to find out what constitutes abusive behaviour, to read survivor stories, to find books on the subject, and follow links to national, state and international websites on the issue (www.cybergrrls.com/views/dv/ 2002).

Many now argue that it should not be the case that we have to view women as *either* the victims of potential cyberviolence *or*, at the other end of the scale, as savvy cybersurfers who are fearlessly marking their spot in cyberspace. Instead, perhaps the most critical and potentially fruitful way of thinking about cybersexploitation is to consider how the growing presence of cyberviolence potentially changes our views as to which types of violence are 'socially acceptable' and those that are not. All forms of intimidation and abuse currently taking place in cyberspace can serve to limit its supposed global, radical and democratic potential for women and men. It is this political commitment to social justice and democratic citizenship that drives many cyberfeminists and others to explore the rich potential of the Internet, despite the dangers of cybersexploitation. Brail implores women not to give up on the Internet, despite risks of experiencing cyberviolence. She insists that, 'Instead of withdrawing from the online world, with all its riches and opportunities, we can form our own networks, online support groups, and places to speak . . . Women cannot be left behind and we cannot afford to be intimidated' (cited in Herman 1999: 204).

It is with this point in mind that we now turn our attention to children, a group that is sometimes regarded as the most vulnerable and at risk of

TOWNHALL   **Forums** **Chat** **Register** **Login**

Voices of Women

help   map

- **Let others learn from your experience!**
Have you been in an abusive relationship and overcome it? Share Your Story

- **Are you in an abusive relationship?**
Find out what behavior constitutes abuse.

- **Domestic Violence Books**
From inspiring survivor's stories to experts advice on escaping abusive relationships, these books offer practical, empowering advice for victims of domestic violence and their friends and family members.

- **Domestic Violence Survivor Stories**
Women who persevered and won their freedom back. Share your personal triumph here!

- **Domestic Violence Links**
Check out National & State Resources, International Websites and Educational & Professionial Websites.

- **How Much Do You Know About Domestic Violence?**
Test your knowledge with our Domestic Violence Quiz.

views archive

@**Cybergrrl**
Cybergrrl
Femina
Webgrrls

@Cybergrrl®

 Search Femina for Domestic Violence Information Online

[Search Femina]

International Websites | Educational and Professional Resources | National and State Resources | Checklist | Your Story | Quiz | CG Safety Net |

©2001 Cybergrrl, Inc. All Rights Reserved. | Terms of Use | Privacy Statement | Question? Email Cybergrrl.

Figure 6.2 Cybergrrl Safety Net.
Source: website contents copyright © 2001 Cybergrrl, Inc.

cybersexual abuse – and – at other times as the smartest and most web savvy today.

Cyberpaedophilia

Any examination of newspaper coverage of cyberrisks and cybercrimes in the 1990s, demonstrates growing public concern around computer-based violence and children. As Lupton (2000) points out, one of the most pressing worries at the moment seems to focus on children's access to the Internet. Here the concerns are basically twofold:

- Children will be exposed to violent websites that may cause them emotional damage.
- Children will become the targets of paedophiles surfing the net for new victims.

It is the latter anxiety which is the focus of this section of the chapter, the former being dealt with already, to some extent, through our discussion of violent cybergames.

Contemporary debates around cyberpaedophilia and child pornography tend to fall into two opposing positions. On the one side are critics who suggest that the Internet's ability to circulate images and information easily, cheaply and globally, potentially means that child pornography and cyberpaedophilia will become more common (Inayatullah and Milojevic 1999). Gregg (1996) contends that the unique character of the Internet, with its apparent ability to quickly and easily access and exchange paedophillic images, has led to widespread outrage and demands in the USA for greater legal vigilance and sanction (Gregg 1996: 160). As is often pointed out, the anonymity of the Internet is one of the features that make this communication technology so potentially dangerous for children. Gregg (1996) insists that:

> The anonymity of online users and their ability to role-play . . . are freedoms which clearly do not exist in face-to-face interactions. The ephemeral online community and the potential for brief contact provide online criminals with safe cover [and beyond this] the free-flowing exchanges of typed conversation and anonymity foster a lack of inhibition.
>
> (Gregg 1996: 169–70)

This situation not only supports a 'distorted view of sexuality within patriarchal societies, but also help[s] predators to find new victims, creating a reverse of civil society, a community of the predatory violent' (Inayatullah and Milojevic 1999: 81). Some media commentators have even suggested that what we are now seeing is the encouragement of the view among some ('deviant') members of the public that paedophilia somehow represents a 'normal' form of sexual interest and activity (McElvoy 2001).

On the other hand, there are commentators who suggest that children are really at no greater risk from cyberpaedophiles than they were in the pre-Internet era. Official statistics in the UK (Home Office 2002), for example, continue to report that children are most at risk of sexual abuse by parents or close relatives (see also Oswell 1999). In 1999, a British rock star was alleged to have a large number of child pornography files on his computer which were discovered when he took it in for repairs. 'This case', argues Hepburn (1999), 'put the issue of Internet censorship and online obscenity back in the public eye. It led those extreme moral minority campaigners who always crop up to call for mass censorship and witch hunts on all Internet sites which could be deemed explicit or offensive.' However abhorrent this case, Hepburn insists, it does not build an argument for restricting access to the Internet so as to ensure that people who are easily offended are not upset. Hepburn (1999) concludes that 'Any call for mass censorship would give those moral crusaders the chance to restrict anything they want'. More-over, he adds, the Internet 'may give them [paedophiles] more explicit material and better ways to distribute it, but, at the end of the day, there is very little there that cannot be found elsewhere'.

Noonan (1998) concurs with this view, arguing that very few paedophillic images are actually available online. Those that are available have been around for quite some time, before the advent of the Internet. In addition, it is very unlikely, in his view, that most children will be exposed to paedophiles in cyberspace. When such incidents do occur journalists tend to cover such stories in a way that encourages the development of a moral panic (see Hamilton 1999; Critcher 2003). By suggesting that there may be many more paedophiles lurking about in cyberspace than actually exist has serious social consequences; it obfuscates the fact that children are much more likely to be assaulted or sexually abused offline. Noonan (1998) emphasizes this point by observing that:

> Sensationalistic panaceas, such as the ubiquitous Megan's Laws [in the US], help to give the public the illusion that politicians are doing some-thing about sexual abuse by focusing on that initiated by strangers. In fact, most data tend to indicate that the majority of sexual abuse is per-petrated by parents . . . with another significant percentage committed by relatives and known friends.
>
> (Noonan 1998: 160)

Such arguments notwithstanding, many parents now feel that the home is no longer a place where children are assured protection from harm. Cyberspace has turned it into a place fraught with danger from outside sources. As Lupton (2000) notes:

> Again, the main anxiety here is in the insidious nature of contact with others through the Internet. The home is now no longer a place of safety or refuge for children, the computer no longer simply an educational tool or source of entertainment but is the possible site of children's corruption. 'Outside' danger is brought 'inside', into the very heart of the home, via the Internet.
>
> (Lupton 2000: 486)

An increasing search for safety has led many parents to install filtering software such as Solid Oak Software's CYBERsitter on their children's computers in order to prevent their access to violent and sexual material (Figure 6.3). CYBERsitter is a Windows programme that stops the user from accessing 'objectionable material' from the Internet. Another strategy now used by some parents is to direct their children to visit 'family friendly' websites like safekids.com, safeteens.com and yahooligans!.com based in the USA and atkidz.com and kidsdomain.co.uk in the UK. SafeKids.com and safeteens.com are operated by 'The Online Safety Project'. Both are free subscription websites set up on 8 September 1998 by the *Los Angeles Times* journalist Larry Magid (2002). Technology journalist and advocate of child online safety, Magid suggests that while filtering software is useful, websites like safekids.com and safeteens.com are resources that can be used by parents to teach their children and teenagers respectively to think critically about safety and privacy on the Internet. On safekids.com, there are tips for parents and children about child safety on the Net and links for more sources of information about this issue (Figure 6.4). There are also lists of child-safe search engines, Internet filtering information and other sites with Internet advice for kids, parents and teachers.

Aside from concerns over children's potential exposure to sex and violence on the Internet, in recent years there has been an increasing awareness of the presence and growing openness of what are referred to as 'hate websites'. These sites, often set up by pre-existing white supremacists groups like the Ku Klux Klan in the USA and the British National Party in the UK are the focus of the next section of this chapter, to which we now turn.

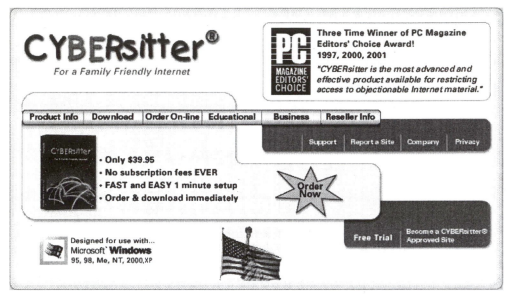

Figure 6.3 CYBERsitter.
Source: CYBERsitter is trademarked and copyrighted by Solid Oak Software,
Incorporated. CYBERsitter is protected by United States Copyright and Trade
Secret Laws.

Cyberhate

Brophy et al. (1999) argue that the enormous growth of the Internet in
the 1990s created a radical new basis for global democratic participation
in the public sphere. While still not available to most around the world, the
Internet has nevertheless already made it possible for increasing numbers of
people to gain access to rapidly expanding bodies of information and to
share experiences in a truly interactive mass medium. However, the Internet
also brings with it the potential to undermine democratic structures by
encouraging the development of interests and organizations keen on promoting forms of racial, ethnic, gender and sexual extremism (Skelton 1994;
Sardar 1996; Capitanchik and Whine 1999; Zickmund 2000; van Zoonen
2001). The authors argue that:

SafeKids.Com

Welcome to SafeKids.Com where you'll find tips, advice and suggestions to make your family's online experience fun and productive!

Daffy Dave Sings
the Safe Kids Online Song
Listen Here

☞ Subscribe to our Free SafeKids/NetfamilyNews Newsletter
Past Issues of Newsletter

Larry's Family Tech Column

Child Safety on the Information Highway	What Are the Risks?
Privacy Issues	Kids' Rules for Online Safety
Guidelines for Parents	Sign the Family Contract for Online Safety (and post it by your computer)

Let Your Kids LISTEN to Kids' Rules for Online Safety

The Online Safety Quiz!
Test your knowledge!"

More Information	Resources
Articles and Issues Understand the issues	Child Safe Search Engines Search engines that are filtered or limited to sites that contain appropriate material
Protecting Your Privacy Sometimes it's OK to Keep Secrets	Tools for Families: Includes Internet filtering options.
SafeTeens.Com Our web site dedicated to keeping teens safe in cyberspace	Other Sites with Internet advice for kids, parents and teachers
The Internet and Computers Everything you need to know	

Online Safety Slide Show (View it online or show it in your community)

SAFETEENS.COM
Keeping teens safe in cyberspace

CyberTipLine
Report Online Crimes Against Children

WebMasters: Link to SafeKids.Com

Contributors

For More Safety Info Visit GetNetWise

Contact us by e-mail

Privacy Policy

Labelled with ...

SafeKids.Com is operated by The Online Safety Project
SafeKids.Com is not affiliated with the National Safe Kids Campaign
Copyright 2002 Online Safety Project
subscribe to SafeKids/NetFamilyNews Newsletter

Figure 6.4 Safekids.com
Source: Safekids.com courtesy of Larry Magid for Safekids.com

Amidst all this glamorous and exciting potential, however, there lurks a darker side. Whilst the Web can be used to heighten a sense of community, and to bring diverse groups closer, it can perform a similar unifying function for those who wish to provoke the fragmentation and disintegration of those communities. Already we can see that extremists of many different persuasions are using the Internet to rally support, preach to the unconverted, and assault targeted groups. Estimates of the number of hate sites vary from 163 to 600; what is certain is that the number is growing.

(Brophy et al. 1999: 9)

As noted in the section on cybersexploitation, email is one of the ways in which the racist individuals and groups can use the Internet to harass and threaten others. In 1996, for example, a California university student was apprehended after having sent a racially abusive email to 59 fellow students, many of whom were of Asian origin. The student's message was anonymous and said 'I personally will . . . find and kill everyone of you' and was signed 'Asian Hater' (cited in Ogilvie 2000: 2).

On 15 May 1999, the *Palm Beach Post* journalist Isger (1999) reported on Rabbi Cooper's search for what he called 'stealth websites' – hate websites that are cleverly hidden within seemingly innocuous ones. Cooper, associate dean of the Los Angeles-based Simon Wiesenthal Center, found that by clicking on a website dedicated to the Reverend Dr Martin Luther King Jr, that it was actually racist (white supremacist). Cooper maintained that it offered a 'slick, attractive and sophisticated presentation', clearly constructed by a web-savvy person. Isger (1999) remarked: 'The people who peddle hate are no slouches when it comes to technology. In a few short years, they've learned to be subtle, hiding in otherwise innocent Web venues – places where teens are likely to bump into them'. Teachers and parents are unlikely to discover homophobic, racist and anti-Semitic websites because these sites are mostly linked to ones that children and young people frequent. Cooper added: 'The average young person is not seeking these sites because they're into Adolf Hitler or looking for a neo-Nazi page. They're more likely looking for alternative music or something, then they're a click away from some of the most dangerous sites promoting hate' (cited in Isger 1999).

Concurring with this point, Fiske (2000) notes how Combat 18 (a breakaway group from the white supremacist British National Party) has an 'orientation toward football and music and more generally establishing a niche within neo-fascist youth culture' (Fiske 2000: 76). The Internet has become an increasingly powerful means of communication between neo-fascist groups around the world. Moreover:

The Net's significance as a new media technology, particularly for the young, lies in the opportunities it provides for new sources and forms of information production, dissemination and consumption . . . These factors and the relative absence of regulation and censorship surrounding the Net has created an important space for extremist views including those of young fascists.

(Fiske 2000: 76)

Such extremist views are linked not only to white supremacist groups such as Combat 18, but also to some fundamentalist religious sites. For example, on 13 January 1999, the *Evening Standard* journalist Adamson (1999) reported that he had found a London-based hate website called 'Supporters of Shariah' or 'SOS' authored by a Muslim Imam. Examining the website's October 1998 newsletter, the journalist claims to have discovered advertisements for 'military training courses, martial arts and map reading for "brothers" and special lectures for "sisters" on the role of women in the field of Jihad holy war'. Also on the site was a photograph of 'one of the world's most wanted men, Sheik Osama bin Laden – the terrorist accused by the US government of masterminding the bombings of US embassies in East Africa' (and later alleged to be behind the attacks on the USA on September 11 2001). Below this image was a 17-page fatwa or 'declaration of war' against the 'enemies of Islam'.

Public concern continues to rise on both sides of the Atlantic regarding the extent to which the Internet can be used for violent purposes. Fears about hate websites, along with cyberpaedophilia, cyberstalking and other forms of cyberviolence, are leading to demands for greater restrictions over the flow of information in cyberspace. With this in mind, in the final section of this chapter, we turn to a discussion of cybersurveillance, looking at specific efforts made by governments in the USA and elsewhere to police the Internet.

Cybersurveillance

In order to understand public responses to cyberviolence such as the ones outlined above, it is important to fully appreciate the debates between those who herald the Internet's radical, democratizing potential and those who are deeply concerned about its potential dangers. As members of British civil liberties group Liberty (the former National Council for Civil Liberties) have pointed out:

The tensions between rights and liberties are thrown into sharp relief by concerns about the use of the net to further anti-social or even potentially harmful aims: children gain access to inappropriate material; far-right organizations circulate racist hatespeech. The benefits of a free market of ideas clearly outweigh the disadvantages, but this does not mean the latter can be easily dismissed.

(Liberty 1999: 1–2)

Since the early 1990s, as government policy-makers and media pressure groups began to show a marked interest in discussing the potential threats posed by the Internet, journalists picked up on public anxieties and provided a platform for discussions (Heins 2000). Typically, the terms of debate have been shaped by the media effects tradition of communication (see Chapter 1), leading to the Internet being blamed for inciting violent behaviour in children. This is nowhere more apparent than in the legislation that the administration of former US President Bill Clinton tried to pass during the 1990s.

On 8 February 1996, President Clinton signed into law the Communications Decency Act (CDA). The principal aim of the Act was to regulate Internet transmissions of 'patently offensive material', particularly in places where children could have access to it. Everard (2000) suggests that attempts to legislate in this area came out of increasingly vociferous debates between those who argued for regulation of pornographic material because of its potential harm to children versus those who fought to support the US constitutional right to free speech (Everard 2000: 136). The CDA was designed to provide the US government with powers to censor online speech and to fine those found in violation of the Act.

The American Civil Liberties Union (ACLU) mounted a challenge to the CDA, arguing that it contravened constitutional amendments that protected free speech. ACLU lawyers suggested that the term 'patently offensive material' was not sufficiently succinct and therefore could be potentially used to censor a wide range of information available on the Internet as well as on other media. An example of the possible abuse of state power the Act would likely permit, ACLU lawyers argued, was that this phrase could lead to the censorship of educational materials on the subject of HIV/AIDS to young people.

While government lawyers tried to defend the legislation by suggesting that the courts would play a key role in interpreting it so that it was applied only to 'real' pornography, the judges were unconvinced by the government's arguments, granting a temporary injunction against the implementation of the CDA. In the following year, 1997, the US Supreme Court declared the bill to be 'unconstitutional' under the Constitution's First Amendment, a right which overrides the state's duty of care for its citizens or any definitions of 'decency' (Everard 2000: 138). In fact, existing legislation designed to regulate the dissemination of pornography was already being applied not only to print and broadcast media, but also to telephonic communication. In the view of the ACLU representatives, the CDA was an unnecessary piece of legislation.

Also in 1996 the US Congress passed the Child Pornography Prevention Act (CPPA). The Act was designed to make illegal the production and distribution of virtual child pornography (images are computer generated rather than actual photographs or video) which many said was so technically sophisticated that it was almost indistinguishable from real child pornography. Those behind the CPPA sought to ban virtual child pornography because they argued that it might encourage paedophiles to sexually abuse children. However, on 16 April 2002, the US Supreme Court held in a six to three decision that the CPPA was too broad and unconstitutional. Writing the majority decision of the Court, Justice Anthony M. Kennedy said, 'The sexual abuse of a child is a most serious crime and an act repugnant to the moral instincts of a decent people . . . Nevertheless . . . if the 1996 law were allowed to stand, the Constitution's First Amendment right to free speech would be "turned upside down" ' (cited in Stout 2002).

In 1998 the Child Online Protection Act (COPA) was signed into law by President Clinton as part of a budget passed by US Congress in October of that year. However, the law did not go into effect as it was immediately challenged by a group of 17 organizations established and led by the ACLU. In February 1999, a temporary injunction blocked the law until a court could hear the appeal from the ACLU. US District Court Judge Lowell Reed Jr granted an injunction noting that it was doubtful that the law would be upheld because it would not be able to withstand legal challenges on the basis of First Amendment guarantees of free speech. Moreover, the judge commented that he 'saw a chilling effect resulting from this act [which] could result in self censorship of constitutionally protected speech' (Drucker and Gumpert 2000: 148). Here we see that the terms of the debate were firmly entrenched within the free speech versus censorship binarism that has held such a firm grip on the terms of debate around pornography.

Overall, discussions in Europe around Internet censorship and regulation have been less turbulent than in the USA. Our newspaper database searches for coverage of this issue in the UK yielded far fewer stories than a similar one for the USA. Where stories showed up in the UK news, most occurred from the late 1990s whereas US reporting went back more than 10 years. However, concerns around Internet violence are now increasing in Europe. In 1997, for example, the European Parliament commissioned an independent study by Smith System Engineering into the possibility of developing technical blocks to pornographic, racist and violent material. The report concluded that while blocks were possible, they could be achieved only by 'comprehensive surveillance of all [Internet] traffic.' This, the report's authors claimed, would be 'politically and socially unacceptable' (Standage 1997).

At the Internet Summit in Munich in September 1999, the German social policy think-tank the Bertelsmann Foundation (linked to the media conglomerate Bertelsmann group) proposed that the Internet could be rated by 12, 15 and 18 certificates like films. The Foundation also proposed that churches, schools and trades unions could be invited to manufacture Internet filters, which Web users could attach to their Internet browser. However, European free speech advocates attacked these proposals, arguing that they contravened the spirit of the Web – namely to provide a greater freedom of information.

In November 2000, French courts ordered the US-based web company Yahoo! to block French users from accessing Nazi memorabilia on its US auction site (by installing filtering technology). Antiracist pressure groups around the world hailed the decision as a positive step forward, while others argued that it set a worrying precedent for censorship, and the imposition of the laws of one country on another. By January 2001, almost two months after the French court ruling and under pressure from groups like the Simon Wiesenthal Center, Yahoo! auctions spokesperson Brian Fitzgerald stated that it would more actively monitor its auction site to keep out items related to hate groups (Guernsey 2001). Before the French court ruling, the site had listed more than a thousand articles related to the Ku Klux Klan and various Nazi groups, including knives, robes and daggers.

In response to the efforts of think-tanks and governments around the world to clamp down on the Internet, University of Edinburgh doctoral student Ian Clarke created FreeNet, a computer system that 'makes it easy to publish information on the Internet anonymously' (Cohen 2000). While FreeNet has alarmed some cultural commentators who claim that it might 'give a free rein to terrorists, software pirates and paedophiles' (Cohen 2000), Clarke insists that FreeNet will not attract such people. In his view, they are more interested in keeping secrets than in putting them on a public network. Child pornographers already publish files on the Internet with impunity, he insists. FreeNet would not make this situation worse or better. Clarke concludes by saying that 'society should not ban a tool which would benefit the majority just because a minority may misuse it' (cited in Talacko 2000).

Conclusion

This chapter examined media and cultural studies research into violence and cyberspace, first by looking at cybergames, followed by cybersexploitation, cyberpaedophilia and cyberhate. The final section of the chapter considered recent efforts to regulate and censor violent Internet content, where we saw that the terms of the debate over cyberviolence are still firmly locked in the free speech versus censorship debates that have long shaped discussions about media violence.

In the final chapter of this book, we return to a direct consideration of the ways in which the media violence debate has been shaped by the binaristic model of free speech versus censorship and methodologically by the 'effects' versus 'no effects' models of communication. We argue that the time is now long overdue for a radical rethink of the terms of this debate in order to construct arguments that can take into account the ways in which media violence may contribute to the re(production) of unequal power relations in society.

Further reading

Bell, D. and Kennedy, B.M. (eds) (2000) *The Cybercultures Reader*. London: Routledge.

Jordan, T. (1999) *Cyberpower: The Culture and Politics of Cyberspace and the Internet*. London: Routledge.

Parratt, L. and Wadham, J. (eds) (1999) *Liberating Cyberspace: Civil Liberties, Human Rights and the Internet*. London: Pluto in association with Liberty.

Porter, D. (ed.) (1997) *Internet Culture*. London: Routledge.

Smith, M.A. and Kollock, P. (eds) (1999) *Communities in Cyberspace*. London: Routledge.

Conclusion

7 | # THE FUTURE OF MEDIA VIOLENCE RESEARCH

The [media violence] debate has been profoundly masculine in orientation. One of the most significant challenges of the future is to shift the terms of debate away from the dominant, but limiting, models of free speech and censorship, which derive from masculine ideas of aggressive journalistic realism on the one hand and of paternalistic protectionism on the other.

(Stuart Cunningham 1992: 71)

The media occupy an important public space in our culture and both reflect and shape public culture as well as our private relationships. In bringing together the discussion of violence across a range of media it has been our intention to identify the many and varied ways in which audiences encounter stories *about* violence, and images *of* violence in the news, films, television, advertising, pornography and cyberspace. By presenting such a broad study, we have been able to show how media violence is the wallpaper of everyday life. To our knowledge, no single text has brought together the discussion of how violence is communicated across such a range of different media technologies and media forms before.

The arguments presented in this book have not followed the behavioural model of media effects. But neither have they fallen into the alternative 'default' position that there are no or only fleeting effects of violent imagery. Our position is that if, as a society, we deny that media violence has *any* real effect on audiences, then we fail to appreciate how that violence shapes wider perceptions about who has, and who should have, power in society. Moreover, the denial of any media effects has to be understood as a political position that contributes to the perpetuation of ideological systems of repression and oppression through the free use of representations of violence. In this respect, the understanding of media violence that we advocate is similar to cultivation theory. We agree with Gerbner et al. (1999: 337) that 'Violence is a social relationship. People hurt or kill to force (or deter) unwanted behaviour, to dominate, to terrorize. Symbolic violence is literally a 'show of force.' It demonstrates power: who can get away with what against whom.' Yet by adding critical feminism and Marxism to the analytical mix presented in this book, we have also illustrated how media violence upholds white heterosexual patriarchal **hegemonic power** structures.

Our perspective has shown how violence and masculinity are promoted as inherently and legitimately linked in, for example, televised sport, action movies, computer games, pornography and advertising. We have also illustrated how expressions of violence by minority groups are subject to heavy condemnation and constructed as a threat to 'civilized' society. Therefore, we are aware that to claim any one expression of violence is worse than another is itself political, and the politics of calls for censorship or sanctions of violence need to be carefully evaluated.

Censorship is of course a very controversial issue. However, an obvious question posed by our discussion of media violence is why we fight so hard to protect the media and artists' freedom to depict sometimes gruesomely brutal images of violence? We are constantly told that artistic expression must be free from censorship and that once we consent to censorship, there will be no knowing what we will be prevented from reading, seeing and knowing. Yet the freedom of speech/freedom of expression argument provides no protection to those portrayed as victims nor to those at whom hate material might be targeted. In fact, free speech is a deeply rooted ideological notion with a historical and political legacy based in white middle-class patriarchal liberal culture. Freedom of speech actually upholds the privilege of white middle-class males by ensuring that their stories, fantasies and desires are freely communicated around the globe. Because non-whites, women, homosexuals, the working classes and children, for example, do not have the same kind of control over the channels of communication and have limited access to the economic resources needed to promote their world-views, the marginalization of their perspectives is assured anyway. As this clearly implies, unofficial censorship, as well as the privileging of particular ideological discourses, operates throughout the whole circuit of communication, from the production of media texts to their systems of representation and reception.

This brings us to the future of media violence research. As Cunningham (1992) argues, media researchers must move beyond, on the one hand, continually attempting to affirm behavioural models of media effects, and, on the other, defending audiences' right to the pleasures of media violence. A concerted effort among researchers to investigate the political basis of the production, distribution, textual representation and appeal to audiences of media violence is required. We need to examine the complex relations of forces that come together to encourage the production and distribution of this material, consider what its representation communicates, how audiences evaluate and respond to it, and how their interpretations are 'related to forms of self and social agency . . . within a variety of cultural sites' (Giroux 1995: 311). Further, we need to identify 'which parts of [the] audience perceive the greatest threat from violent content, and reasonably focus on responding to them' (Cunningham 1992: 71). Therefore, this also requires consideration of the role that media policy needs to play in that response.

Likewise, there is a need to conduct audience research into a wider variety of media texts and genres that circulate violence. For example, we need to know more about the reception of newspapers, advertising, sports programming, films, crime dramas, reality television, pornography, computer games, Internet material, and so on. We would argue that a number of audience studies significantly contribute to knowledge about how media representations of violence are engaged with, and the role that these play in the lives of individuals and in social culture more generally. But much more research of this kind is needed to gain a nuanced and politically engaged understanding of how media violence might contribute to particular ideological structures, beliefs and identities. We need to investigate in more detail the extent to which masculinity may be linked to enjoyment of media violence, in what variety of contexts, exactly what is it in media texts that encourages this enjoyment, and whether its privileging works to deter women, for example, from enjoying the text. We also need to examine when women do find pleasure in media texts containing violence and what are the discursive conditions of reception on which that pleasure is based? Thus, reception research must attend not only to how media audiences interpret representations of violence, but also to how these representations inform and/or contribute to wider social and cultural relationships.

As we hope to have made clear throughout this book, we firmly believe that media violence significantly contributes to how we think about, and negotiate, our identities and social positions whether we are marginalized or powerful. In each of the chapters we have tried to address many of the concerns expressed so succinctly by feminist critic hooks (2000a). How do the media contribute to cultures of domination in which violence comes to be regarded as an inevitable and accepted way of controlling some (usually marginalized) groups in society?

Social, political and economic hierarchies are not ever simply nor unproblematically produced or reproduced by the media. Dominant groups cannot maintain their power simply through coercion as Italian political theorist Antonio Gramsci (1971) has so convincingly argued. Instead, they are structurally reproduced through *persuasion* (while not perfect, this is the best of all possible political-economic systems, so enjoy!) as well as by the threat of *coercion* (reject this system at your peril – we have jails into which you can be thrown!). As hooks suggests,

> In a culture of domination everyone is socialized to see violence as an acceptable means of social control. Dominant parties maintain power by the threat (acted upon or not) that abusive punishment, physical or psychological, will be used whenever the hierarchical structures in place are threatened.
>
> (hooks 2000a: 64)

It is easier to persuade someone of something when it is backed up by the threat of possible punishment.

In September 2001, for example, journalists around the world reported US President George W. Bush's address calling for global support for the US military intervention in Afghanistan in retaliation for the events of September 11. Failure to support this effort, Bush informed the world, would be construed by the American government and people as an implicit endorsement for 'global terrorism'. In February 2002, Bush declared that the new enemy of the 'free world' is an 'axis of evil' comprising 'terrorist networks' like that of al-Qa'ida and states such as Iran, Iraq and North Korea. Bush's position leaves no room for counter-argument or sensitivity to social and historical context or political interpretation. It demands a simplistic response to a binaristic question – are you 'with us' (with the 'good guys') or 'against us' (with the 'bad guys')?

We have found over the years that feminist theories, in particular, have helped us to better understand such sociopolitical binarisms and the sexist, classist and racist assumptions that underpin them. It is through these mechanisms that various forms of human violence become normalized in western societies. According to hooks (2000a: 65), the narrative of 'good guys versus the bad guys' – so typical of fictional and factual media in the west – helps to socialize children into a world in which violence deeply structures social relations (see also hooks 2000c). After September 11, people in the west have been encouraged in very stark terms to accept without any qualification the view that George W. Bush is the 'good guy' and Osama bin Laden the 'bad guy' and that bad guys deserve to die.

hooks (2000a) makes a salient point about the need to connect media violence and 'patriarchal thinking or male domination':

As long as sexist thinking socializes boys to be 'killers', whether in imaginary good guy, bad guy fights or as soldiers in imperialism to maintain coercive power over nations, **patriarchal violence** will continue . . . Women and men must oppose the use of violence as a means of social control in all its manifestations: war, male violence against women, adult violence against children, teenage violence, racial violence, etc. . . . In our nation masses of people are concerned about violence but resolutely refuse to link that violence to patriarchal thinking or male domination.

(hooks 2000a: 65–6)

hooks further argues for the necessity of connecting patriarchal thinking with racist, classist and homophobic assumptions so prevalent in US society. As Thoman (1993) suggests, social inequalities and problems such as 'pervasive life-long poverty, hunger, joblessnesss and drug addiction – as well as ready availability of guns' are at the root of rising violence in the US (see also Gitlin 1997).

Of course, the media are not the only influence on all of us – other key sites of power and influence include the family, schools, peers, church, workplace, and so on. However, the media play an increasingly important role in everyday socialization processes in many countries around the world, many of which are experiencing enormous growth in the availability of and access to an ever widening array of media forms. As many media critics have pointed out, much of what is now being distributed around the world comes from the USA or is heavily influenced by US cultural values. Kamalipour and Rampal (2001: 1) suggest, for example, that 'At the dawn of the twenty-first century, the dominance of America's cultural products globally remains unparalleled' (2001: 1). For Gitlin (1997) this begs the question, 'Is market-driven culture a reflection of the population, or a toxic side-effect of global capitalism?' Just what this means for research on media violence is now a crucial question that urgently needs to be addressed.

While western media research primarily continues to address surface manifestations of media violence to either prove direct, harmful effects on people or, conversely, to say that there are no (or limited) effects (other than, perhaps, positive ones), a much more salient point will be missed. As Gitlin (1997) argues, 'The cheapening of violence – not so much the number of incidents as their emptiness and lightweight gruesomeness – leads to both paranoia and anesthesis . . . Whiz-bang new technologies like high-definition TV will offer sharper images of banality'. It is the very 'banality', 'everydayness' or 'normalcy' of media violence that surrounds us and its connections to social inequalities and actual violence that is at issue. We need to ask how media violence socializes and directs our thinking and actions in a range of hierarchical, complex, nuanced, insidious, gratifying, pleasurable and largely imperceptible ways. This task now needs our undivided and radically politicized attention.

GLOSSARY

Audience reception research: the study of how media audiences make sense of and interpret media texts in relation to their social positions and identities.

British Board of Film Censors/British Board of Film Classification (BBFC): the advisory body established in 1912 to oversee the certification of films for exhibition, renamed in 1985.

Censorship: the official prohibition, suppression or deletion of material on the grounds that it is objectionable or unsafe for public consumption. Unofficial censorship is caused by people not having the power or resources to create and distribute texts or materials.

Civil libertarian: see **liberal humanism**.

Cognitive perspective: see **cognitive theory**.

Cognitive theory: a theory of comprehension based upon acquired knowledge enabling the prediction and interpretation of narrative. Argues that through previous encounters with characters and their motivations, media audiences are rapidly able to understand new characters and events. The theory is critiqued for neglecting to consider how ideology informs the process of interpretation.

Columbine High School shootings: in 1999 in Littleton, Colorado, Eric Harris, 18, and Dylan Klebold, 17, shot and killed 12 of their fellow high school students and 1 teacher and wounded 23 others in the deadliest school shooting to date in the USA. At the end of an hour-long rampage, the teenagers killed themselves. It was suggested that their actions were influenced by violent media content, and especially computer games.

Cultivation theory: see **Cultural Indicators Project**.

Cultural Indicators Project: the project developed by George Gerbner and his colleagues that theorizes the consequences of living in a mass mediated cultural and symbolic world. It is argued that the violence encountered in the media affects the conception of social reality and who has power and who does not in that reality.

Cultural studies: an interdisciplinary research tradition that grew out of Marxist theory and leftist politics that is primarily concerned with investigating relations of power within institutions, in textual representation and in audience interpretation of texts.

Desensitization theory: the theory that the more audiences see violence in the media, the less they are emotionally effected by it.

Discourse: language expression (speaking, writing and representation) that produces particular understandings of the object referred to.

Dominant ideological readings: the notion that media texts privilege the worldviews of those with the most power in society.

Federal Communications Commission (FCC): the independent US government agency established in 1934 to regulate interstate and international communications by radio, television, wire, satellite and cable. The FCC's jurisdiction covers the 50 states, the District of Columbia and US possessions; it is responsible to Congress.

Federal Trade Commission (FTC): 'enforces . . . US federal antitrust and consumer protection laws. [It] seeks to ensure that the nation's markets function competitively, and are vigorous, efficient, and free of undue restrictions. The Commission also works to enhance the smooth operation of the marketplace by eliminating acts or practices that are unfair or deceptive. In general, the Commission's efforts are directed toward stopping actions that threaten consumers' opportunities to exercise informed choice' (Federal Trade Commission 2002).

Fetish/fetishism: the worshipping of a person, parts of the body or objects in sexual terms to the extent that the person or object is seen only in these terms and any other power they may hold is denied.

First Amendment of the US Constitution: established in 1791, this states that 'Congress shall make no law respecting an establishment of religion, or prohibiting the free exercise thereof, or abridging the freedoms of speech, or of the press; or the right of the people peaceably to assemble, and to petition the Government for redress of grievances.' This is significant defence of freedom of speech. In Britain, which does not have a written constitution, there are no laws that grant rights to freedom of speech in the same way as the US Constitution.

Flaming: defined as a situation in cyberspace in which someone says something hostile to someone else where they would not say it in person. Such attacks often shut down conversation. Flaming has also been defined as offering a blunt opinion in newsgroups of chat sites. This sort of flaming does not tend to end conversations.

Freedom of speech: the right to freely express thoughts, opinions and ideas without interference or fear of government reprisal, even to spend your money in any way you see fit (see also **First Amendment of the US Constitution**).

Gangsta rap: rap music commonly critiqued as advocating violence, especially gun violence. Contains explicit and usually highly misogynistic lyrics.

Hays Office: the name by which the MPPDA is often called, from the office of Will Hays, the President of the MPPDA.

Hegemonic power: see **hegemony**.

Hegemony: Italian political theorist Antonio Gramsci's (1971) notion of 'hegemony' suggests that the 'dominant' classes in society have to constantly renegotiate their position with the 'subjugated' classes. To maintain power, they must rule by winning people's consent to the economic system that privileges those already in positions of power, rather than through coercion or repression.

Ideology: a concept associated with Marxist theorizing which conceives of the dominant social group's worldview as conditioning the meanings through which all groups understand the world in which they live.

James Bulger: the 2-year-old child murdered by two 10-year-olds in Bootle, near Liverpool in 1993. At the boys' trial the judge speculated as to whether the killers actions had been prompted by their watching the video *Child's Play 3* in which a possessed child/mannequin terrorizes children. No evidence of the murderers having seen the film was ever found.

Legion of Decency: the pressure group set up to campaign against, and boycott movies considered indecent by the Catholic Church.

Liberal humanism: a political ideology centred on the belief in the rights of the individual, as against the rights of government. The position espouses the rights to freedom of expression and free speech, and freedom from ideological constraints.

Longitudinal studies: research studies conducted over a number of years to assess, for example, the long-term effects of engagement with media violence.

Male gaze: the male point of view or way of looking that is privileged in patriarchal culture and which constructs women as objects of male desire.

Moral panic: the theory that agents and institutions of control, including the media, exaggerate and amplify forms of deviance in order to justify the control of those portrayed as 'deviant'.

Motion Picture Association of America (MPAA): the new name given to the Motion Picture Producers and Distributors Association in 1945.

Motion Picture Producers and Distributors Association (MPPDA): the self-regulatory body formed in 1922 by the US film industry to monitor the production of films to ensure that they did not contain 'morally objectionable' content. See also **Hays Office**.

MUDs: MUDs are 'networked, multi-user virtual reality systems which are widely available on the Internet' (Reid 1999: 5). In these systems or communities, users often adopt new identities (gender, ethnic, class and sexuality) to establish and construct imagined communities. Users speak to each other by typing questions, answers and comments.

National Association of Motion Picture Industries (NAMPI): the US body established by the movie industry in 1916 to respond to public complaints about film content and impose written standards on its members.

National Board of Censorship of Motion Pictures, later the **National Board of Review (NBR):** established in 1909, the National Board of Censorship of Motion Pictures was renamed the NBR in 1915 to encourage a wider appreciation of its function in the promotion of 'respectable' films, and to rid it of the perception of being singularly concerned with film censorship. Nevertheless, one of its roles was to oversee film content by passing films for exhibition and granting seals of approval to film theatres. Industry conformity to NBR requirements began to collapse after 1915 and in 1922 the MPPDA took over the role of censoring film content. The NBR exists to this day, though now as a film appreciation society.

Neo-conservatism: the recent resurgence in calls for a return to 'traditional' morals and behaviours. A position that supports censorship on the basis that it protects social morals and the well being of society.

Netiquette: cyberspace rules of proper behaviour for exchanges between participants to support friendly, open and non-threatening exchanges. Examples include refraining from using capital letters when typing messages as this constitutes shouting.

Objectification/objectify: to reduce something to the status of an object rather than a conscious living subject. Most often used with reference to the representation of women as objects of men's desires.

Paedophile: a person who is sexually attracted to children.

Patriarchal violence: violence that functions to maintain male ideological domination of society.

Patriarchy/patriarchal ideology: a social system in which men have dominant power in society and its social institutions such as the family, church, media and educational system. The meanings ascribed to phenomena are determined by the patriarchy, and thus become the dominant ideology.

Payne Fund Studies (PFS): an extensive set of research studies investigating the effects of film viewing upon youth audiences in the USA in the late 1920s and early 1930s. Published in eight volumes, the studies remain to this day the largest audience research investigation of film effects. It was concluded that crime and violence in films had a direct influence on the likelihood of juvenile delinquency in viewers. The studies were largely discredited because of their simplistic assertion of a cause–effect relationship between film viewing and acts of crime and violence (see Jowett et al. 1996).

Populist view of audiences: the argument that audiences actively construct their own meanings of texts according to their particular social identities and desires. Such conclusions about audience interpretation were especially common in the late 1980s and 1990s when media researchers focused on exploring 'pleasures' of media reception. The approach is criticized for failing to consider the ideological bases on which pleasure is premised.

Postmodern/postmodernism: in media and cultural studies this term is predominately used to refer to the postindustrial period marked by the ascendancy of consumer culture in which grand narratives of truth have been rejected. Consequently, a sense of meaninglessness can lead to social discontentment and fear of the loss of social and moral order.

Power relations: social relations differentiated according to ideologically ascribed positions of power.

Production Code Administration (PCA): established by William Hays in response to the Legion of Decency campaign. The PCA approved, rejected or censored films produced by the Hollywood studios and maintained control over film content 1934–66.

Psychoanalytic theory: a theory of human psychology based on the belief that our gender identities, and how these identities developed, structure our unconscious desires which in turn underlie all human activity. Media texts are theorized as structured according to these desires in terms of both production and reception. First developed by Freud, the theory was modified by Lacan, who translated it into linguistic terms and theorized language as the expression of patriarchal desire.

Representation: all kinds of media texts and imagery and which are necessarily produced from a specific and selective physical and social point of view.

Semiotic analysis: the ('scientific') analysis of media texts as 'signs' and the processes through which meaning is created from these.

Sexualization: the representation of a person or object in sexual terms.

SM (sadomasochism): some regard it as obtaining pleasure from a power exchange and/or pain in consensual sex play or sexual fantasies for mutual pleasure, not violence or cruelty. Others see it as a humiliating and degrading form of sexual perversion where the dominant person (sadist) gains sexual pleasure by degrading, humiliating or inflicting pain upon a submissive partner (masochist), who claims to derive sexual pleasure from this mistreatment.

V-chip: software that provides the means to block television and video reception by either ratings codes or specified age appropriate programming.

Video nasties: a term coined by the UK tabloid press and applied to uncertified horror films on video released in Britain during the early 1980s which the Director of the Department of Public Prosecutions considered potentially obscene.

Williams report: the 1979 Report on obscenity and film censorship was produced by a committee chaired by British philosopher Bernard Williams.

REFERENCES

Aaronovitch, D. (2000) Pornography is a danger to children, *Independent*, 24 May.

ABCNEWS.com (2002) Virtual violence: are violent video games too real for kids? http://abcnews.go.com/sections/GMS/AmericanFamily/GMA011015War_Games.htm (accessed 21 Mar. 2002).

Adamson, C. (1999) London preacher who weaves web of hate and terror, *Evening Standard* (London), 13 January.

Ali, M. (2002) The media violence debate in review – defining media violence: multiple understandings.
www.stanford.edu/class/comm217/projects/mariam/definingviolence.htm (accessed 12 Feb. 2002).

Allan, S. (1999) *News Culture*. Buckingham: Open University Press.

Allan, S., Adam, B. and Carter, C. (eds) (2000) *Environmental Risks and the Media*. London: UCL Press.

Alloway, L. (1971) *Violent America: The Movies 1946–64*. New York: Museum of Modern Art.

Alloway, N. and Gilbert, P. (1998) Video game culture: playing with masculinity, violence and pleasure, in S. Howard (ed.) *Wired Up: Young People and the Electronic Media*. London: UCL Press.

ANANOVA (2002) European computer games market 'overtaking US'. http://www.ananova.com/news/story/sm_543678.html (accessed 18 Apr. 2002).

Anderson, A. (1997) *Media, Culture and the Environment*. London: UCL Press.

Anderson, R. (1995) *Consumer Culture and TV Programming*. Boulder, CO: Westview Press.

Assister, A. (1989) *Pornography: Feminism and the Individual*. London: Pluto.

Assister, A. and Carol, A. (eds) (1993) *Bad Girls and Dirty Pictures: The Challenge to Reclaim Feminism*. London: Pluto.

Baird, R.M. and Rosenbaum, S.E. (eds) (1998) *Pornography: Private Right or Public Menace?* New York: Prometheus.

Ballard, I.M. (1995) See no evil, hear no evil: television violence and the First Amendment, *Virginia Law Review*, 81: 175–222.

Bandura, A., Ross, D. and Ross, S.A. (1963) Imitation of film-mediated aggressive models, *Journal of Abnormal and Social Psychology*, 66: 3–11.

Barker, J. (2000) Shock: the value of emotion, in D. Berry (ed.) *Ethics and Media Culture: Practices and Representations*. Oxford: Focal Press.

Barker, M. (2001) The Newson report: a case study in 'common sense', in M. Barker and J. Petley (eds) *Ill Effects: The Media/Violence Debate*, 2nd edn. London: Routledge.

Barker, M. and Petley, J. (2001) Introduction: from bad research to good – a guide for the perplexed, in M. Barker and J. Petley (eds) *Ill Effects: The Media/Violence Debate*, 2nd edn. London: Routledge.

Barry, D.S. (1999) Growing up violent, in R.E. Hiebert (ed.) *Impact of Mass Media: Current Issues*. New York: Addison Wesley Longman.

Bassett, G. (1991) Ninjas under the bed: the television violence debate, *Delta*, 45: 73–83.

BBC Broadcasting Research (1988) *Crimewatch UK*. London: BBC Special Projects Research.

Beck, U. (1992) *Risk Society: Towards a New Modernity*, trans. Mark Ritter. London: Sage.

Beck, U. (1999) *World Risk Society*. Cambridge: Polity.

Bell, D. and Kennedy, B.M. (eds) (2000) *The Cybercultures Reader*. London: Routledge.

Belton, J. (1996) The production code, in J. Belton (ed.) *Movies and Mass Culture*. New Brunswick, NJ: Rutgers University Press.

Benedict, H. (1992) *Virgin or Vamp: How the Press Covers Sex Crimes*. Oxford: Oxford University Press.

Berenstein, R.J. (1996) *Attack of the Leading Ladies: Gender, Sexuality, and Spectatorship in Classic Horror Cinema*. New York: Columbia University Press.

Berkowitz, L. and Rawlings, E. (1963) Effects of film violence on inhibitions against subsequent aggression, *Journal of Abnormal and Social Psychology*, 66: 405–12.

Black, G.D. (1998) *The Catholic Crusade against the Movies: 1940–1975*. Cambridge: Cambridge University Press.

Bork, R.H. (1998) Slouching towards Gomorrah, in R.M. Baird and S.E. Rosenbaum (eds) *Pornography: Private Right or Public Menace?* Amherst, NY: Prometheus.

Boyle, R. and Haynes, R. (2000) *Power Play: Sport, the Media and Popular Culture*. London: Longman.

Branscombe, A. (1997) Panel: who owns the Internet?, in O'Reilly and Associates (eds) *The Internet and Society*. Cambridge, MA: Harvard University Press.

Brophy, P., Craven, J. and Fisher, S. (1999) *Extremism and the Internet*. Manchester: Centre for Research in Library and Information Management, Manchester Metropolitan University.

Brunsdon, C. (1998) Structure of anxiety: recent British television crime fiction, *Screen*, 39(3): 223–43.

Buckingham, D. (1996) *Moving Images: Understanding Children's Emotional Responses to Television*. Manchester: Manchester University Press.

Buckingham, D. (2000) *After the Death of Childhood: Growing Up in the Age of the Electronic Media*. Cambridge: Polity.

Buckingham, D., Davies, H., Jones, K. and Kelley, P. (1999) Public service goes to the market: British children's television in transition, *Media International Australia incorporating Culture and Policy*, 93: 65–76.

Burch, N. (1978–79) Porter or ambivalence, *Screen*, 19 (Winter): 91–105.

Burchill, J. (1986) *Girls on Film*. London: Virgin.

Burke, K. (1999) AVIVA: the women's World Wide Web, in J. Parratt and L. Wadham (eds) *Liberating Cyberspace: Civil Liberties, Human Rights and the Internet*. London: Pluto in Association with Liberty.

Burstyn, V. (1985) *Women against Censorship*. Vancouver: Douglas McIntyre.

Burstyn, V. (1999) *The Rites of Men: Manhood, Politics, and the Culture of Sport*. Toronto: University of Toronto Press.

Bushman, B.J. and Huesmann, L.R. (2001) Effects of televised violence on aggression, in D.G. Singer and J.L. Singer (eds) *Handbook of Children and the Media*. Thousand Oaks, CA: Sage.

Calcutt, A. (1999) *An A–Z of Cyberculture*. London: Macmillan.

Cameron, D. and Frazer, E. (1987) *The Lust to Kill: A Feminist Investigation of Sexual Murder*. Cambridge: Polity.

Cameron, D. and Frazer, E. (2000) On the question of pornography and sexual violence: moving beyond cause and effect, in D. Cornell (ed.) *Feminism and Pornography*. Oxford: Oxford University Press.

Cannon, L. (1998) Official negligence: Lou Cannon dissects the Rodney King case and the LA riots. http://www.pbs.org/newshour/authors_corner/jan-june98/cannon_4–7.html (accessed 14 Apr. 2002).

Cantor, J. (1998) Children's attraction to violent television programming, in J.H. Goldstein (ed.) *Why We Watch: The Attractions of Violent Entertainment*. Oxford: Oxford University Press.

Capitanchik, D. and Whine, M. (1999) The governance of cyberspace: racism on the Internet, in J. Parratt and L. Wadham (eds) *Liberating Cyberspace: Civil Liberties, Human Rights and the Internet*. London: Pluto in Association with Liberty.

Caputi, J. (1988) *The Age of Sex Crime*. London: Women's Press.

Caputi, J. (1992) Femicide: lethal violence against women in pornography and gorenography, in J. Radford and D.E.H. Russell (eds) *Femicide: The Politics of Woman Killing*. Buckingham: Open University Press.

Caputi, J. (1999) Pornography of everyday life, in M. Meyers (ed.) *Mediated Women: Representations in Popular Culture*. Cresskill, NJ: Hampton Press.

Carroll, N. (1990) *The Philosophy of Horror, or Paradoxes of the Heart*. London: Routledge.

Carroll, N. (1998) The professional western: south of the border, in E. Buscombe and R.E. Pearson (eds) *Back in the Saddle Again: New Essays on the Western*. London: British Film Institute.

Carter, C. (1995) Nuclear family fall-out: postmodern family culture and media studies, in B. Adam and S. Allan (eds) *Theorizing Culture: An Interdisciplinary Critique after Postmodernism*. London: UCL Press.

Carter, C. (1998) When the extraordinary becomes ordinary: everyday news of sexual violence, in C. Carter, G. Branston and S. Allan (eds) *News, Gender and Power*. London and New York: Routledge.

Carter, C., Branston, G. and Allan, S. (1998) (eds) *News, Gender and Power*. London: Routledge.

Cavender, G. (1998) In 'the shadow of shadows': television reality crime programming, in M. Fishman and G. Cavender (eds) *Entertaining Crime: Television Reality Programs*. New York: Aldine de Gruyter.

Cavender, G. and Fishman, M. (1998) Television reality programs: context and history, in M. Fishman and G. Cavender (eds) *Entertaining Crime: Television Reality Programs*. New York: Aldine de Gruyter.

Chalaby, J.K. (2000) New media, new freedoms, new threats, *Gazette*, 62(1): 19–29.

Christensen, F.M. (1998) Elicitation of violence: the evidence, in R.M. Baird and S.E. Rosenbaum (eds) *Pornography: Private Right or Public Menace?* Amherst, NY: Prometheus.

Clark, K. (1992) The linguistics of blame: representations of women in *Sun*'s reporting of crimes of sexual violence, in M. Toolan (ed.) *Language, Text and Context: Essays in Stylistics*. London: Routledge.

Clover, C. (1992) *Men, Women and Chainsaws*. London: Routledge.

CNN (1997) Russian crime goes to mass market. http://www.cnn.com/WORLD/9708/07/russian.crime.shows/ August 7.

CNN (2001a) Is Osama bin Laden still in Tora Bora? Do British and Middle Eastern journalists cover the war differently than Americans? Donald Rumsfeld charms the press corps. *CNN Reliable Sources*. http://www.cnn.com/TRANSCRIPTS/0112/16/rs.html (accessed 23 Apr. 2002).

CNN (2001b) Has the media changed since September 11? *CNN Reliable Sources*. http://www.cnn.com/TRANSCRIPTS/0112/29/rs.00.html (accessed 23 Apr. 2002).

Cohen, D. (2000) The Internet is about to get even harder to police, *New Scientist*, 25 March.

Cohen, J. (2001) The myth of the media's role in Vietnam. http://www.fair.org/articles/kerrey-vietnam.html (accessed 23 Apr. 2002).

Combs, R. (1981) Sam Peckinpah: the bloody balladeer, *The Movie: The Illustrated History of the Cinema*, 71: 1414–16.

Comstock, G. and Paik, H. (1991) *Television and the American Child*. San Diego, CA: Academic Press.

Cook, D.A. (2000) *Lost Illusions: American Cinema in the Shadow of Watergate and Vietnam, 1970–1979*. New York: Charles Scribner's Sons.

Cook, P. (1985) Authorship and cinema, in P. Cook (ed.) *The Cinema Book*. London: British Film Institute.

Cook, P. (1989) *The Accused, Monthly Film Bulletin*, 56(661): 35–6.

Cornell, D. (2000a) Pornography's temptation, in D. Cornell (ed.) *Feminism and Pornography*. Oxford: Oxford University Press.

Cornell, D. (2000b) Introduction, in D. Cornell (ed.) *Feminism and Pornography*. Oxford: Oxford University Press.

Corner, J., Richardson, K. and Fenton, N. (1990) *Nuclear Reactions: Form and Response in Public Issue Television*. London: John Libbey.

Cottle, S. (1993) *TV News, Urban Conflict and the Inner City*. Leicester: Leicester University Press.

Cottle, S. (ed.) (2000) *Ethnic Minorities and the Media*. Buckingham: Open University Press.

Coventry Evening Telegraph (2000) Internet stalker's threat to Titanic star Kate, *Coventry Evening Telegraph*, 22 June.

Coward, R. (1982) Sexual violence and sexuality, *Feminist Review*, 11: 9–22.

CPMA (1997) In 1990s TV news turns to violence and show biz. http://www.cmpa.com/pressrel/mm78pr.htm (accessed 14 Apr. 2002).

Craig, T. and Petley, J. (2001) Invasion of the Internet abusers: marketing fears about the information superhighway, in M. Baker and J. Petley (eds) *Ill Effects: The Media/Violence Debate*. London: Routledge.

Crane, J.L. (1994) *Terror and Everyday Life: Singular Moments in the History of Horror Film*. London: Sage.

Creed, B. (1993) *The Monstrous Feminine: Film, Feminism, Psychoanalysis*. London: Routledge.

Creed, B. (1998a) Film and psychoanalysis, in J. Hill and P.C. Gibson (eds) *The Oxford Guide to Film Studies*. Oxford: Oxford University Press.

Creed, B. (1998b) The *Crash* debate: anal wounds, metallic kisses, *Screen*, 39(2): 175–9.

Critcher, C. (2003) *Moral Panics and the Media*. Buckingham: Open University Press.

Cromartie, M. (1998) Give me liberty but don't give me filth, in R.M. Baird and S.E. Rosenbaum (eds) *Pornography: Private Right or Public Menace?* Amherst, NY: Prometheus.

Cuklanz, L.M. (1996) *Rape on Trial: How the Mass Media Construct Legal Reform and Social Change*. Philadelphia, PA: University of Pennsylvania Press.

Cuklanz, L.M. (2000) *Rape on Prime Time: Television, Masculinity, and Sexual Violence*. Philadelphia, PA: University of Pennsylvania Press.

Culf, A. (1993) BBC defends 'voyeuristic' crime series, *Guardian*, 23 June.

Culf, A. (1994) ITV axes winner *True Crime* series, *Guardian*, 30 August.

Cumberbatch, G. (1989) Violence and the mass media: the research evidence, in G. Cumberbatch and D. Howitt, *A Measure of Uncertainty: The Effects of the Mass Media*. London: John Libbey.

Cummings, B. (1992) *War and Television*. London: Verso.

Cunningham, S. (1992) A neverending story? The TV violence debate, *Media Information Australia*, 64: 67–72.

Curran, J. (1990) New revisionism in mass communication research: a reappraisal, *European Journal of Communication*, 5(2–3): 135–64.

Cybergrrl Safety Net (2002) http://www.cybergrrl.com/views/dv (accessed 15 Apr. 2002).

Czitrom, D. (1996) The politics of performance: theatre licensing and the origins of movie censorship in New York, in F.G. Couvres (ed.) *Movie Censorship and American Culture*. Washington, DC: Smithsonian Institution Press.

Davies, M.M. (1997) *Fake, Fact or Fantasy: Children's Interpretations of Reality*. Mahwah, NJ: Lawrence Erlbaum.

Davies, M.M. (2001) *'Dear BBC': Children, Television Storytelling and the Public Sphere*. Cambridge: Cambridge University Press.

Dietz, S., Blackwell, K. and Daley, P. (1982) Measurement of empathy toward rape victims and rapists, *Journal of Personality and Social Psychology*, 43: 372–84.

Dines, G. (1997) *Pornography: The Consumption of Inequality*. London: Routledge.

Doane, M.A. (1991) *Femmes Fatales: Feminism, Film Theory, Psychoanalysis*. London: Routledge.

Docherty, D. (1990) *Violence in Television Fiction: Public Opinion and Broadcasting Standards 1*. London: John Libbey.

Doyle, A. (1998) *Cops*: television policing as policing reality, in M. Fishman and G. Cavender (eds) *Entertaining Crime: Television Reality Programs*. New York: Aldine de Gruyter.

Drucker, S.J. and Gumpert, G. (2000) CyberCrime and Punishment, *Critical Studies in Media Communication*, 17(2): 133–58.

Duff, M. (1993) Gun videos nominate for MTV's highest awards, *Human Events*, 53(32): 11.

Dworkin, A. (1981) *Pornography: Men Possessing Women*. London: Women's Press.

Dworkin, A. (1997) *Life and Death: Unapologetic Writings on the Continuing War against Women*. London: Virago.

Dworkin, A. (1998) Against the male flood: censorship, pornography, and equality, in R.M. Baird and S.E. Rosenbaum (eds) *Pornography: Private Right or Public Menace?* Amherst, NY: Prometheus.

Dworkin, A. (2000) Pornography and grief, in D. Cornell (ed.) *Feminism and Pornography*. Oxford: Oxford University Press.

Dworkin, R. (1998) Liberty and pornography, in R.M. Baird and S.E. Rosenbaum (eds) *Pornography: Private Right or Public Menace?* Amherst, NY: Prometheus.

Dyson, R.A. (2000) *Mind Abuse: Media Violence in an Information Age*. Montreal: Black Rose.

Easton, S.M. (1994) *The Problem of Pornography*. London: Routledge.

Eaton, M. (1995) A fair cop? Viewing the effects of the canteen culture in *Prime Suspect* and *Between the Lines*, in D. Kidd-Hewitt and R. Osborne (eds) *Crime and the Media: The Post-modern Spectacle*. East Haven, CT: Pluto.

ELSPA (2002) Computer and video games sales rocketed. http://www.elspa.com/pr/pressrelease.asp?mode=view&t=1+id=278 (accessed 18 Apr. 2002).

Evans, W. (1984) Monster movies: a sexual theory, in B.K. Grant (ed.) *Planks of Reason: Essays on the Horror Film*. Metuchen, NJ: Scarecrow Press.

Everard, J. (2000) Internet censorship: US, Europe and Australia, in *Virtual States: The Internet and the Boundaries of the Nation-State*. London: Routledge.

Faludi, S. (1992) *Backlash: The Undeclared War against Women*. London: Chatto and Windus.

Federal Trade Commission (2000) FTC releases report on the marketing of violence entertainment to children. FTC press release. Washington, DC: FTC.

Federal Trade Commission (2002) Federal Trade Commission vision, mission and goals. http://www.ftc.gov/ftc/mission.htm (accessed 19 July 2002).

Feilitzen, C.V. (1998) Media violence – four research perspectives, in R. Dickinson, R. Harindranath and O. Linné (eds) *Approaches to Audiences: A Reader*. London: Arnold.

Finn, G. (1989–90) Taking gender into account in the 'Theatre of Terror': violence, media, and the maintenance of male dominance, *Canadian Journal of Women and the Law*, 3(2): 375–94.

Fishman, M. and Cavender, G. (eds) (1998) *Entertaining Crime: Television Reality Programs*. New York: Aldine de Gruyter.

Fisk, R. (2001) Lost in the rhetorical fog of war. http://www.zmag.org/fogwar.htm (accessed 14 Apr. 2002).

Fiske, J. (1987) *Television Culture*. London: Methuen.

Fiske, J. (2000) White watch, in S. Cottle (ed.) *Ethnic Minorities and the Media*. Buckingham: Open University Press.

Fiske, J. and Hartley, J. (1978) *Reading Television*. London: Methuen.

Fowles, J. (1999) *The Case for Television Violence*. Thousand Oaks, CA: Sage.

French, K. (1996) Introduction, in K. French (ed.) *Screen Violence*. London: Bloomsbury.

Gauntlett, D. (1995) *Moving Experiences: Understanding Television's Influences and Effects*. London: John Libbey.

Gauntlett, D. (1998) Ten things wrong with the 'effects' model, in R. Dickson, R. Harindranath and O. Linné (eds) *Approaches to Audiences: A Reader*. London: Arnold.

Geen, R.G. (1994) Television and aggression: recent developments in research and theory, in D. Zillman, J. Bryant and A.C. Huston (eds) *Media, Children, and the Family: Social Scientific, Psychodynamic, and Clinical Perspectives*. Hillsdale, NJ: Lawrence Erlbaum.

Gerbner, G. (1983) The importance of being critical in one's own fashion, in special *Ferment in the Field* issue of *Journal of Communication*, 33(3): 355–62.

Gerbner, G. (1995) The hidden message in anti-violence public service announcements, *Harvard Educational Review*, 65(2): 292–8.

Gerbner, G. (1994) Television violence and the art of asking the wrong question. www.medialit.org/Violence/articles/televisionviol.htm (accessed 12 Feb. 2002).

Gerbner, G. and Gross L. (1976) Living with television: the violence profile, *Journal of Communication*, 26(2): 173–99.

Gerbner, G., Gross L., Jackson-Beeck, M., Jeffries-Fox, S. and Signorielli, N. (1978) Cultural indicators: violence profile no. 9, *Journal of Communication*, 28(3): 176–207.

Gerbner, G., Gross L., Signorielli, N., Morgan, M. and Jackson-Beeck, M. (1979) The demonstration of power: violence profile no. 10, *Journal of Communication*, 29(3): 177–96.

Gerbner, G., Gross, L., Morgan, M. and Signorielli, N. (1995) Violence on television: the Cultural Indicators Project, *Journal of Broadcasting and Electronic Media*, 39(2): 278–83.

Gerbner, G., Morgan, M. and Signorielli, N. (1999) Profiling television violence, in K. Nordenstreng and M. Griffin (eds) *International Media Monitoring*. Cresskill, NJ: Hampton Press.

Gibson, P.C. and Gibson, R. (eds) (1993) *Dirty Looks: Women, Pornography, Power*. London: British Film Institute.

Giddens, A. (1992) *The Consequences of Modernity*. Cambridge: Polity.

Giroux, H.A. (1995) *Pulp Fiction* and the culture of violence, *Harvard Educational Review*, 65(2): 299–314.

Gitlin, T. (1980) *The Whole World is Watching: Mass Media in the Making and Unmaking of the New Left*. Berkeley, CA: University of California Press.

Gitlin, T. (1994) *Inside Prime Time*. London: Routledge.

Gitlin, T. (1997) Is media violence free speech? A debate between George Gerbner and Todd Gitlin. http://www.media-awareness.ca/eng/issues/violence/resource/articles/gerbner.htm (accessed 12 Feb. 2002).

Gitlin, T. (2001) The ordinariness of American feelings. http://www.opendemocracy.net/forum/document-details.asp?DocID=723&CatID=98 (accessed 14 Apr. 2002).

Glasgow University Media Group (1976) *Bad News*. London: Routledge and Kegan Paul.

Glasgow University Media Group (1980) *More Bad News*. London: Routledge and Kegan Paul.

Glasgow University Media Group (1982) *Really Bad News*. London: Writers and Readers.

Gledhill, C. (1985) Genre, in P. Cook (ed.) *The Cinema Book*. London: British Film Institute.

Goffman, E. (1976) *Gender Advertisements*. London: Macmillan.

Goldman, R. (1992) *Reading Ads Socially*. London: Routledge.

Goldman, R. and Papson, S. (1996) *Sign Wars: The Cluttered Landscape of Advertising*. New York: Guilford Press.

Gomery, D. (1996) The economics of horror film, in J.B. Weaver III and R. Tamborini (eds) *Horror Films: Current Research on Audience Preferences and Reactions*. Mahwah, NJ: Lawrence Erlbaum.

Goodman, J. (1989) The taboo busters, *Guardian*, 8 February.

Gracyk, T.A. (1998) Pornography as representation: aesthetic considerations, in R.M. Baird and S.E. Rosenbaum (eds) *Pornography: Private Right or Public Menace?* Amherst, NY: Prometheus.

Grade, M. (1989) *Report of the Working Group on the Fear of Crime*. London: Standing Conference on Crime Prevention, Home Office.

Grainger, A. and Jackson, S. (1999) Resisting the swoosh in the Land of the Long White Cloud, *Peace Review*, 11(4): 511–16.

Gramsci, A. (1971) *Selections from the Prison Notebooks of Antonio Gramsci*, ed. and trans. Q. Hoare and G. Nowell Smith. New York: International Publishers.

Grant, B.K. (1999) American psycho/sis: the pure products of America go crazy, in C. Sharrett (ed.) *Mythologies of Violence in Postmodern Media*. Detroit, MI: Wayne State University Press.

Greenman, C. (1999) The V-chip arrives with a thud, *New York Times*. 4 November.

Gregg, J. (1996) Caught in the web: entrapment in cyberspace, *Hastings Communication/Entertainment Law Journal*, 19: 157–97.

Grier, S.A. (2001) The Federal Trade Commission's Report on the marketing of violent entertainment to youths: developing policy-tuned research, *Journal of Public Policy and Marketing*, 20(1): 123–32.

Griffin, S. (1981) *Pornography and Silence: Culture's Revenge against Nature*. London: Women's Press.

Grisham, J. (1996) Natural bred killers, in K. French (ed.) *Screen Violence*. London: Bloomsbury.

Guernsey, L. (2001) Yahoo to try harder to rid postings of hateful material, *New York Times*, 3 January.

Guerrero, E. (2001) Black violence as cinema: from cheap thrills to historical agonies, in J.D. Slocum (ed.) *Violence and American Cinema*. London: Routledge.

Guerrilla Girls (2002) Homepage. http://www.guerrillagirls.com/ (accessed 23 Feb. 2002).

Gunning, T. (1994) An aesthetic of astonishment: early film and the (in)credulous spectator, in L. Williams (ed.) *Viewing Positions: Ways of Seeing Film*. New Brunswick, NJ: Rutgers University Press.

Gunter, B. (1985) *Dimensions of Television Violence*. Aldershot: Gower.

Gunter, B. and McAleer, J. (1997) *Children and Television*, 4th edn. London and New York: Routledge.

Hall, S. et al. (eds) (1978) *Policing the Crisis: Mugging, the State, and Law and Order*. London: Macmillan Education.

Hallin, D. (1986) *The Uncensored War*, Berkeley, CA: University of California Press.

Hamilton, A. (1999) The Net out of control – a new moral panic: censorship and sexuality, in L. Parratt and J. Wadham (eds) *Liberating Cyberspace: Civil Liberties, Human Rights and the Internet*. London: Pluto in Association with Liberty.

Hamilton, J.T. (1998) *Channeling Violence: The Economic Market for Violent Television Programming*. Princeton, NJ: Princeton University Press.

Hansen, A. (ed.) (1993) *The Mass Media and Environmental Issues*. Leicester: Leicester University Press.

Haraway, D. (2000). A cyborg manifesto: science, technology and socialist-feminism in the late twentieth century, in D. Bell and B.M. Kennedy (eds) *The Cybercultures Reader*. London: Routledge.

Hartley, J. (2000) Communicative democracy in a redactional society: the future of journalism studies, *Journalism: Theory, Practice and Criticism*, 1(1): 39–48.

Haskell, M. (1987) *From Reverence to Rape: The Treatment of Women in the Movies*, 2nd edn. Chicago: University of Chicago Press.

Hawkins, M.A. and Nakayama, T.K. (1992) Discourse on women's bodies: advertising in the 1920s, in L.A.M. Perry, L.H. Turner and H.M. Sterk (eds) *Constructing and Reconstructing Gender: The Links among Communication, Language and Gender*. Albany, NY: State University of New York Press.

Hebert, H. (1988) The nightmare of nark's corner, *Guardian*, 2 June.

Hebert, H. (1993) The people's peep show, *Guardian*, 23 November.

Heins, M. (2000) Blaming the media: would regulation of expression prevent another Columbine?, *Media Studies Journal*, fall: 14–23.

Hepburn, I. (1999) Case to censor Net not proven, *Aberdeen Press and Journal*, 6 December.

Herman, C. (1999) Women and the Internet, in L. Parratt and J. Wadham (eds) *Liberating Cyberspace: Civil Liberties, Human Rights and the Internet*. London: Pluto in Association with Liberty.

Herman, E.S. and Chomsky, N. (1988) *Manufacturing Consent: The Political Economy of the Mass Media*. New York: Pantheon.

Herring, S. (1999) Posting in a different voice: gender and ethics in computer-mediated communication, in P.A. Mayer (ed.) *Computer Media and Communication: A Reader*. Oxford: Oxford University Press.

Hill, A. (1997) *Shocking Entertainment: Viewer Response to Violent Movies*. Luton: University of Luton Press.

Hill, A. (2001) Women's responses to shocking entertainment, in M. Barker and J. Petley (eds) *Ill Effects: The Media/Violence Debate*, 2nd edn. London: Routledge.

Hitchens, C. (2001) Still standing in the ruins of a dream, *Sunday Star Times*, 16 September.

Hoberman, J. (1998) A test for the individual viewer: *Bonnie and Clyde*'s violent reception, in J.H. Goldstein (ed.) *Why We Watch: The Attractions of Violent Entertainment*. Oxford: Oxford University Press.

Holland, P. (1992) *What is a Child? Popular Images of Childhood*. London: Virago.

Holland, P. (2001) Living for libido: or, 'Child's Play IV', in M. Barker and J. Petley (eds) *Ill Effects: The Media/Violence Debate*, 2nd edn. London: Routledge.

Hollingsworth, M. (1986) *The Press and Political Dissent: A Question of Censorship*. London: Pluto.

Home Office (2002) *Criminal Statistics, England and Wales, 2001*. London: HMSO.

hooks, b. (1992) *Black Looks: Race and Representation*. Boston, MA: South End Press.

hooks, b. (1993) Power to the pussy: we don't wannabe dicks in drag, in L. Frank and P. Smith (eds) *Madonnarama: Essays on Sex and Popular Culture*. Pittsburgh, PA: Cleis Press.

hooks, b. (2000a) *Feminism is for Everybody: Passionate Politics*. London: Pluto.

hooks, b. (2000b) Good girls look the other way, in D. Cornell (ed.) *Feminism and Pornography*. Oxford: Oxford University Press.

hooks, b. (2000c) *Where We Stand: Class Matters*. London: Routledge.

Hubbard, B. (1999) Researchers say Harris reconfigured video game boy turned 'Doom' into school massacre, investigators claim, *Denver Rocky Mountain News*, 3 May.

Hunt, D.M. (1997) *Screening the Los Angeles 'Riots'*. New York: Cambridge University Press.

Hunt, K. and Kitzinger, J. (1996) Public place, private issue? The public's reaction to the Zero Tolerance campaign against violence against women, in H. Bradby (ed.) *Defining Violence: Understanding the Causes and Effects of Violence*. Aldershot: Avebury.

Huntley, R. (1998) Slippery when wet: the shifting boundaries of the pornographic (a class analysis), *Continuum: Journal of Media and Cultural Studies*, 12(1): 69–81.

Hurd, G. (1981) The television presentation of the police, in T. Bennett, S. Boyd-Bowman, C. Mercer and J. Woollacott (eds) *Popular Television and Film*. London: British Film Institute in association with The Open University.

Huesmann, L.R. (1986) Psychological processes promoting the relation between exposure to media violence and aggressive behavior by the viewer, *Journal of Social Issues*, 42: 125–39.

Inayatullah, S. and Milojevic, I. (1999) Exclusion and communication in the Information ERA: from silences to global conversation, in W. Harcourt (ed.) *Women@Internet: Creating New Cultures in Cyberspace*. London: Zed.

Isger, S. (1999) Rabbi to unveil hate's hideouts on the Internet, *Palm Beach Post*, 15 May.

Itzin, C. (ed.) (1992) *Pornography: Women, Violence and Civil Liberties*. Oxford: Oxford University Press.

Izod, J. (1988) *Hollywood and the Box Office 1895–1986*. London: Macmillan.

Jacobs, J. (2000) Gunfire, in J. Arroyo (ed.) *Action/Spectacle Cinema: A Sight and Sound Reader*. London: British Film Institute.

Jacobs, L. (1939) *The Rise of the American Film: A Critical History*. New York: Harcourt, Brace.

Jermyn, D. (2001) 'Death of the girl next door': celebrity, femininity, and tragedy in the murder of Jill Dando, *Feminist Media Studies*, 1(3): 343–59.

Jhally, S. (1987) *The Codes of Advertising: Fetishism and the Political Economy of Meaning in the Consumer Society*. London: Frances Pinter.

Johnson, E. and Scheafer, E. (1993) Soft core/hard gore: *Snuff* as a crisis in meaning, *Journal of Film and Video*, 45(2–3): 40–59.

Jones, A. and Adeniji-Adele, T. (2001) Chatrooms are great – except for the liars, *Observer*, 18 March.

Jordan, T. (1999) *Cyberpower: The Culture and Politics of Cyberspace and the Internet*. London: Routledge.

Jowett, G. (1996) A significant medium for the communication of ideas: *The Miracle* decision and the decline of motion picture censorship, 1952–1968, in F.G. Couvares (ed.) *Movie Censorship and American Culture*. Washington, DC: Smithsonian Institute Press.

Jowett, G.S., Jarvie, I.C. and Fuller, K.H. (1996) *Children and the Movies: Media Influence and the Payne Fund Controversy*. Cambridge: Cambridge University Press.

Juffer, J. (1998) *At Home with Pornography: Women, Sex, and Everyday Life*. New York: New York University Press.

Kael, P. ([1974] 1996a) Killing time, in K. French (ed.) *Screen Violence*. London: Bloomsbury.

Kael, P. (1996b) *Raising Kane and Other Essays*. London: Marion Boyars.

Kamalipour, Y.R. and Rampal, K.R. (eds) (2001) *Media, Sex, Violence and Drugs in the Global Village*. Lanham, MD: Rowman and Littlefield.

Kappeller, S. (1988) *The Pornography of Representation*. Cambridge: Polity.

Karp, H. (2000) Angels online, *Reader's Digest*, April: 34–40.

Katz, J. (1995) Advertising and the construction of violent white masculinity, in G. Dines and J.M. Humez (eds) *Gender, Race and Class in Media*. Thousand Oaks, CA: Sage.

Kerekes, D. and Slater, D. (1995) *Killing for Culture: An Illustrated History of Death Film from Mondo to Snuff*. London: Creation.

Kermode, M. (1997) Horror: on the edge of taste, in R. Peitrie (ed.) *Film and Censorship: The Index Reader*. London: Cassell.

Kilbourne, J. (1995) Beauty and the beast of advertising, in G. Dines and J.M. Humez (eds) *Gender, Race and Class in Media*. Thousand Oaks, CA: Sage.

Kilbourne, J. (1999) *Deadly Persuasion: Why Women and Girls Must Fight the Addictive Power of Advertising*. New York: Free Press.

King, S.R. (1999) Game blocker to be installed on Windows, *New York Times*, 25 June.

Kipnis, L. (1996) *Bound and Gagged: Pornography and the Politics of Fantasy in America*. Durham, NC: Duke University Press.

Kitzinger, J. and Hunt, K. (1993) *Evaluation of Edinburgh District Council's Zero Tolerance Campaign: Full Report*. Edinburgh: Edinburgh District Council Women's Committee.

Klein, N. (2000) *No Logo*. London: Flamingo.

Klite, P. (1999) TV news and the culture of violence. http://www.bigmedia.org/texts6.html (accessed 23 Apr. 2002).

Knightly, P. ([1975] 1999) *The First Casualty*. London: Quartet.

Kolata, G. (2002) A study finds more links between TV and violence. http://www.nytimes.com/2002/03/29/health/29VIOL.html (accessed 29 Mar. 2002).

Krafka, C. and Linz, D. (1997) Women's reactions to sexually aggressive mass media depictions, *Violence against Women*, 3(2): 149–82.

Kramarae, C. and Taylor, H.J. (1993) Women and men on electronic networks: a conversation or a monologue, in H.J. Taylor, C. Kramarae and M. Ebben (eds)

Women, Information Technology and Scholarship. Urbana, IL: Center for Advanced Study.

Kramer, P. (2001) 'Clean, dependable slapstick': comic violence and the emergence of classical Hollywood cinema, in J.D. Slocum (ed.) *Violence and American Cinema.* London: Routledge.

Kuhn, A. (1982) *Women's Pictures: Feminism and Cinema.* London: Routledge and Kegan Paul.

Kuhn, A. (1985) History of the cinema, in P. Cook (ed.) *The Cinema Book.* London: British Film Institute.

Kuhn, A. (1988) *Cinema, Censorship and Sexuality 1909–1925.* London: Routledge.

Kunkel, D. and Wilcox, B. (2001) Children and media policy, in D.G. Singer and J.L. Singer (eds) *Handbook of Children and the Media.* Thousand Oaks, CA: Sage.

LaHaye, T. (1998) The mental poison, in R.M. Baird and S.E. Rosenbaum (eds) *Pornography: Private Right or Public Menace?* Amherst, NY: Prometheus.

Lande, N. (ed.) (1996) *Dispatches from the Front: A History of the American War Correspondent.* New York: Oxford University Press.

Lang, K. and Lang, G.E. (1983) The 'new' rhetoric of mass communications research: a longer view, in special *Ferment in the Field* issue of *Journal of Communication,* 33(3): 128–40.

Lang, M. (2000) America faces tolerance vs. hate battle, Dees warns crowd at MU, *Lancaster New Era,* 10 November.

Laughren, J. (2000) Cyberstalking awareness education. www.acs.ucalgary.ca/~dabrent/380/webproj/jessica.html (accessed 3 Apr. 2002).

Leibovich, L. (1998]) Rethinking Rodney King. http://www.salon.com/news/1998/03/13.html (accessed 14 Apr. 2002).

Levine, M. (1996) *Viewing Violence: How Media Violence Affects your Child and Adolescent's Development.* New York: Doubleday.

Lewis, J. (1982) The story of a riot: the television coverage of civil unrest in 1981, *Screen Education,* 40: 15–33.

Lewis, R. and Rolley, K. (1997) (Ad)dressing the dyke: lesbian looks and lesbians looking, in M. Nava, A. Blake, I. MacRury and B. Richards (eds) *Buy this Book: Studies in Advertising and Consumption.* London: Routledge.

Liberty (ed.) (1999) *Liberating Cyberspace: Civil Liberties, Human Rights and the Internet.* London: Pluto.

Linné, O. and Wartella, E. (1998) Research about violence in the media: different traditions and changing paradigms, in R. Dickinson, R. Harindranath and O. Linné (eds) *Approaches to Audiences: A Reader.* London: Arnold.

Linz, D., Donnerstein, E. and Penrod, S. (1984) The effects of multiple exposures to filmed violence against women, *Journal of Communication,* 34(3): 130–47.

Lowery, S.A. and DeFleur, M.L. (1995) *Milestones in Mass Communication: Media Effects,* 3rd edn. London: Longman.

Lupton, D. (2000) The embodied computer/user, in D. Bell and B.M. Kennedy (eds) *The Cybercultures Reader.* London: Routledge.

Lupton, D. and Tulloch, J. (1999) Theorizing fear of crime: beyond the rational/irrational opposition, *British Journal of Sociology,* 50(3): 507–23.

Lyman, R. (2000) Hollywood insiders give thumbs-down to critics, *New York Times*, 18 September.

Lynch, J. (2002) *Reporting the World*. Tatlow, UK: Conflict & Peace Forums.

Lynch, J. and McGoldrick, A. (2000) What a peace journalist would try to do. www.mediachannel.org/originals/warandpeace2.shtml (accessed 23 Apr. 2002).

Lyons, C. (1997) *The New Censors: Movies and the Culture Wars*. Philadelphia, PA: Temple University Press.

McBride, J. (1995) *War, Battering, and Other Sports: The Gulf between American Men and Women*. Atlantic Highlands, NJ: Humanities Press.

MacCann, R.D. (1962) *Hollywood in Transition*. Boston, MA: Houghton Mifflin.

McElvoy, A. (2001) When 'just looking' is no excuse, *Independent*, 15 February.

MacKay, F. (1996) The Zero Tolerance campaign: setting the agenda, *Parliamentary Affairs: A Journal of Comparative Politics*, 49(1): 206–20.

McKinney, D. (1993) Violence: the strong and the weak, *Film Quarterly*, 46(4): 16–22.

MacKinnon, C.A. (2000a) Only words, in D. Cornell (ed.) *Feminism and Pornography*. Oxford: Oxford University Press.

MacKinnon, C.A. (2000b) Not a moral issue, in D. Cornell (ed.) *Feminism and Pornography*, Oxford: Oxford University Press.

McLaughlin, L. (1998) Gender, privacy and publicity in media event space, in C. Carter, G. Branston and S. Allan (eds) *News, Gender and Power*. London: Routledge.

McLaughlin, T. (1999) The ethics of basketball, *Continuum: Journal of Media and Cultural Studies*, 13(1): 13–28.

McLeod, J.M., Kosicki, G.M. and Pan, Z. (1991) On understanding and misunderstanding media effects, in J. Curran and M. Gurevitch (eds) *Mass Media and Society*. London: Arnold.

McLuhan, M. (1964) *Understanding Media: The Extensions of Man*. London: Sphere.

Magid, L. (2002) About Larry Magid. http://www.larrysworld.com/larrybio.html (accessed 15 Apr. 2002).

Maguire, B., Sandage, D. and Weatherby, G.A. (2000) Violence, morality and television commercials, *Sociological Spectrum*, 20: 121–43.

Malcolm, D. (1989) The lust picture show, *Guardian*, 16 February.

Male, A. (1997) 100 years' gore, *Neon*, September.

Maltby, R. (2001) The spectacle of criminality, in J.D. Slocum (ed.) *Violence and American Cinema*. London: Routledge.

Medved, M. (1992) *Hollywood vs America: Popular Culture and the War on Traditional Values*. New York: HarperCollins.

Medved, M. (1996) Hollywood's four big lies, in K. French (ed.) *Screen Violence*. London: Bloomsbury.

Meloy, J. and Gothard, S. (1995) A demographic and clinical comparison of obsessional followers and offenders with mental disorders, *American Journal of Psychiatry*, 152: 259–63.

Meyers, M. (1995) News of battering, *Journal of Communication*, 44(2): 47–63.

Meyers, M. (1997) *News Accounts of Violence against Women: Engendering Blame.* Thousand Oaks, CA: Sage.

Microsoft (2000) Using content ratings. http://www.microsoft.com/windows2000/techinfo.reskit/en/ierk/Ch08_b.thm (accessed 13 Apr. 2002).

Miller, C. (2000) The perfect storm. http://www.geocities.com/iraqinfo/gulfwar/gulfdocs/perfect/html (accessed 23 Apr. 2002).

Miller, D. and Philo, G. (1996) Against orthodoxy: the media do influence us, *Sight and Sound*, 12: 18–20.

Miller, D., Kitzinger, J., Williams, K. and Beharrell, P. (1998) *The Circuit of Mass Communication.* London: Sage.

Millum, T. (1975) *Images of Women: Advertising in Women's Magazines.* London: Chatto and Windus.

Minogue, T. (1990) Putting real crime in the picture, *Guardian*, 3 September.

Mitchell, E. (2001) Good at action films: maybe too good, *New York Times*, 18 September.

Modleski, T. (1988) *The Women Who Knew Too Much.* London: Methuen.

Moore, S. (1993) On crime and crime reporting, *Observer Magazine*, 16 May.

Morrison, D.E. and Tumber, H. (1988) *Journalists at War: The Dynamics of News Reporting during the Falklands Conflict.* London: Sage.

Morrison, D.E with MacGregor, B., Svennevig, M. and Firmstone, J. (1999) *Defining Violence.* Luton: University of Luton Press.

Mortimer, B. (1997) The postmodern person in *Taxi Driver*, *Raging Bull* and *The King of Comedy*, *Journal of Film and Video*, 49(1–2): 28–38.

Mourão, M. (1999) The representation of female desire in early modern pornographic texts, 1660–1745, *Signs: Journal of Women in Culture and Society*, 24(3): 573–602.

Mullen, P., Pathé, M., Purcell, R. and Stuart, G. (1999) Study of stalkers, *American Journal of Psychiatry*, 156(8): 244–9.

Murdock, G. (2001) Reservoirs of dogma: an archaeology of popular anxieties, in M. Barker and J. Petley (eds) *Ill Effects: The Media/Violence Debate.* London: Routledge.

Murray, J.P. (1993) The developing child in a multimedia society, in G.L. Berry and J. Keiko Asamen (eds) *Children and Television: Images in a Changing Sociocultural World.* Newbury Park, CA: Sage.

Musser, C. (1990) *The Emergence of Cinema: The American Screen to 1907.* New York: Charles Scribner's Sons/Macmillan.

National Television Violence Study (1997) *National Television Violence Study*, vol. 2. Thousand Oaks, CA: Sage.

Naureckas, J. (1990) Media on the march. http://www.fair.org/extra/9011/media-march.html (accessed 23 Apr. 2002).

Nelson, R. (1997) *TV Drama in Transition: Forms, Values and Cultural Change.* London: Macmillan.

Nightingale, V. (1996) *Studying Audiences: The Shock of the Real.* London: Routledge.

Noonan, R.J. (1998) The psychology of sex: a mirror from the Internet, in J.

Gakenbach (ed.) *Psychology and the Internet: Intrapersonal, Interpersonal and Transpersonal Implications*. San Diego, CA: Academic Press.

Office for National Statistics (2002) *Social Trends 32*. London: Stationery Office.

Ogilvie, E. (2000) Cyberstalking, *Australian Institute of Criminology*, Trends and Issues in Crime and Criminal Justice series, September.

Osborne, R. (1995) Crime and the media: from media studies to post-modernism, in D. Kidd-Hewitt and R. Osborne (eds) *Crime and the Media: The Post-modern Spectacle*. East Haven, CT: Pluto.

Oswell, D. (1999) The dark side of cyberspace: Internet content regulation and child protection, *Convergence*, 5(4): 42–62.

O'Toole, L. (1998) *Pornocopia: Porn, Sex, Technology and Desire*. London: Serpent's Tail.

Owen, O. (2001) Our worst nightmare, *Observer*, 18 March.

Paik, H. and Comstock, G. (1994) The effects of television violence on antisocial behaviour: a meta-analysis, *Communication Research*, 21(4): 516–46.

Parker, T. (1998) The impact of pornography on marriage, in R.M. Baird and S.E. Rosenbaum (eds) *Pornography: Private Right or Public Menace?* Amherst, NY: Prometheus.

Parratt, L. and Wadham, J. (eds) (1999) *Liberating Cyberspace: Civil Liberties, Human Rights and the Internet*, London: Pluto in association with Liberty.

Paul, D. and McJannet, J. (2000) Dando suspect: was he driven mad by sexy pose?, *Daily Star*, 26 May.

Petley, J. (2001) Us and them, in M. Barker and J. Petley (eds) *Ill Effects: The Media/Violence Debate*, 2nd edn. London: Routledge.

Phelps, G. (1997) Britain: out of fear and ignorance, in R. Peitrie (ed.) *Film and Censorship: The Index Reader*. London: Cassell.

Philo, G. (1990) *Seeing and Believing: The Influence of Television*. London: Routledge.

Pinedo, I. (1996) Recreational terror: postmodern elements of the contemporary horror film, *Journal of Film and Video*, 48(1–2): 17–31.

Pines, J. (1995) Black cops and black villains in film and TV crime fiction, in D. Kidd-Hewitt and R. Osborne (eds) *Crime and the Media: The Post-modern Spectacle*. East Haven, CT: Pluto.

Plant, S. (1996) On the matrix: cyberfeminist simulations, in R. Shields (ed.) *Cultures of the Internet: Virtual Spaces, Real Histories, Living Bodies*. Thousand Oaks, CA: Sage.

Poole, O. (2001) Hollywood combat movies sate bullish national mood, *New Zealand Herald*, 8 November.

Porter, D. (ed.) (1997) *Internet Culture*. London: Routledge.

Potter, W.J. (1999) *On Media Violence*. Thousand Oaks, CA: Sage.

Prasad, V.K. and Smith, L.J. (1994) Television commercials in violent programming: an experimental evaluation of their effects on children, *Journal of the Academy of Marketing Sciences*, 22(4): 340–51.

Prince, S. (2000a) *A New Pot of Gold: Hollywood under the Electronic Rainbow, 1980–1989*. New York: Charles Scribner's Sons.

Prince, S. (2000b) Graphic violence and the cinema: origins, aesthetic design, and social effects, in S. Prince (ed.) *Screening Violence*. London: Athlone Press.

Prince, S. (2000c) The aesthetic of slow-motion violence in the films of Sam Peckinpah, in S. Prince (ed.) *Screening Violence*. London: Athlone Press.

Pringle, H. and Thompson, M. (1999) *How Cause Related Marketing Builds Brands*. Chichester: Wiley.

Rae, F. (2002) It's a kid's world, *New Zealand Herald 'e.g. Magazine'*, 18–24 April.

Randall, R. (1976) Censorship: from *The Miracle* to *Deep Throat*, in T. Balio (ed.) *The American Film Industry*. Madison, WI: University of Wisconsin Press.

Reid, E. (1999) Hierarchy and power: social control in cyberspace, in M.A. Smith and P. Kollock (eds) *Communities in Cyberspace*. London: Routledge.

Rhodes, J. (2001) Journalism in the new millennium: what's a feminist to do?, *Feminist Media Studies*, 1(1): 49–53.

Rich, B.R. (1992) Art house killers, *Sight and Sound*, 2(8): 5–6.

Rich, M., Woods, E.R., Goodman, E., Emans, J. and Durant, R.H. (1998) Aggressors or victims: gender and race in music video violence, *Pediatrics*, 101(4): 669–75.

Riggs, L.W. and Willoquet, P. (1989) Up against the looking glass! Heterosexual rape as homosexual epiphany in *The Accused*, *Film and Literature Quarterly*, 17(14): 214–23.

Roberts, D.F. and Christenson, P.G. (2001) Popular music in childhood and adolescence, in D.G. Singer and J.L. Singer (eds) *Handbook of Children and the Media*. Thousand Oaks, CA: Sage.

Robertson, J.C. (1989) *The Hidden Cinema: British Film Censorship in Action: 1913–1972*. London: Routledge.

Rockwell, L.H. Jr (2000) Don't believe them. http://www.geocities.com/iraqinfo/gulfwar/gulfdocs/believe.html (accessed 23 Apr. 2002).

Rodgerson, G. and Wilson, E. (eds) (1991) *Pornography and Feminism*, London: Lawrence and Wishart.

Rosenbaum, D.E. (2000) Hollywood executives go to Washington, *New York Times*, 28 September.

Rowland, W.D. (1983) *The Politics of Television Violence: Policy Uses of Communication Research*. Beverly Hills, CA: Sage.

Royalle, C. (2000) Porn in the USA, in D. Cornell (ed.) *Feminism and Pornography*. Oxford: Oxford University Press.

Rubin, G. (1993) Misguided, dangerous and wrong: an analysis of anti-pornography politics, in A. Assister and C. Avedon (eds) *Bad Girls and Dirty Pictures: The Challenge to Reclaim Feminism*. London: Pluto.

Rubin, M. (1999) *Thrillers*. Cambridge: Cambridge University Press.

Russell, D.E.H. (ed.) (1993) *Making Violence Sexy: Feminist Views on Pornography*. New York: Teacher's College Press.

Russell, D.E.H. (1998) *Dangerous Relationships: Pornography, Misogyny, and Rape*. London: Sage.

Russell, D.E.H. (2000) Pornography and rape: a causal model, in D. Cornell (ed.) *Feminism and Pornography*. Oxford: Oxford University Press.

Sabo, D. and Jansen, S.C. (1998) Prometheus Unbound: constructions of masculinity in the sports media, in L.A. Wenner (ed.) *Media Sport*. London: Routledge.

Sack, K. (2000) Federal report criticizes entertainment marketing, *New York Times*, 10 September.

Said, E. (2001) The necessity of skepticism backlash and backtrack. http://www.zmag/org.saidcalam2.htm (accessed 14 Apr. 2002).

Sardar, Z. (1996) alt.civilizations.faq: cyberspace as the darker side of the West, in Z. Sardar and J.R. Ravetz (eds) *Cyberfutures*. London: Pluto.

Schaefer, E. (1999) *Bold! Daring! Shocking! True! A History of Exploitation Films, 1919–1959*. Durham, NC: Duke University Press.

Schechter, D. (2001) Covering violence: how should media handle conflict? http://www.mediachannel.org/views/dissector/coveringviolence.shtml (accessed 4 Apr. 2002)

Schindler, C. (1996) *Hollywood in Crisis: Cinema and American Society 1929–1939*. London: Routledge.

Schlesinger, P. and Tumber, H. (1993) Fighting the war against crime: television, police and audience, *British Journal of Criminology*, 33(1): 19–32.

Schlesinger, P. and Tumber, H. (1994) *Reporting Crime: The Media Politics of Criminal Justice*. Oxford: Clarendon Press.

Schlesinger, P., Tumber, H. and Murdock, G. (1991) The media politics of crime and criminal justice, *British Journal of Sociology*, 42(3): 397–420.

Schlesinger, P., Dobash, R.E., Dobash, R. and Weaver, C.K. (1992) *Women Viewing Violence*. London: British Film Institute.

Schlesinger, P., Haynes, R., Boyle, R. *et al.* (1998) *Men Viewing Violence*. London: Broadcasting Standards Commission.

Schlolar, S. (2002) Pat Califia – a three part interview. http://www.technodyke.com/features/patcalifa1.asp (accessed 24 Feb. 2002).

Scott, A., Semmens, L. and Willoughby, L. (1999) Women and the Internet: the natural history of a research project, *Information, Communication and Society*, 2(4): 541–65.

Segal, L. (1993) Does pornography cause violence?, in P.C. Gibson and R. Gibson (eds) *Dirty Looks: Women, Pornography, Power*. London: British Film Institute.

Segal, L. and McIntosh, M. (eds) (1992) *Sex Exposed: Sexuality and the Pornography Debate*. London: Virago.

Sharrett, C. (1984) The idea of apocalypse in *The Texas Chainsaw Massacre*, in B.K. Grant (ed.) *Planks of Reason: Essays on the Horror Film*. Metuchen, NJ: Scarecrow Press.

Sharrett, C. (1999) Afterword, in C. Sharrett (ed.) *Mythologies of Violence in Postmodern Media*. Detroit, MI: Wayne State University Press.

Shen, F. and Prinsen, T. (1999) Audience responses to TV commercials embedded in violent programmes, in M.S. Roberts (ed.) *The Proceedings of the 1999 Conference of the American Academy of Advertising*. Gainesville, FL: University of Florida.

Signorielli, N. (1991) *A Sourcebook on Children and Television*. Westport, CT: Greenwood Press.

Silverman, K. (1988) *The Acoustic Mirror: The Female Voice in Psychoanalysis and Cinema*. Bloomington, IN: Indiana University Press.

Simpson, P.L. (1999) The politics of the apocalypse in the cinema of serial murder, in C. Sharrett (ed.) *Mythologies of Violence in Postmodern Media*. Detroit, MI: Wayne State University Press.

Skal, D.J. (1993) *The Monster Show: A Cultural History of Horror*. New York: W.W. Norton.

Skelton, C. (1994) Network of hate: the dark side of cyberspace, *id Magazine*, 3(2): 15.

Slocum, J.D. (ed.) (2001) *Violence and American Cinema*. London: Routledge.

Sloop, J.M. (1997) Mike Tyson and the perils of discursive constraints: boxing, race, and the assumption of guilt, in A. Baker and T. Boyd (eds) *Sports Media, and the Politics of Identity*. Bloomington, IN: Indiana University Press.

Smith, A. (1995) By women, for women and about women rules OK?, in P. Burston and C. Richardson (eds) *A Queer Romance: Lesbians, Gay Men and Popular Culture*. London: Routledge.

Smith, G. (2000) Oliver Stone: why do I have to provoke?, in J. Arroyo (ed.) *Action/Spectacle Cinema: A Sight and Sound Reader*. London: British Film Institute.

Smith, M.A. and Kollock, P. (eds) (1999) *Communities in Cyberspace*. London: Routledge.

Smith, P. (1995) Eastwood bound, in M. Berger, B. Wallis and S. Watson (eds) *Constructing Masculinity*. London: Routledge.

Smith, S.L. and Boyson, A.R. (2002) Violence in music videos: examining the prevalence and context of physical aggression, *Journal of Communication,* 52(1): 61–83.

Snow, N. (2001) Social implications of media globalization, in Y.R. Kamalipour and K.R. Rampal (eds) *Media, Sex, Violence and Drugs in the Global Village*. Lanham: Rowman and Littlefield.

Solomon, S.J. (1972) *The Film Idea*. New York: Harcourt Brace Jovanovich.

Soothill, K. and Walby, S. (1991) *Sex Crime in the News*. London: Routledge.

Sparks, R. (1992) *Television and the Drama of Crime: Moral Tales and the Place of Crime in Public Life*. Buckingham: Open University Press.

Spender, D. (1995) *Nattering on the Net: Women, Power and Cyberspace*. Sydney: Spinfex.

Spitzer, M.L. (1998) A first glance at the constitutionality of the V-chip ratings system, in J. Hamilton (ed.) *Television Violence and Public Policy*. Ann Arbor, MI: University of Michigan Press.

Springer, C. (2001) The seduction of the surface: from *Alice* to *Crash, Feminist Media Studies*, 1(2): 197–213.

Springhall, J. (1998) *Youth, Popular Culture and Moral Panics: Penny Gaffs to Gangster-Rap, 1830–1996*. London: Macmillan.

Standage, T. (1997) CONNECTED: Internet censorship is feasible, but . . ., *Daily Telegraph*, 7 October.

Starker, S. (1989) *Evil Influences: Crusades against the Mass Media.* New Brunswick, NJ: Transaction.

Steinem, G. (1998) Erotica and pornography: a clear and present difference, in R.M. Baird and S.E. Rosenbaum (eds) *Pornography: Private Right or Public Menace?* Amherst, NY: Prometheus.

Steiner, L. (1999) The *New York Times* coverage of Anita Hill as a female cipher, in M. Meyers (ed.) *Mediated Women: Representations in Popular Culture.* Cresskill, NJ: Hampton Press.

Stone, A.R. (1991) Will the real body please stand UP@ boundary stories about virtual cultures, in M. Benedikt (ed.) *Cyberspace: First Steps.* Cambridge, MA: MIT Press.

Stout, D. (2002) Supreme Court strikes down ban on virtual child pornography, *New York Times.* www.nytimes.com/2002/04/16/national/16CND-PORN.html (accessed 16 Apr. 2002).

Sutherlin, J. (2001a) Have things improved? What has changed, if anything since the Rodney King beating? (Interview with Earl Caldwell). http://www.newswatch.sfsu.edu/qa/030501king_qa_caldwell.html (accessed 14 Apr. 2002).

Sutherlin, J. (2001b) Have things improved? What has changed, if anything since the Rodney King beating? (Interview with Austin Long-Scott). http: //www.newswatch.sfsu.edu/qa/030501king_qa_long-scott.html (accessed 14 Apr. 2002).

Sweeney, J. (1992) Where fear and loathing stalk the set, *Observer*, 10 May.

Talacko, P. (2000) INSIDE TRACK: the publisher with no name: decentralised networks such as FreeNet allow users to post material and not be traced, *Financial Times* (London), 28 July.

Tasker, Y. (1993) *Spectacular Bodies: Gender, Genre and the Action Cinema.* London: Routledge.

Taubin, A. (1991) Killing men, *Sight and Sound*, 1(1): 14–19.

Taylor, J. (1995) War in the British press, in J. Walsh (ed.) *The Gulf War did not Happen: Politics, Culture and Warfare Post-Vietnam*, Aldershot: Arena.

Taylor, J. (1998) *Body Horror: Photojournalism, Catastrophe and War.* Manchester: Manchester University Press.

Thoman, E. (1993) Making connections: media's role in our culture of violence. www.medialit.org/Violence/articles/make_conn.htm (accessed 12 Feb. 2002).

Tomasulo, F.P. (1999) Raging bully: postmodern violence and masculinity in *Raging Bull*, in C. Sharrett (ed.) *Mythologies of Violence in Postmodern Media.* Detroit, MI: Wayne State University Press.

Torrens, K. (1998) I can get any job and feel like a butterfly! Symbolic violence in the TV advertising of Jenny Craig, *Journal of Communication Inquiry*, 22(1): 27–47.

Travis, A. (2002) *Straw Dogs* video ban lifted, *Guardian* 2 July: 5.

Tulloch, J. and Tulloch, M. (1993) Understanding TV violence: a multifaceted cultural analysis, in G. Turner (ed.) *Nation, Culture, Text: Australian Cultural and Media Studies.* London: Routledge.

Turkle, S. (1999) Tinysex and gender trouble, in L. Parratt and J. Wadham (eds)

Liberating Cyberspace: Civil Liberties, Human Rights and the Internet, London: Pluto in association with Liberty.

Twitchell, J.B. (1989) *Preposterous Violence: Fables of Aggression in Modern Culture*. New York: Oxford University Press.

UCLA Television Violence Monitoring Report (1995) UCLA Center for Communication Policy.

van Zoonen, L. (1994) *Feminist Media Studies*. Thousand Oaks, CA: Sage.

van Zoonen, L. (2001) Feminist Internet studies, *Feminist Media Studies*, 1(1): 67–72.

Walker, P. (1991) U.S. bombing: the myth of surgical bombing in the Gulf War. http://www.geocities.com/iraqinfo/gulfwar/gulfdocs/wc-myth.html (accessed 23 Apr. 2002).

Walkerdine, V. (1997) *Daddy's Girl: Young Girls and Popular Culture*. Cambridge, MA: Harvard University Press.

Walter, N. (1999) *The New Feminism*. London: Virago.

Washington Post (1994) Commitments: 'game' remains the same – even in cyberspace, *Los Angeles Times*, 20 June.

Watson, R. and Easterbrook, G. ([1991] 1996) A new kind of warfare, *Newsweek*, 28 January, in N. Lande (ed.) *Dispatches from the Front: A History of the American War Correspondent*. New York: Oxford University Press.

Weaver, C.K. (1995) Representations of men's violence against women: audio-visual texts and their reception. Unpublished PhD thesis, University of Stirling.

Weaver, C.K. (1996) The television and violence debate in New Zealand: some problems of context, *Continuum: Australian Journal of Media and Culture*, 10(1): 64–75.

Weaver, C.K. (1998) *Crimewatch UK*: keeping women off the streets, in C. Carter, G. Branston and S. Allan (eds) *News, Gender and Power*. London: Routledge.

Weaver, C.K. and Michelle, C. (1999) Public communication compromised: the impact of corporate sponsorship on a pro-social media campaign, *Australian Journal of Communication*, 26(3): 83–97.

Weaver, C.K., Carter, C. and Stanko, E. (2000) The female body at risk: media, sexual violence and the gendering of public environments, in S. Allan, B. Adam and C. Carter (eds) *Environmental Risks and the Media*. London: Routledge.

Weaver, M.J. (1998) Pornography and the religious imagination, in R.M. Baird and S.E. Rosenbaum (eds) *Pornography: Private Right or Public Menace?* Amherst, NY: Prometheus.

Whannel, G. (1992) *Fields in Vision: Television Sport and Cultural Transformation*. London: Routledge.

White, R.A. (1983) Mass communication and culture: transition to a new paradigm, in special *Ferment in the Field* issue of *Journal of Communication*, 33(3): 279–301.

Whitney, C. and Wartella, E. (2000) On US journalism and education, *Journalism: Theory, Practice and Criticism*, 1(1): 52–5.

Whittle, S. (2002) Working the web: surfing police, *Guardian*, online section, 11 April: 4.

Wiegman, R. (1998) Race, ethnicity, and film, in J. Hill and P. Church Gibson (eds) *The Oxford Guide to Film Studies*. Oxford: Oxford University Press.

Will, G.F. (1998) America's slide into the sewer, in R.M. Baird and S.E. Rosenbaum (eds) *Pornography: Private Right or Public Menace?*, Amherst, NY: Prometheus.

Williams, B. (1979) *Report on Obscenity and Film Censorship*. London: HMSO.

Williams, D. (2001) Have things improved? What has changed, if anything since the Rodney King beating? (Interview with Hector Tobar). http://www.newswatch.sfsu.edu/qa/030501king_qa_tobar.html (accessed 14 Apr. 2002).

Williams, L. (1989) *Hard Core: Power, Pleasure, and the 'Frenzy of the Visible'*. Berkeley, CA: University of California Press.

Williams, L. (1991) Film bodies: gender, genre and excess, *Film Quarterly*, 44(4): 2–13.

Williams, L. (1996) When the woman looks, in B.K. Grant (ed.) *The Dread of Difference: Gender and the Horror Film*. Austin, TX: University of Texas Press.

Williamson, J. (1978) *Decoding Advertisements: Ideology and Meaning in Advertising*. London: Marion Boyars.

Wills, N. (2001) '110 per cent woman': the crotch shot in the Hollywood musical, *Screen*, 42(2): 121–41.

Wilson, B.J., Donnerstein, E., Linz, D. et al. (1998a) Content analysis of entertainment television: the importance of context, in J. Hamilton (ed.) *Television Violence and Public Policy*. Ann Arbor, MI: University of Michigan Press.

Wilson, B.J., Smith, S.L., Potter, T. et al. (1998b) Content analysis of entertainment television: the 1994–1995 results, in J. Hamilton (ed.) *Television Violence and Public Policy*. Ann Arbor, MI: University of Michigan Press.

Wilson, C.C. II (2000) The paradox of African American journalists, in S. Cottle (ed.) *Ethnic Minorities and the Media*. Buckingham: Open University Press.

Winerip, M. (1995) Making peace with the *Power Rangers*, *Parenting*, February: 77–82.

Winship, J. (2000) Women outdoors: advertising, controversy and disputing feminism in the 1990s, *International Journal of Cultural Studies*, 3(1): 27–55.

Wlodarz, J. (2001) Rape fantasies: Hollywood and homophobia, in P. Lehman (ed.) *Masculinity: Bodies, Movies, Culture*. London: Routledge.

Wober, M. and Gunter, B. (1990) *Crime Reconstruction Programmes: Viewing Experiences in Three Regions, Linked with Perceptions of and Reactions to Crime*. London: IBA Research Paper.

Wolf, N. (1990) *The Beauty Myth*. London: Chatto and Windus.

Wolfsfeld, G. (1997) *Media and Political Conflict: News from the Middle East*. Cambridge: Cambridge University Press.

Wood, R. (1984) An introduction to the American horror film, in B.K. Grant (ed.) *Planks of Reason: Essays on the Horror Film*. Metuchen, NJ: Scarecrow Press.

Woodruff, K. (1996) Alcohol advertising and violence against women: a media advocacy case study, *Health Education Quarterly*, 23(3): 330–45.

Woodward, W., Kelso, P. and Vidal, J. (2000) Protests erupt in violence: 'guerrilla gardening' action turns ugly with looted shops and battles with police, *Guardian*, 2 May.

Wykes, M. (2000) The burrowers: news about bodies, tunnels and green guerrillas, in S. Allan, B. Adam and C. Carter (eds) *Environmental Risks and the Media*. London: Routledge.

Yaquinto, M. (1998) *Pump 'em Full of Lead: A Look at Gangsters on Film*. New York: Twayne.

Young, A. (1990) *Femininity in Dissent*. London: Routledge.

Young, P. and Jesser, P. (1997) *The Media and the Military*. London: Macmillan.

Young Women's Christian Association (YWCA) (1996) *Imagine Life without Violence: A Practical Guide to Reducing Violence in our Lives*. Seattle: YWCA.

Zelizer, B. and Allan, S. (eds) (2002) *Journalism after September 11*. London: Routledge.

Zickmund, S. (2000) Approaching the radical other: the discursive culture of cyber-hate, in D. Bell and B.M. Kennedy (eds) *The Cybercultures Reader*. London and New York: Routledge.

Zwick, E. and Herskovitz, M. (2001) When the bodies are real, *New York Times*, September 23.

INDEX